THE STUDENT PARAMEDIC SURVIVAL GUIDE

Your Journey from Student to Paramedic

Second edition

THE STUDENT PARAMEDIC SURVIVAL GUIDE

Your Journey from Student to Paramedic

Second edition

Edited by Amanda Blaber

Open University Press

Open University Press
McGraw Hill
Unit 4,
Foundation Park
Roxborough Way
Maidenhead
SL6 3UD

email: emea_uk_ireland@mheducation.com
world wide web: www.openup.co.uk

First published 2015
First published in this edition 2023

A catalogue record of this book is available from the British Library

ISBN-13: 9780335251926
ISBN-10: 0335251927
eISBN: 9780335251933

Library of Congress Cataloging-in-Publication Data
CIP data applied for

Typeset by Transforma Pvt. Ltd., Chennai, India

PRAISE FOR THIS BOOK

"The student paramedics survival guide is an essential read for those interested in a career within paramedicine and currently studying towards. This book assists in the knowledge and understanding of what this journey looks like from that initial interest to completion and has invaluable key points to assist all students and prospective applicant throughout and maintain a well balance view and approach to all aspects for their forthcoming journey."
Mark Willis, Programme Lead – BSc (Hons) Paramedic Science and
Out of Hospital Care, Faculty of Health Sciences & Well-Being,
University of Sunderland, UK

"This superb book will help prospective and student paramedics to prepare for their studies and manage the professional expectations of their programmes, as well as providing great tips to help along the way. This book allows readers access to the reality of student paramedic life, which is essential in considering a career as a paramedic. Highly recommended."
Kath Jennings, Section Lead for Paramedic Science programmes,
School of Health Sciences, University of Greenwich, UK

"I thought the book was an excellent resource, not only for current students but also for anyone who is considering applying to join the profession. It is detailed and informative, providing a real world view of what being a student paramedic entails and incorporates good advice for every element of the journey. It covers those aspects that potential students may have already considered and many more that they potentially haven't even thought about."
Tracey Brickell, Deputy Course and
Placement Lead, University of Portsmouth, UK

"An excellent text and invaluable resource - not only for current paramedic students but also those looking to apply for a paramedic programme. This book has been comprehensively updated from the previous edition with helpful chapters on the application

journey, advice for the undergraduate years, the transition to becoming registered and getting that all important first job. Expertly edited & authored by Amanda, the chapter authors/contributors add significant gravitas to the book, ensuring it reflects the ever-changing profession and developments in paramedic education. A must have publication"

Aidan Ward, Professional Lead: Paramedic Programmes,
University of Northampton, UK

CONTENTS

LIST OF TABLES

LIST OF AUTHORS AND CONTRIBUTORS

Amanda Blaber: Senior Fellow Higher Education Academy (SFHEA, Advance HE), MSc, PG DipHE, BSc (Hons), DipHE (A&E), ENB 998 (Teaching and Assessing), RGN. Honorary Fellow of the College of Paramedics. Senior Lecturer, School of Sport and Health Sciences, University of Brighton, UK.

Helen Abrahams: Student Advice Manager, University of Brighton, UK.

Kevin Barrett: RN, PgCHSCE, MRes SFHEA. Senior Lecturer, University of Brighton, UK.

Mark Durell: Senior Lecturer, University of Brighton and Specialist Paramedic (Critical Care), University Hospital Southampton/Hampshire and Isle of Wight Air Ambulance, UK.

Gemma Howlett: MSc, BSc (Hons), FdSc, MCPara, SFHEA. Principal Lecturer, University of Cumbria, UK.

Dan Jarman: BSc (Hons). Lecturer, Paramedic, School of Sport and Health Sciences, University of Brighton, UK.

Dr Aimee McKinnon: Research Clinical Psychologist, Oxford Centre for Anxiety Disorders and Trauma, University of Oxford, UK. Aimee also works in the NHS as a Specialist Clinical Psychologist, Berkshire Traumatic Stress Service.

Jo Mildenhall: MA MBACP. Paramedic Psychological Health and Wellbeing Manager, College of Paramedics.

Jessica Rimmer: Frontline Paramedic. Lecturer and Placement Lead, School of Sport and Health Sciences, University of Brighton, UK. Paramedic on the British Superbikes (BSB) Medical Team.

Paul Saunders: BSc (Hons), BA (Hons). Lecturer, School of Sport and Health Sciences, University of Brighton, UK. Paramedic and Practice Educator, South East Coast Ambulance Service NHS Foundation Trust.

Kim Tolley: RN, BSc, PGCAE, MSc. Professional Liaison Consultant, The Health and Care Professions Council.

Gabriella Tyson: DPhil researcher and psychologist, University of Oxford, UK.

Dr Jennifer Wild: Professor of Military Mental Health, University of Melbourne, Australia.

Abbie Wilkins: Lead Well-being Practitioner and Senior Research Assistant, University of Oxford, UK.

FOREWORD

A long time ago I was a gardener nurseryman, and I chose to join my local ambulance service, which happened to be the capital. It wasn't possible to become a paramedic, they didn't exist, only Intubation and Infusion crews known as I&I of which I became one in 1984. But walking into the job centre in Northwest London was a massive decision for me to step into what would become my new career and vocation lasting over forty years. You see, my Mum had been a nurse and my Dad an ambulance driver/attendant in the 1950s. Later, in the next century, my son would go to university to be educated and trained to become a paramedic for ten years on the front line, before re-training as a vicar. My daughter became a doctor specialising in Cardiology after significant education and clinical development.

Careers change and adapt and indeed many of you reading this will be mature students switching job roles for a variety of reasons and trying to find out, is this the best path for you? Many more of you, will join the 8,000 student paramedics in the many HCPC approved university-based programmes, whether via an apprenticeship or a direct entry UCAS application. Gaining information is key, not just for your next steps, but for your entire career. Every patient intervention requires you to problem solve based on information you discover in quality history taken from a patient or a career.

I came home from my ambulance training (eight-week course) and told my Dad, that I had learnt the three Ps of ambulance aid: - preserve life, promote recovery and prevent the condition from deteriorating. My Dads repost (two-week Civil Defence training course) was ah yes, pull up, pop them into the back and push on to the hospital. My son's approach was closely aligned to becoming a professional, (joining the College of Paramedics) paramedicine, (not every paramedic wears green) Preparedness, (accepting lifelong learning not just passing the course) practice education, (receiving and later becoming a great supporter of students) placements (not just ambulances, but all aspects of patient care pathways) and preceptorship, settling into your new role and becoming fully autonomous and independent in practice.

Every journey starts with a first step. Maybe buying this book is yours, but soon you will want to plan ahead and take with you all you need for the entirety of the journey. The wisdom in this book is perfectly sound. Listen and reflect on the student's feedback, grasp the information proffered by the expert authors. Many of the contributors who have crafted exceptional chapters in this book and are at the very top of the profession and work with students daily, to help them, guide them, pick up them up and to care for students as they strive to become the very best next generation of paramedics into the 21st century.

My journey is nearly done and as I reflect and look back, I know who helped me the most to achieve all that I could be. They were inspirational leaders and managers, but at their heart they were educators. Why don't you aspire to be one very soon.

Bob Fellows FCPara
Head of Education
College of Paramedics
Visiting Professor University of Ulster

ACKNOWLEDGEMENTS

I dedicate this book specifically to people I have taught across the years. We have learned together and worked together and had fun while doing so. It is a pleasure to be in contact with many of you still and to call you colleagues and friends now, rather than students. Working in healthcare is a very demanding career, but one thing that is certain is that we make strong friendships and can rely on each other to 'be there'.

Tragically, this bond is sometimes not enough, and we have all unfortunately experienced loss of friends and colleagues who have either had their lives cut short by underlying disease or who have found life too overwhelming to find a way through the complexity and pain. There are several people who are in my mind as I write this, who are no longer with us and who we miss terribly. But they also make us smile when they come into our thoughts. We hold onto the positive memories of you all – thank you for being part of our lives.

THANK YOU

Thank you to the families of paramedics who have taken the time to be honest and open and who have responded to a request for their insight into the profession.

A huge thank you to Bénédicte Deutsch for reading the chapters and commenting from a paramedic's perspective.

Thank you to Graham Harris for reading some chapters and being my critical friend, as well as my fellow editor on several other textbooks.

HOW TO USE THIS BOOK

This book will provide you with a realistic view of the journey from student to paramedic. The information, comments, responses, case studies and reflection points offered will interest you, and may sometimes surprise you, but will leave you wanting to learn and investigate more. The intention is that this text will act as a valuable resource to guide you from the initial consideration of your journey and throughout that journey, culminating in the start of a successful career as a paramedic.

A variety of approaches have been taken in order to elicit useful and realistic information for the reader. The contributors include student paramedics, academics, paramedics and paramedic practice educators (PEds). These contributors come from higher education institutions, National Health Service Trusts covering many regions of England, the College of Paramedics (CoP) and the Health and Care Professions Council (HCPC). This text is inclusive and useful for students studying towards paramedic registration across all areas of England, and the book will also be of use beyond this, in the rest of the United Kingdom.

In all chapters, within each part of this text, the contributors have had the freedom to make specific comments relating to the subject being discussed. Throughout the text there are sections that offer comments/ responses to questions. The contributions are identified as follows:

📖   denotes comments/responses to questions from students

🚨   denotes responses to questions from paramedics and/or paramedic practice educator (PEd)

🎓   denotes responses to questions from academics

👪 family   denotes responses to questions from family members

The symbols will make the comments from the contributor easy to find and will enable readers to compare and contrast the views of each of them. Some of the comments are short, others have been summarised, and some are longer, with greater explanation. For visual aesthetic reasons quotation marks have been removed. The symbol for student comments has been used in some chapters, so it can be clearly seen that views have been voiced by many and not just one or two students. Some chapters are more heavily reliant on student comments than others, this was an intentional decision, to give students the opportunity to share their experiences and advice. Some of the comments/responses to questions may contradict each other; this is not surprising, considering the different roles and experiences the contributors will have had. Some comments/responses to questions may be quite controversial and may present a different reality than that expected or experienced by the reader.

The contributors have been asked to respond to specific questions, and you will be able to read the questions posed and the individual responses. In most chapters, the questions and responses have been collated from students in specific cohorts at various points in their academic studies and from various routes of academic study. Their comments represent a wide range of views, some conflicting, and as unique as each individual student, in order to provide the reader with the diversity of opinion based on experience.

The intention is that many of the comments will encourage you to think more deeply about aspects of your study and practice. This text will endeavour to present a realistic view within its chapters, and in some areas may challenge your assumptions and impressions, with regard to studying in a higher education environment and working in a clinical environment.

Throughout this text anonymity is maintained, names used are pseudonyms, and all experiences recalled and commented on have been adapted and are included for illustrative purposes only.

In addition, there are:

- case studies
- sections linked to each other, for easy cross-referencing
- reflection points
- references, suggested reading and actions at the end of the chapters.

It is hoped the reader will find this format engaging and useful.

INTRODUCTION

I want to thank all of the students, clinicians and academics who have worked with me across the years and have helped make this a 'go to' text. A special 'thank you' to students who have provided such positive feedback about the first edition to me personally; it really is appreciated. I would also like to thank all the people who have taken time to write reviews about this book; it is very reassuring to know that it is useful. You have all initiated the motivation within me to produce this second edition.

Embarking on a new journey, in the form of a different or new career move, could make a significant change to your life. Whatever your individual journey, your decision to want to become a paramedic is not one that can be taken lightly. This career may be something you have worked towards while at school or college. For others, you may be working for an ambulance trust or other healthcare provider and want to embark on a career as a paramedic. For some, it will be a total change of career direction.

In terms of your studies, this may mean:

- direct entry from school/college into higher education for a graduate-level course;
- taking the apprenticeship route, with some study in a higher education institution (HEI);
- exiting your job (after obtaining any additional qualifications that you may have needed) and starting an apprenticeship or HEI-based course;
- and for others it may be re-entry into higher education, after a previous degree in a different subject.

As can be seen from the list above, there are various routes to becoming a student paramedic, all of which bring richness and a variety of experiences into the workplace and classroom. This profession is not specifically one for young people or just for mature students – your success is entirely dependent on you as an individual: your personal qualities, attitudes, self-awareness and behaviours. All of these aspects will be explored in the various chapters of the book.

This text is the culmination of relevant experiences from students and professionals as they have reflected on their own journeys to becoming a paramedic. The text specifically includes the comments, thoughts and suggestions of students and colleagues from the practice and academic environment.

The contributors aim to bring you, the reader, some of their insights and experiences, in order that you can be as prepared as possible for your academic and professional journey towards your career as a paramedic. The cross-section of students (junior and senior), paramedics, paramedic practice educators (PEds) and academics making comments throughout the text represent a wide geographical area, variety of higher education institutes and NHS trusts. By adopting this inclusive approach, the text will be largely representative of the educational and clinical practice experiences of students across England. There are some variations across Scotland, Wales, and Northern and Southern Ireland in respect of the types of programmes offered (both higher education institutions and ambulance service in-house routes in some areas). These differences also encompass funding, and specific guidance should be sought from the region concerned.

This text is not specific to any particular National Health Service (NHS) acute or community trust, ambulance trust or higher education institution. As the text is not specific to any one geographical location, you should expect to undertake further research for yourself on the geographical areas that you are considering. Further research should be specific and focused on your chosen institution or institutions, and ambulance and acute/community NHS trusts.

This book **does not** address specific study skills, such as time management, writing at university level, note-taking, writing essays or managing revision. This is intentional, as to address such subjects (and more besides) in the detail required would require a book in itself. I strongly advise that you use the suggested reading to read a selection of the excellent study skills texts that are listed, to find a few that suit your learning style and needs. The reader should, therefore, supplement the information discussed in this text with more generic study skills texts.

The text has chapters which are situated within specific parts; this is in direct response to students' comments about their studies. Students' comments can be categorised in five areas, which form the five parts of the text:

1   Is this the right career for me?
2   Preparing to apply
3   Making the most of your academic study
4   Placement: preparing for it and making the most of it
5   Transition to registration

The chapters within each part have been carefully selected to reflect the specific issues related to being a student paramedic. The issues and subjects addressed in this text do not relate to any other subject area.

PART 1
Is this the right career for me?

1 THE REALITY OF THE ROLE OF A STUDENT PARAMEDIC

Jo Mildenhall

It is inescapable that the dramas on TV and films at the cinema often portray paramedics as rushing around in ambulances, blue lights flashing and screeching to a halt at the scene of a near-disaster and trauma on a regular basis. When not dealing with major trauma, they are often fictionally depicted as resuscitating patients who make an almost miraculous and instantaneous recovery. All in all, these paramedics are whizzing around, pants on the outside of their trousers, being the epitome of a super-hero.

Hmm. Thankfully, some 'on the wall' documentaries bring the role a little more down to earth and show the realities of the work. Sadly, if you thought the job was like the above, then I am sorry to disappoint you! Paramedicine is not all trauma and resuscitation. In fact, less than 4 per cent of all 999 calls are trauma related.

Much of the work is rather more routine and includes assessment and treatment of people with acute and chronic medical conditions, such as chest infections, asthma, epileptic seizures, and injuries including those sustained by elderly fallers, horse riders, and children. Certainly, one of the draws of the job is that no two shifts are the same. While as a paramedic you will see a lot of the above kinds of incidents, you will also be exposed to social and emotional situations. For example, people who are lonely and isolated, people at the end of life, or family who have been bereaved. You will see much vulnerability and social deprivation, and individuals who may live life in a completely different way to that which you've experienced. Call outs to those who use alcohol and/or drugs or other chemical stimulants are also a core part of our work.

Sometimes, these situations can be risky. Sometimes, we can face individuals experiencing heightened emotions or who have an altered state of consciousness which is affecting their behaviour. Sometimes, we can face violence and challenging situations – something discussed later in this book. Sometimes, situations can resonate with us, emotionally and psychologically – perhaps because the incident rings true of our own life experiences, or a patient reminds us of someone we are/were close to. Sometimes, we can see things that truly are horrific, and yet, in the face of such adversity, we remain calm, collected, and professional, to provide care and help to those who have been affected at the scene.

In this way, the job of a paramedic can be stressful. Providing care for individuals who are distressed, sometimes angry, unwell, or may be dying, is not easy. Added factors such as working shifts across different hours of the day and night, can be exciting but can also be extremely tiring and lower your tolerance and raise your stress levels.

One of the most important aspects of the role of being a paramedic is keeping yourself psychologically healthy and well. While resilience – dealing with and growing from adversity, will be covered in Chapter 18, this chapter will explore stress and psychological well-being, self-awareness, and preparing for what you'll see and deal with, as a paramedic.

Stress

So, what does stress actually mean? The Mental Health Foundation (2021) states that stress is 'the feeling of being overwhelmed or unable to cope with mental or emotional pressure'. This is particularly relevant to the ambulance sector where paramedics often work in time-critical situations, as already discussed. In pressured environments where there is a lot going on, lots to think about, and/or where we do not feel we have control over events, it's normal to feel a level of stress and/or anxiety. However, when these feelings become sustained and/or overwhelming, then the impact upon your body may start to affect your overall health.

Sources of stress vary for each person and stresses that may affect a student may well be different to those of an employed registered health professional (see Table 1.1). While over time your role may change, it is almost a given that at some point, you will experience a stress response. It may be one significant event or multiple smaller events that build up and cause stress.

Recognising stress in ourselves can be a challenge. Sometimes, it can creep up on you, at other times, it may be very obvious. Having self-awareness, that is, having awareness of your body's physical, emotional, behavioural, and psychological responses is vital for understanding how you respond to stressors. To have control over your thoughts, feelings, and behaviours, you need to be aware of them, giving yourself a chance to consider how you respond. The more self-aware you are, the more likely you will be able

Table 1.1 Potential sources of stress

Potential sources of stress

Student-related factors:

- Financial burdens/money management
- Work/life/study imbalance
- Tiredness from shift placements and university work
- Social relationships: friendship cliques, romantic partnerships, relationship breakdowns
- Exams, and Objective Structured Clinical Examinations (OSCEs: practical examinations)
- Poor/overcrowded housing
- Limited privacy/noisy environment
- Poor sleep schedule
- Transitioning to a new town/city
- Isolation and loneliness

Work-related factors:

- Work/life imbalance: rota and relief working versus days off
- Working long hours/late finishes
- Adapting to shift work: physical and mental tiredness
- Lack of available resources/support
- Preceptorship requirements
- Professional relationships
- Bureaucracy and admin
- Exposure to clinical/critical incidents
- Redeployment and/or retirement
- Working with less experienced/less clinically qualified staff
- Lack of teamwork
- Inefficient systems of work
- Organisational restructuring
- Managers who are perceived as unsupportive
- Little control over events at work
- Working in dangerous/risky settings
- Facing harassment/discrimination at work
- No opportunity for personal or professional growth
- Transitioning from being a student (third person on the vehicle) to being a newly qualified paramedic (NQP) making clinical decisions
- Having to manage and make decisions (without appropriate education/ training) for patients with complex medical histories, who may be better cared for by their GP, but cannot access the GP

Home-related/social life factors:

- Financial constraints/expenditures
- Getting used to living independently

(Continued)

Table 1.1 Continued

- Competing demands for time
- Family/friend relationships
- Shift work impacting social/family events
- Overwhelming responsibilities
- Periods of change/uncertainty
- Worrying about world events such as terrorism or war
- Bereavement/loss/divorce
- Moving house and/or housing issues
- Caring for elderly/vulnerable family members
- Traumatic event such as theft, rape, domestic violence, stalking
- Natural disaster or incidents affecting your community, including fire and flooding
- Managing/adjusting to long-term health conditions or experiencing ill health
- Life transitions: menopause, ageing, retirement, gender transition

to protect and maintain your well-being. Boxes 1.1, 1.2 and 1.3 may help you to assess your own self-awareness of stress and your own individual reaction/s.

These lists are not exhaustive, and you can probably think of your own responses that you experience.

In the short term, stress can be manageable, and even helpful in motivating us – for example, in preparing for and taking exams, or interviews. Feeling a little stress raises your adrenaline, heightens your awareness and reactions, and makes you ready for action. However, too much stress over a longer period of time – prolonged stress – is when we see problems arise.

Box 1.1 How you might feel when you are stressed

- Anxious
- Frustrated
- Afraid
- Angry
- Defensive
- Irritable
- Tearful
- Down, depressed, of low mood
- Up and down
- Isolated
- Loss of confidence/self-esteem

Box 1.2 How you might react physically to stress

- Tense, sore, achy muscles
- Headaches
- Indigestion/upset stomach
- Sweating/night sweats
- Heart racing/palpitations
- Hyperventilation
- Overtiredness/insomnia
- Unable to concentrate or focus
- Easily distracted
- Reduced memory

Box 1.3 Behaviour you might display when stressed

- Upset
- Increased use of cigarettes, alcohol or other drugs
- Pacing
- Indecisiveness
- Inflexibility with decisions
- Withdrawing from social situations/relationships
- Sexual problems
- Over- or under-eating
- Not taking an interest in usual activities – such as sports/ exercise

Being aware of the effects of stress also allows you to recognise indicators in your colleagues, patients, family, or friends. Working closely with colleagues offers a unique opportunity to identify any changes in each other's behaviours, personality, or emotional responses. This is an important informal strategy, and one that can be highly effective in enabling someone to reflect on how they are feeling, evaluate any issues, and make any changes to improve their psychological well-being, including accessing support.

Reflection: Points to consider

1   Thinking about your life so far, have you experienced any really stressful moments/situations?
2   Were these short term in nature?
3   How did you manage the situation/stressors?
4   Do you recognise the feelings, physical reactions or associated behaviours listed in Boxes 1.1–1.3? Can you add to the lists?
5   Have you ever experienced stress on a long-term basis?
6   How was this different?
7   Would you want to go through it again?
8   What coping strategies did you use? Did they help?

Burnout

Burnout is a term that has been frequently used, particularly during the COVID-19 pandemic. It refers to the long-term impact of stress, where a person feels no longer able to cope. Generally, people experiencing burnout feel emotionally and physically drained, are exhausted, and feel unable to keep up with the demands of life. They may feel like there is not enough time for things, they don't have the energy, they experience cynicism about their work or study, or they appear very negative about work or their working environment which may show as frustration, distrust, or hopelessness. They may be easily distracted, disengaged – and not wishing to engage, lack care and compassion, are critical of themself and others, and avoid work or study, or on the contrary, display behaviours of workaholism.

Early recognition of stress and seeking to rebalance well-being can counteract the development of burnout. But this can generally only be the case if you are self-aware enough to recognise there is a potential stress-related problem. Low mood associated with burnout may lead to depression and for some, can lead to suicidal thinking as life may not seem worth living.

If you notice these descriptions in yourself, it's really important to talk to others about how you're feeling. Talk to your GP, trusted family or friends and/or work colleagues, your manager, and reach for more specific support from professional agencies (see the list towards the end of this chapter).

Moral distress and moral injury

Without going into the technicalities, moral distress and moral injury are two terms that have entered into the world of paramedicine following the start of the COVID-19 pandemic, when paramedics were forced to make tough decisions around patient care and treatment that would otherwise be considered inconceivable and outside of normal practice. Subsequently, the impact on practitioners has included experiencing guilt, frustration, anger and shame at not being able to provide the level of care that a patient may have needed, whether that be due to insufficient resources, lack of equipment and personal protective equipment (PPE), preventing families from being with their loved ones who were dying or critically unwell, or following guidance which required patients to stay at home even though they may have been seriously ill.

While these terms have been used within other professional circles for some time, in the healthcare environment, moral distress is, as noted above, associated with the feelings of emotional unease or distress that occur when a practitioner is unable to provide the care or treatment that they know a patient needs but are prevented from doing so, and prevented from doing what they believe is right. Moral injury, on the other hand, goes much deeper. This is a form of intense and prolonged psychological harm where our concepts of morality (things that are right and wrong) and beliefs are completely disrupted. This then impacts our sense of self, our view of others and the world. This can lead to distrust, feelings of betrayal or abandonment, and can negatively affect our mental health in the longer term (British Medical Association 2021).

In dealing with moral distress or moral injury, it is important to recognise that often this will be in response to a situation that has required you to make decisions in the face of ethical dilemmas. No matter which decisions you have made, there is a chance that this could lead to feelings of guilt about it and/or distress at wondering if you have done something wrong or if a different decision would have prompted a more favourable out-come. This is generally, in the short term, a natural response. Consider talking with colleagues or others in the healthcare team about your con-cerns and worries, or utilise counselling as a means of having a safe space to talk things through. Some ambulance and healthcare trusts also use Schwartz Rounds or Action Learning Sets, where staff can come together to speak in confidence about the ethical challenges and emotional aspects of an incident or event that has been experienced in the workplace.

Post-traumatic stress

You may have read about, or watched on TV, reports which highlight the numbers of paramedics and ambulance staff being affected by post-traumatic stress, much in the way that military personnel have. Currently, research literature from across the globe indicates that approximately 11 per cent of ambulance personnel experience post-traumatic stress symptoms (Petrie et al. 2018). While we could debate whether or not more (or less) are affected is a discussion for another day. However, what the research does indicate is that generally, the prevalence of post-traumatic response symptoms in ambulance staff is higher than for the general population. But – and this is an important but – this research suggests that around 89 per cent of ambulance staff do not develop post-traumatic symptomology (and may in fact experience post-traumatic growth).

Post-traumatic stress is a heightened anxiety-fear response following exposure to adverse experiences, whether witnessed first hand, or from hearing or observing the traumatic situation through others who witnessed it, including from individuals' narratives, stories published in the media, video footage of an incident, and so on.

After a truly distressing incident, it is a perfectly normal human response to feel affected by it (see Case study 1.1). It is normal to think about it, to run the incident through in your mind to try to make sense of it, or perhaps, in contrast, to try to shut it out of your mind completely and avoid thinking about it. In the short term, these responses are completely normal. At this stage, one of the best mediators to help with this response is to talk with trusted others.

If a person experiences heightened levels of anxiety, as well as some other indicators shown in Box 1.4 for a month or more, then it is possible that they may trigger the diagnosis of post-traumatic stress disorder, which may be determined by their doctor, a psychologist or psychiatrist.

Post-traumatic growth

While paramedics and ambulance staff may be deeply affected by an incident, this does not always mean that they will experience difficulties. Research shows that following an adverse event, some people experience positive growth, meaning that they may have a greater appreciation of life and their relationships with others. They may also find that they develop

Box 1.4 Post-traumatic stress response presentations

- Having memories of the event that are recurrent, intrusive, and distressing
- Disrupted sleep and nightmares
- Feeling on edge and anxious
- Heightened physical, mental, and emotional reactions to reminders of the event
- Avoiding the location where the incident happened, and avoiding people or activities that act as reminders of the event
- Avoiding thinking about, or talking about, the event or similar events
- Hiding away parts of the body that were injured or exposed
- Feeling low and experiencing negative thoughts about yourself
- Feeling hopeless about the future
- Loss of trust in others which may lead to difficulty with maintaining close relationships or having negative thoughts about others
- Feeling numb – not knowing how you feel, or like 'there is nothing there' in terms of your feelings
- Drinking excessive alcohol, using drugs, over- or under-eating, driving recklessly, engaging in risky behaviours that are out of character
- Difficulty concentrating and remembering things
- Feeling completely overwhelmed
- Finding that you're easily startled or frightened
- Feeling that you're always on the look-out, unable to relax, or feel safe

personal strength and insight into themselves, enhanced compassion, and they may experience spiritual change.

Developing psychological ill-health while in practice

Life is unpredictable and adverse events happen. Many people, within the course of their lifetime will experience psychological ill health, for example, developing depression due to the end of a relationship, or becoming psychologically unwell due to a bereavement or physical condition, such as postnatal depression, or from burnout, stress, or post-traumatic stress as mentioned above. Developing psychological ill health while in the role of a student or qualified paramedic does not mean that your career is over. However, at times like this, it can sometimes help to take time out, even if only for a short period to give yourself time to breathe and become well. Universities and employers are used to supporting students/employees who find themselves facing life challenges, and/or developing symptoms of psychological distress and/or illness. Later in this chapter, we will talk further about the help and support available for student paramedics and qualified paramedics.

Prior psychological health and neurodivergent conditions

Having a diagnosed mental health condition is unlikely to stop you from taking up a position as a paramedic. Indeed, many paramedics do have lived experience of depression, anxiety, obsessive compulsive disorder, as well as neurodivergent conditions including autism, dyslexia, and dyspraxia. To join the ambulance service or another healthcare provider, you (as a potential employee) are required to have an assessment with the occupational health department who will discuss aspects of the work with you and how you may cope with this. They may require a report from your GP, psychiatrist, and/or psychologist to gain further understanding of any treatment you are receiving. This may also include requesting information from the DVLA if your condition has impacted your driving, or an education report if you have a specific learning disability. See Case study 1.1 for a student's experience.

CASE STUDY 1.1

I am writing this as a registered paramedic, but reflecting on my experiences as a student paramedic. Being dyslexic as a student paramedic comes with a range of challenges. One main difficulty was being asked in practice, what support I wanted. I wanted people to give me ideas and options of support instead of asking me and working this out as I progressed. Some staff have a poor understanding of dyslexia. At university, things were okay, my friends had an understanding and there was a range of support (dyslexia support tutor, personal tutor, student union). Although I wished I had approached the student union earlier, they were really helpful and provided materials/ workshops for practice staff, so they had more insight into dyslexia.

Things in practice that helped me were: sitting in silence when I did my paper work; researching handover formulas; writing acronyms to help me formulate my handover; writing my paperwork in the same way each time; ensuring staff understood that sometimes it takes me longer to write, especially when I am tired; having cues for different questions when I become tired; and asking others to make notes for me.

Being dyslexic strengthens many aspects of paramedic practice, such as thinking outside the box and scene management. People often only focus on the challenges. Celebrating differences puts a focus on the benefits of being dyslexic.

It is important that you have the insight into your own condition(s) to know when you may need to seek help. Hopefully, this book will help you to decide whether the role is one which will be suited to you, whether you feel realistically that you would be able to care for patients who may be critically unwell, whether you can keep your own psychological well-being in check alongside working demanding shift patterns. As the student comment below demonstrates, it is really important to consider such issues before applying. Be realistic and honest with yourself. Are you in *the best shape* possible (mentally and physically) to be able to cope with both the academic and clinical demands of the programme.

Student paramedic comment: Placement can be stressful and you need to be in the right headspace yourself in order to care and look after others. This is something I have really struggled with.

Preparing for the role and looking after your well-being

So, you're all set and signed up for your paramedic degree, and it's time to go out on your ambulance service placement. You're excited and positive about finally getting out to experience the job that you're being educated for, but know that you'll need to be prepared to go into unknown or unpredictable situations. So, how do you do this, and what do you need to know in terms of looking after your well-being?

The most important source of information and support will come from those whom you meet who are doing the work, especially your practice educator/facilitator, clinical mentor, or link-lecturer. They will be able to provide you with a wealth of information about how to deal with different situations in practice, including where to find help and support, dealing with patients with challenging behaviour, and coping with shift working and nights. Being informed can help to alleviate any anxieties or worries and give you confidence and insight into coping strategies that may be useful.

Helpful and positive coping techniques include physical activities such as running, swimming, or team sports, mindfulness meditation, hobbies that you enjoy, or just simply getting out into the fresh air (Mental Health Foundation 2022). There is a significant amount of research that indicates the positive benefits of talking with those that you trust and feel comfortable with. If you would prefer to talk with someone you don't know, details of resources and professional agencies that can help can be found towards the end of this chapter.

To develop self-awareness and to identify if your psychological well-being is affected, the mental health continuum (AACE 2022) is an easy-to-use ambulance-specific tool that also gives pointers on supportive ways that can help you to feel well. Some university courses include specifically focused mental health awareness short courses as part of their undergraduate courses. Ones to look out for are Mental Health First Aid or MIND blue light courses.

Physically, the role of paramedic is a demanding one. I'm not going to lie, it can be really, really difficult to keep eating well when on shift – especially at 3am on a night shift when you have only just got your break and are starving hungry. It can be all too tempting to eat a takeaway or fill up on sweets and crisps. Obviously in moderation, this is unlikely to prove too much of an issue, but on a regular basis, this is likely to become problematic. It can include effects such as stomach issues, weight gain, cardiovascular disease, headaches, tiredness, and metabolic issues from sugar highs and lows, and caffeine overload. Keeping hydrated may seem a really basic thing to state, but it is all too common that ambulance staff moderate their fluid intake so that they do not get caught short in needing the toilet, given it could be a few hours before you are able to access facilities. A top tip is to take at least one flask out with you on shift, and sip water or such like regularly, but avoid an excess of caffeine, as some student comments in Box 1.5 illustrate.

Box 1.5 Is there anything you wish you had known or considered before starting the programme?

📖 It feels quite intense and overwhelming to start with and can take a while to adjust.

📖 Being a paramedic has to be something you REALLY want, otherwise you will find it too hard and distressing.

📖 I feel that having some healthcare experience would have helped me. It is quite a lot to take on board; having had some patient contact beforehand would have improved my confidence just talking to people.

📖 How mentally and physically exhausted I would be.

📖 I am worried about qualifying. I have needed all the university support mechanisms to keep mentally well; will I have those available to me from my employer?

📖 I wish I had learned to cook before going to university. I spent Year 1 eating rubbish while on shift which affected my weight, my skin and my opinion of myself.

📖 Cook and freeze healthy food in bulk, so you can take it with you or eat it when you wake up, otherwise you will be tempted with the easy, fattening option of takeaways. Get used to making things that do not need cooking, in case you are off base for the whole shift.

📖 Water is so important; being slightly dehydrated can make you feel awful.

📖 I feel that having a job where you have to communicate and possibly touch, move or handle other people would have helped me not feel so awkward on my shifts early in the programme.

📖 Practise speaking to people of all ages, it is your main skill and fundamental to everything that you do.

📖 I wish I had expected, and known about, the emotional and physical toll it has taken on me.

Psychological well-being support for student paramedics – who can you talk to, and what if it all becomes too much?

In the sixth edition of the Paramedic pre-registration curriculum, due for publication (by the College of Paramedics) in 2023, psychological well-being education will be embedded with the paramedic curriculum. Therefore, forthcoming students will have greater access to information and associated support and coping strategies.

If you find that you are struggling while on placement or at university, the most important thing is to realise that you're not alone and that you don't have to struggle. Universities have a wealth of support services available for students including counselling, financial advice, practice educator (PEd), and academic support. While this is generic to cater for all, your paramedic sciences lecturing team will be able to give more specific ambulance-orientated advice. Some paramedic programmes offer peer support by those in academic Years 2 and 3. This is a great way to chat through worries with someone who likely understands the pressures and demands of study within your particular programme. Alternatively, although not available in all institutions, informal social networks such as reflective groups, clinical supervision groups, or peer-review groups allow students to meet to chat through their practice experiences in confidence.

Universities may also have a Student Paramedic Society which encourages interaction between students of different years and this helps to promote learning and wider networking with students from other universities/areas of the UK. These groups not only give an outlet to talk through how you are feeling, but can also enhance your confidence and learning about a particular area of practice, such as obstetrics or paediatrics, and in this way may reduce stress and worries, as you build greater knowledge and incidents begin to feel less intimidating or anxiety provoking.

When undertaking your placement within the ambulance service, you may be eligible to access support services that employees are entitled to, again an important question to ask. This includes counselling and occupational health. Some services also provide less formal support such as trauma risk management or peer support, which can be helpful to access, particularly after attending a difficult incident. Chatting to your mentor, manager, or other ambulance colleagues is also recommended, as not only can they provide local support, but they will also know what formal services are available to you in your area, as Case study 1.2 demonstrates.

CASE STUDY 1.2

During my first year, I was on a night shift. Nearing the last hour of our shift, we got called to an area that was known locally to be a suicide 'hotspot'. When we arrived, a police officer came and told us what was going on. A young girl, the same age as me, had driven 40 minutes from her home and got out of her car. Something about this attracted the attention of a passer-by, who got out of their car to see if she was okay. The girl ran off and jumped off the edge of the cliff. By the time we arrived, coastguards were searching, helicopters searching the sea with floodlights, other ambulance crews were on their way. We had all our equipment, but were just waiting. We were told they had found her and she was to be airlifted to the top of the cliff. We were anxious but ready but then we were 'stood down' as the girl had died. So we packed everything away, left the scene, went back to base, had a chat on the way and we went home after our shift.

During the call, I experienced the anxiety of potentially treating her, then not, which was stressful. Immediately afterwards, I am not sure how I felt. I was obviously sad, but didn't feel that affected. With hindsight, I think I was maybe a bit numb as I hadn't fully processed what had happened. When I woke up it was the first thing on my mind. I received an email from the chaplain service of the ambulance trust, inviting me to talk if I wanted. I declined – I had not even seen the young girl. At home I was struggling to focus on anything, distract myself effectively, so I went for a walk. I ended up crying unexpectedly, which really surprised me. This then sent me into a bit of a tailspin thinking 'How will I cope with actual traumatic scenes, if this is my response now. I didn't even see her   can I do this job?'

Something that one of the other crew said just kept playing in my mind. They commented on how neatly she had parked her car and said 'She probably sat for a good while thinking about what she was about to do.' Now, I can see that I was very deeply saddened that she would take the time to consider her life and still see death as her best option. My mum phoned me later that day and seemed to know something was up. I hadn't intended to tell her what was happening as I didn't want to worry her or seem like I wasn't coping with the job.

But I ended up telling her that I'd been to a call last night with a girl a similar age to me who had taken her own life. My mum didn't hear all the details, but actually sharing with her that I wasn't doing too well really helped me. She validated my feelings and reiterated that this will be a difficult job and I will come across things that impact me, so it is important to process them in a healthy way rather than try to hold it all in.

My mentor checked in with me too, which I really appreciated, but at that point I did not want to appear weak or incompetent. On our next shift they broached the subject again and I was more honest and said it had affected me. They were really supportive and shared their own experiences which completely changed my perspective about not wanting to talk. It was nice to know you can be an incredible paramedic, but things will get to you, and often it's not what or how you will expect them to get to you.

I wish I had realised there is no shame in sharing what's going on in your head; talking it through helped me so much. Especially, with my mentor, as they had been there and had the understanding that other people can't. I was so focused on proving to myself (and others) I could cope, that I neglected what was going on, which if it had continued would have been no benefit to me or my future patients.

Other helpful sources of support include:

- The Ambulance Staff Charity (TASC) provides independent confidential mental health support and counselling for students from their second year onwards. https://www.theasc.org.uk
- The national body, the College of Paramedics, provides professional advice and guidance for students as well as registered members. https://collegeofparamedics.co.uk
- Mind Blue Light Together has a dedicated web-hub for coping with student life as a trainee paramedic. https://bluelighttogether.org.uk/ambulance/coping-with-student-life-for-trainee-paramedics/
- Shout UK – a free, 24-hour text service for emergency services' workers. Text 'BLUELIGHT' to 85258. https://giveusashout.org/get-help/bluelight/

If you find yourself in crisis and things have become overwhelming and too much, it is really wise to talk to someone, whether this is a loved one, friend, fellow student, tutor, ambulance colleague, lecturer, manager, or someone you do not know, perhaps via a support line. As the comments below and in Box 1.6 demonstrate, you are not on your own; people are there to help you or to signpost you to expert help, should you need it; but if you do not talk to them, how can they help you?

> **Student paramedic comment:** I think we all had a wobble at one time or another during our programme, wondering if we could, or wanted to do this job. I think this is pretty natural at times, but if it is a constant feeling, it will be stressful. We had a few people who were self-aware enough and brave enough to say this career wasn't for them and left to do something else. I say brave, as they made the right choice, some of my other colleagues were really affected by the job and have suffered as a result. No programme of study is worth being unhappy for. What is going to happen when you are doing the job full time, with no breaks for university time? It will be worse, and it is unlikely to get better.

> **Box 1.6 Do you have any suggestions about sources of support?**
>
> 📖 Be honest with your practice educator (PEd) about any struggles or any extreme emotions you may be experiencing; they were students once too.
>
> 📖 It's fine to ask for support if you are struggling. This might be the first time you have seen certain things – it can be scary. Don't be afraid to talk to your PEd, university support staff, lecturers, other people at the ambulance station; they see this sort of stuff all the time and will know how to help you or where to get help. Depending on the situation, family and friends may be able to listen and help, but sometimes you feel you don't want to burden them and make them worry – this is a personal decision. But whoever you choose: Keep Talking.

Summary

Being a paramedic has many, many positives, and can lead to a fulfilling, rewarding, and meaningful career of meeting and treating a diversity of patients, injuries, and illnesses in a variety of locations. It can be deeply satisfying to know that you have provided care and made a difference to another human being. Sometimes, however, the role of caring for others can be personally challenging, psychologically and physically. Therefore, it's right to weigh up and consider how you may deal with this and if this career is the right choice for you.

At some points in life things may feel too much; this affects our psychological health and we may need help ourselves. This is part of our humanness. You are not alone in this, and you certainly won't be the first to be feeling this way. Academic and placement staff would rather that students share their concerns around aspects of the programme and life in practice that are difficult, than to have students who bottle things up and try to keep going, and in doing so neglect their own needs and care.

References

Association of Ambulance Chief Executives (2022) *Mental Health Continuum*. Available at: https://aace.org.uk/mental-health-continuum/ (accessed 10 May 2022).

British Medical Association (2021) *Moral Distress and Moral Injury: Recognising and Tackling It for UK Doctors*. Available at: https://www.bma.org.uk/media/4209/bma-moral-distress-injury-survey-report-june-2021.pdf (accessed 18 October 2022).

Bryant, R.A., Calvo, R.A., Deady, M. et al. (2018) Prevalence of PTSD and Common Mental Disorders Among Ambulance Personnel: A Systematic Review and Meta-Analysis, *Social Psychiatry & Psychiatric Epidemiology*, 53: 9, 879–909.

Mental Health First Aid website. Available at: https://mhfaengland.org/

Mental Health Foundation (2021) *Stress*. Available at: https://www.mental-health.org.uk/a-to-z/s/stress#:~:text=Stress%20is%20the%20feeling%20of,with%20mental%20or%20emotional%20pressure (accessed 20 April 2022).

Mental Health Foundation (2022). *Physical Health and Mental Health.* Available at: https://www.mentalhealth.org.uk/a-to-z/p/physical-health-and-mental-health (accessed 10 May 2022).

Some useful resources and professional agencies:

No Panic (0844 967 4848) run a helpline between 10am and 10pm every day of the year for support with managing anxiety.

Samaritans (116123) are available 24/7 and offer a safe space for anyone who is having a difficult time.

SANEline (0300 304 7000) are available from 4.30pm–10.30pm. SANEline is a national mental health helpline to anyone affected by mental illness, including friends and carers.

The Mix (text THEMIX to 85258) offer a crisis messenger text service which is available 24/7 for all under 25s. They offer support with urgent issues such as suicidal thoughts, abuse or assault, self-harm, bullying or a relationship breakdown. They also have a helpline available daily to under 25s between 4pm–11pm which can be accessed on 0808 808 4994.

Togetherall is an anonymous community where members can support each other. Access 24 hours a day, 365 days a year. Trained professionals available 24/7 to keep the community safe.

PART 2
Preparing to apply

2 CONSIDERATIONS BEFORE APPLYING

Amanda Blaber

- Students when in ambulance clinical environments will be supported by Registered Paramedics who have undertaken additional education in order to become Practice Educators (PEds). PEds support, coach, supervise and assess student paramedics. You will see this abbreviation throughout the text.
- When in wider NHS clinical placements (non ambulance environments) you will supported by other health care professionals (e.g. Nurses, Midwives, Physiotherapists) who commonly use the term 'Mentor' to describe Registered staff who have undertaken additional education in order to supervise, support, coach and assess a variety of healthcare students.
- Paramedics who have recently completed their educational programme of study are referred to as Newly Qualified Paramedics (NQPs). NQPs will undergo a period of 'preceptorship' once they are employed by a healthcare Trust. This is referred to as Foundation Preceptorship.

A note about terminology

Some institutions use the word *programme* to explain the overall subject, other institutions use the word *course*. For example, the study of paramedic science may be called a programme or course. For ease of reading, the study of student paramedic will be referred to as a programme. The programme will be made up of building blocks that may be called modules, units or courses. This can be confusing. Our tip would be to make sure you understand the terminology, so you will understand how your programme of study will progress.

Some basics you need to be aware of

The title *paramedic* is a legally protected title; only professionals registered with the governing body, the Health and Care Professions Council (HCPC 2023), are able to use the title of paramedic.

All higher education programmes that educate students to become paramedics have been through a stringent process of approval with the HCPC and adhere to their educational regulations and standards. Some higher education institutions (HEIs) have also obtained endorsement from the College of Paramedics (CoP), as the professional body for paramedics, and this will usually be visible in the institution's information about their paramedic programme.

All student paramedics are required to adhere to the *Guidance on Conduct Performance and Ethics for Students* (HCPC 2016a) throughout their period of study. Students need, as a requirement for public safety and protection, to be checked by the Disclosure and Barring Service (DBS). Instruction on the process will be provided by your university. This process identifies any criminal convictions and for some applicants will mean their application cannot proceed. A criminal conviction does not automatically preclude a candidate from applying to study for a paramedic qualification. However, it should be disclosed (as per statutory requirements) to the HEI which may discuss it with the partner placement provider(s) and make a decision on whether you would be suitable, depending on local policies. The candidate will also be screened by occupational health, in line with current Department of Health guidance. This will be organised by your university and/or your ambulance trust, if your programme of study involves employment by the ambulance service.

If successful in both academic and practical aspects of their studies, the student will exit the institution with the award and eligibility to apply for registration as a paramedic. Once registered, the paramedic must adhere to their employer's policies and procedures and demonstrate competence in the HCPC Standards of Proficiency for Paramedics (HCPC 2023) and abide by the HCPC Standards of Conduct, Performance and Ethics (HCPC 2016b).

All healthcare roles are 'front facing' and demand interaction with people and their families. For this reason, one of the most important personal attributes, if not **the** most important, is the ability to communicate effectively.

The importance of communication

The ability to communicate effectively goes far beyond just talking to people. There is a need to consider non-verbal communication, including your own positioning. For example, are you standing over the person, or do you need to kneel down to their level/height? The therapeutic use of touch may be appropriate in certain situations. The healthcare professional needs to be culturally aware and mindful of cultural communication differences. Communication is key to the overall role and success in that role. It is really worth undertaking some wider reading around the subject of communication (see suggested reading at the end of this chapter). See Box 2.1 to see what students feel about communication skills.

𝒞 Refer to Chapter 13 for more on caring for patients and their families.

Communication is essential and is one of the six Cs rolled out by the NHS in December 2012 as part of the Compassion in Practice national nursing strategy (now widely known and used). Communication was consistently discussed in the government's response to the Francis Report (Department of Health 2013b) as requiring improvement, and should hold a central role in any education provided to healthcare professionals. It remains a central theme and effective communication between patients and healthcare staff is further highlighted in the NHS England Report (2021). As a vital and ongoing area that will always benefit from improvement, communication

---

Box 2.1 Students' views on communication skills

📖 I did have some experience talking to people, but I could have done with more.

📖 Dialogue is the single most important part of the paramedic's role, not 'cool' skills. Make sure you are comfortable talking to strangers.

📖 I wish I had some medical experience or experience working with patients before I started, to help develop my communication skills.

📖 Get as much experience in 'people-facing' roles as possible. Any experience is good experience.

📖 As a mature student, I feel communication is one of my strong points because I have some life experience.

📖 Build up your social confidence by talking to people of all ages.

📖 As a first-year student you should focus on communication skills. This is the foundation of your patient care and a key skill throughout your career. Good communication skills will help you talk to patients about your clinical findings and will help you to organise onward care with other healthcare staff. Additionally, great communication skills can really put a patient at their ease – this should not be underestimated.

skills will be discussed as part of your studies, but it is worth noting these skills generally take time to develop, hone and practise. A caring nature cannot be taught. Of course, patients are best placed to distinguish between a healthcare professional that cares and one that does not. Many programmes will work with patients and carers in the teaching and assessment of students in order to help students develop communication skills in a safe environment.

The NHS is under constant scrutiny from politicians and the media. Since 2010 attention has been focused on issues with the quality of care and the professionals who provide the care (Department of Health 2013a, 2013b). While the cases highlighted within the media spotlight were predominantly hospital-based, the changes and focus for all NHS trusts highlighted in the Francis Report (Department of Health 2013a) equally apply to NHS ambulance trusts and employees. This level of scrutiny is ongoing and is something about which you need to be aware. If you keep abreast of local and national news, there is not a week that goes by where the health service is not in the news and, more often than not, the issues are around communication and/or quality of care. Communication is at the heart of the NHS and is a crucial element of patient care. Gaining experience in an environment where you need to communicate with people is, therefore, extremely valuable.

& Refer to Chapter 13 for current issues in healthcare and more information on the six Cs.

Gaining 'appropriate' experience

Appropriate is a term that students report is widely used by staff at HEIs. It is an ambiguous term, and academics use the term in different ways. Box 2.2 presents some interpretations of the term.

What is 'appropriate' experience?

The term *appropriate* can encompass many experiences. One of the most important skills to acquire through experience is being able to communicate with a stranger. It is possible to improve your communication skills, and indeed it will be essential to become more aware of the ways in which you can do this. Having experience of talking and establishing a rapport with strangers is a great starting point.

Box 2.2 Interpretations of the word 'appropriate', in respect of gaining appropriate experience

🎓 **Academic response:** In academic terms and particularly when talking about prior 'appropriate' experience, this is taken to mean 'suitable'. Just because your prior experience may not be of a medical nature, that does not mean it is not appropriate and will not be valuable to your role as a paramedic. Students who have some experience of life tend to fare better in caring and health professions. In this context, then, the life experience of the student would be deemed appropriate if this can be communicated in an application form or at interview. The important thing is that you can recognise how the knowledge, skills and attributes that you have developed through prior experience can be transferable to the role of paramedic.

🚨 **Paramedic educator (PEd) response:** The term 'appropriate', particularly in placement, is often used in the context of behaviour. Ask yourself: Is something suitable in the circumstances? This can apply to any number of things from humour, dress, the way in which you communicate with your patients or how you behave towards your colleagues.

🚨 **Paramedic educator (PEd) response:** The term 'appropriate' refers to transferable and learned behaviours, actions, attitudes and knowledge acquired from healthcare environments, where patient, relative, and staff interactions occur.

📖 **Student paramedic response:** 'Appropriate' means having or doing something which brings a positive outcome or advantage to you or a situation.

🚨 **Paramedic educator (PEd) response:** 'Appropriate' is being able to adapt to the situation and change attitude depending on what the patient is expecting and how they are responding to the interaction.

Any participative role where you communicate with strangers on a regular basis will be valuable. This could include working in a shop, volunteer work, or working with vulnerable members of the community on a voluntary/paid basis, such as at a residential care home. There are many more, as can be seen by the student comment below.

Student paramedic comment: Obviously paramedic practice involves caring for people in a pre-hospital setting . . . however, so much of this involves non-clinical aspects such as communication, empathy, listening skills and decision-making. Though I gained some experience of basic healthcare working with disabled pupils, in my previous job as a special needs teaching assistant, I learned just as much about effective communication, persuasiveness and conflict resolution through working with the able-bodied children who were also pupils at the school.

Appropriate experience is not just knowing how to put someone's arm in a sling, it's as much about learning how to listen, talk, reassure and bring calm to people . . . and you don't need to get a Saturday job in a hospital to develop these things, you can develop your 'people skills' just as much working in a retail environment as in a clinical one.

The practical skills that a paramedic needs to possess will be taught to you throughout your programme. In many respects, this is the easy part; the more complex part is most definitely fine-tuning and excelling at communication in all its forms (see the suggested reading at the end of this chapter).

ℰ Refer to Chapters 8 and 9 for more information on the importance of communication skills.

What sorts of things can be classified as 'appropriate' experience?

The simple answer to this question is anything that involves you demonstrating effective communication with people. This may be achieved in the following ways:

Volunteering

This can take many forms, but try to focus on any volunteering opportunity where you mix with people and peers. If you can access volunteering that is focused in a public service environment it would be more relevant to your chosen career, such as hospitals, social care and schools. This will obviously involve talking to people across the lifespan, which will be beneficial, as paramedics care for people before birth and through to old age-related death.

Building up a regular programme of volunteering will help you to demonstrate your reliability, and your commitment to your volunteering opportunities.

Work experience

Some of you will have the opportunity to undertake work experience as part of the course/qualification you are studying. This may mean that you do not have much choice about what or where your work experience will be. It is usually the case that educational facilities such as schools and colleges identify appropriate places for work experience to be undertaken according to the course or subjects being studied. Again, your attendance and reliability are important transferable skills. See the suggested reading list at the end of this chapter for the NHS web address relating to work experience.

Paid work

Paid employment and your attendance/sickness record demonstrates reliability (or lack of it). Any paid job is good experience, even if it is a weekend or evening job. A job in social care or healthcare will, of course, mean you have direct communication with clients and/or patients and the opportunity to learn and hone a variety of communication skills. But it is important to note that this is not the only place where communication skills are central to the job. Any job that is customer facing (for example, shopwork or hospitality) will enable you to develop your communication skills accordingly.

Transferable skills

At university open days, lecturers and paramedic lecturer practitioners/ associate lecturers are often asked what experience candidates need before applying. This is not an easy question to answer and to some extent is subjective. Each candidate is unique and, as such, will have varied experiences. The easiest way to answer this question is to think about *transferable skills*. What attributes, skills and personality traits do you possess that you think will be required for your chosen career? (See the reflection points below.) While some candidates will have direct experience with patients and providing patient care, others may not, and this is not necessarily a negative; for example, see the student comments in Box 2.3. Think about the career you are considering. It is fundamentally about communicating with, and caring for, people of all ages. So if you have any experience working with people (as an employee or on a voluntary basis), it could be considered appropriate.

It is also important that you consider your own personal qualities and compare these to those you believe a paramedic should possess. Self-awareness is also an important part of being able to help others. Being 'in tune' with yourself may enable you to be more astute and responsive to others' needs.

Reflection: Points to consider

- Clarify for yourself what you think the role of a paramedic is. Make a list of your answers.
- What personal attributes would you say are valuable?
- Think about any voluntary or paid work you have done. What personal attributes are transferable to the paramedic role as you described it above?

Why is gaining experience important?

Generally, patients do not call for ambulance assistance lightly; it is a conscious decision that is for many patients a last resort. Many patients will be frightened, anxious and unwell. Your ability to communicate effectively with them will help to put them at their ease, reduce their anxiety, instil confidence in your ability to help them, and make their overall experience as positive as possible (Street 2019). But handling patients badly can have long-lasting consequences for patients and their carers.

Shouldn't I be getting experience with the ambulance service?

Due to insurance, health and safety issues and ambulance trust policy, it is sometimes difficult to obtain experience observing on ambulance vehicles. But although you may not be able to gain prior experience, it may benefit you to speak to people who are paramedics, by asking them about their study and how they progressed to the role of paramedic. Ask what they do during the course of a shift: this should provide a realistic picture (and more realistic than the media portrays). Find out if your region employs paramedics in areas other than the ambulance service. You may be able to observe their working practices and discuss with them how this differs from the role of the paramedic working for an ambulance service.

Television documentaries usually focus on the ambulance service paramedic and are heavily edited, as their role is primarily to entertain the viewer. What you will see in documentaries are snippets of care episodes that are usually not realistic in terms of the amount of time you spend with patients; they mostly include footage of dramatic patient interactions/incidents and are not a true reflection of what happens during the course of a shift. Speak to student paramedics and paramedic lecturers when you visit university open events. Visit the College of Paramedics website, and read the section about ambulance trusts, and the frequently asked questions. You may also find the reading list at the end of this chapter useful.

Doing this research yourself should help you prepare for the programme and also be ready with questions that are focused and specific to the university you wish to apply to.

Is there competition for a place to study for a paramedic qualification?

The short answer to this question is yes. Competition is fierce, but there are many more HEIs commissioned to run paramedic programmes now than there were a few years ago. However, healthcare courses generally are extremely popular since the COVID-19 pandemic, but this may change over time.

Box 2.3 Advice for prospective candidates on how they can 'prepare' before applying for an academic programme of study

📖 I wish I had spent more time in a healthcare role before starting this programme. There is no rush and it may have made my grades better and my clinical care better, making the whole experience less stressful and more enjoyable.

📖 Try to understand the job role. There are many rewarding jobs in the ambulance service (and healthcare generally) that do not require a university qualification.

📖 Get physically fit and stay fit. Learn how to cook the basics of healthy food; shifts are tough and you cannot eat fast food and take-aways all the time.

📖 Make sure you can take care of yourself (washing, ironing, cook-ing). This will make it easier to manage university demands and placement shifts. Make sure you practise time management – it is a vital skill.

📖 Make sure you take care of yourself mentally and physically; you will need to do this for the entire duration of the programme.

📖 Don't come to this thinking it is like any other academic pro-gramme. You just can't scrape by, as it is your patients' best inter-ests at stake. The things you see and conversations you have will make you grow up quite a lot. This is not necessarily a bad thing for your career, but it may mean you have less in common with your friends who are doing other things – they will have different priorities to you.

🚨 **Newly-qualified paramedic response:** Spend time before and during university getting the most experience you can. Work in a nursing home or for a care agency, understand why these roles are so difficult and why no-one seems to ever know what's really going on. Once you have worked in such an environment you will under-stand and it won't cause you the frustration that it will do having never worked in this area of care.

Student paramedic comment: Our programme leader told us that four other people were interviewed for my place. I had been given the opportunity. We were told to 'look after our place' as it had already been hard won. This really motivated me to do my best, I didn't want to squander the place that someone else didn't get the chance to have.

Popularity

The role of paramedic is very popular as a choice for career. It is a dynamic, multi-functional role within the NHS and one which can be developed into a career path for paramedics much more so now than ever before. The career choices for individuals once registered as a paramedic are numerous, and personal development is expected. These opportunities lead to paramedics going to work overseas, working with general practitioners, in walk-in centres, in emergency departments, or in research or education. Much more than ever before, paramedics can choose to focus their career in a way that evolves to suit their interests and expertise and ultimately benefits patient care.

The interview process

The purpose of this section is to give an overview of what may happen at interview. This information is deliberately quite generic and more detail would be provided by the institution that is inviting you to interview. All HEIs will interview prospective candidates across the academic year before the programme begins. Candidates will usually be sent details of the type of interview process the university uses. Some HEIs use face-to-face panel interviews (with university and/or ambulance trust staff), others use mini multiple interviews (MMIs), while others' processes are all online. MMIs involve candidates rotating around a series of simulation stations and being asked questions by a number of different interviewers. The HEI will usually provide details as required.

Student paramedic comment: Like everyone, I prepared for my university interviews by trying to second-guess what the interviewers would want to know and swotting in those areas. I probably had a load of rehearsed answers which tried to show that even my hobbies had some element of 'transferable skill' to being a paramedic. I did four interviews and got two offers. I think now that the offers I got came out of those interviews where I got away from my 'prepared speeches' and was able to show something of who I actually am while talking to the interviewers. 'Knowing your stuff' is obviously important, but 'being yourself' is just as important – interviewers want to see who you are, not just what you know.

Student paramedic comment: Because the interview is time limited, you cannot think too much, and just have to be yourself. The interview is likely to be designed to test different sides of your personality, so even if you feel you didn't do well for one question, you can make up for it with answers to other questions. So if you don't answer all questions well, it does not mean you will fail to get through.

Some HEIs may require candidates to sit a short mathematics and English paper in addition to the interview. Some HEIs and partner ambulance trusts also require candidates to pass a fitness test, and this may take place before or after the interview. There may be additional requirements that are specific to the institution; again details/guidance would be given to candidates before the interview. Make sure you read all the information that you are given, so you are as prepared as you can be.

What to do if I am not successful?

Although it may seem like the end of the world, it may not be the end of your journey. With the popularity of paramedic education, it is not surprising that many candidates are unsuccessful on the first occasion.

If you still wish to pursue this career choice, try to obtain some feedback on why you were not successful. Bear in mind that due to the vast numbers of candidates, many universities are not able to resource staff to provide dedicated, personalised feedback. If you do gain this information, reflect on what you have been told, across the course of the year.

If you are not able to gain this information:

- Review your personal statement.
- Be realistic about your previous experiences (voluntary and employed).
- Reflect on the experiences other people had whom you met at interview.
- Perhaps think about widening your experience.
- Gain a better and more realistic view of what paramedics actually do. It is nothing like television portrayal of the role.

You may want to consider if this is what you really want, and how much you are prepared to commit to attaining a place. Review your supporting statement and update it, in line with your added year of experience(s) before reapplying to UCAS.

Use your time constructively. Think about what other candidates may have (in terms of experience) that you may not have; paid care work experience is always a good option, if possible. You may find other doors open for you and that you find something you unexpectedly enjoy doing – who knows? If not, you will still be developing and practising your communication and care skills during this time.

The positive is that, should you reapply, you will know what to expect from the interview process!

How is studying for a paramedic qualification different from other subjects?

There are several main differences that may (or may not) be applicable to the programme you wish to apply to:

- You are receiving an academic and professional qualification; consequently, these types of programmes (mainly in healthcare subjects) are longer than non-professionally regulated programmes. You may find that most programmes involve a longer academic year than subjects that do not end with the eligibility to register with a profession, for example a History, English or Maths degree. Professional programmes may be around 40–45 weeks in length.
- Some programmes involve employment with a National Health Service (NHS) ambulance trust, so you may not receive the same university holidays as other students.

- You may be required to undertake shift work while studying.
- You may be required to work shifts in the wider NHS in areas highlighted in the College of Paramedics Curriculum Guidance.
- The programme will cover a vast array of subjects that are relevant to the role. In addition, you will study specific clinical skills and associated anatomy and physiology.

⌀ Refer to Chapters 7, 8 and 9 for more information on subjects covered briefly in this chapter.

Having provided a brief summary of how paramedic programmes differ from other programmes of study, the reality of student paramedic study requires careful consideration.

References

Blaber, A.Y. (ed.) (2019) *Foundations for Paramedic Practice: A Theoretical Perspective* (2nd edn). Maidenhead: Open University Press.

College of Paramedics: *Become a Paramedic*. Available at: https://collegeofparamedics.co.uk/COP/Become_a_Paramedic/COP/BecomeAParamedic/Become_a_Paramedic.aspx?hkey=f10838de-b67f-44a0-83b7-8140d8cdba83 (accessed 8 April 2022).

College of Paramedics (2019). *Paramedic Curriculum Guidance* (5th edn). Available at: https://collegeofparamedics.co.uk/COP/ProfessionalDevelopment/Paramedic_Curriculum_Guidance.aspx (accessed 24 May 2022).

College of Paramedics website. Available at https://www.collegeofparamedics.co.uk/ (accessed 12 April 2022).

Department of Health (2013a) *Report of the Mid Staffordshire NHS Foundation Trust Public Inquiry: Executive Summary*. London: The Stationery Office.

Department of Health (2013b) *Patients First and Foremost: The Government's Initial Responses to the Francis Inquiry*. London: The Stationery Office.

Health and Care Professions Council (2016a) *Guidance on Conduct and Ethics for Students*. Available at: https://www.hcpc-uk.org/globalassets/

resources/guidance/guidance-on-conduct-and-ethics-for-students.pdf (accessed 25 May 2022).

Health and Care Professions Council (2016b) *Standards of Conduct, Performance and Ethics*. Available at: https://www.hcpc-uk.org/standards/standards-of-conduct-performance-and-ethics/ (accessed 25 May 2022).

Health and Care Professions Council (2023) *Standards of Proficiency for Paramedics*. Available at: https://www.hcpc-uk.org/standards/standards-of-proficiency/paramedics/ (accessed 25 May 2022).

NHS Careers: *Paramedic*. Available at: https://www.healthcareers.nhs.uk/explore-roles/allied-health-professionals/roles-allied-health-professions/roles-allied-health-professions/paramedic/paramedic (accessed 8 April 2022).

NHS England (2021) *Improving communication between healthcare professionals and patients in the NHS in England*. London: NHS England (accessed 23 May 2022).

Step into the NHS: *Finding Work Experience in the NHS*. Available at: https://www.stepintothenhs.nhs.uk/work-experience (accessed 8 April 2022)

Street, P.A. (2019) Interpersonal communication: a foundation of practice. In A.Y. Blaber (ed.) *Blaber's Foundations for Paramedic Practice: A Theoretical Perspective* (3rd edn). Maidenhead: Open University Press.

Useful websites:

Guidance on Conduct and Ethics for Students: https://www.hcpc-uk.org/globalassets/resources/guidance/guidance-on-conduct-and-ethics-for-students.pdf

HCPC Communication and Social Media: https://www.hcpc-uk.org/standards/meeting-our-standards/communication-and-using-social-media/

HCPC Guidance on Health and Character: https://www.hcpc-uk.org/resources/guidance/guidance-on-health-and-character/

HCPC Guidance on Social Media: https://www.hcpc-uk.org/globalassets/resources/guidance/guidance-on-social-media.pdf

HCPC Student Hub: https://www.hcpc-uk.org/students/

Standards of Proficiency for Paramedics: https://www.hcpc-uk.org/standards/standards-of-proficiency/paramedics/

3 THE REALITY OF STUDENT PARAMEDIC STUDY

Amanda Blaber

The focus of this chapter is on giving student paramedics a voice, in order that you can read their study advice based on reality. As individuals, students will view experiences differently; they will each have their own coping mechanisms and may have different motivations for studying for a paramedic qualification. The comments are from students in Years 1, 2 and 3 of their studies (depending on the length of their programme). This is because the realities of the student paramedic role and your priorities do alter as time progresses throughout the programme of study. As the student paramedic comment below illustrates, there are some significant differences between the various paramedic programmes of study and some things to seriously consider.

> **Student paramedic comment:** You will not have a traditional university experience. Some of the things you will experience will be very challenging. Seriously consider if you are personally ready (everyone is different), maybe take a gap year, earn some money, get a job in healthcare … there are so many options, you do not need to do this straight from school or college.

Preparation for study

Your programme will vary in the intensity with which it starts. Some programmes will begin quite slowly and flexibly, others will be *full on* for five days per week, with copious amounts of information being given at the beginning of the programme. One thing that most students have in common is that the learning environment will be different from what they are used to. Box 3.1 reflects that Year 1 students generally wished they had

Box 3.1 Things Year 1 students wished they had done to prepare for their academic studies

📖 Learn the basics of anatomy and physiology (A&P). I read lots and studied a lot, but there is so much to learn and at a high speed. A&P plays a much larger part than I ever realised.

📖 Use the study skills and resources suggested by your university before starting your studies. If I had done this, I may have been quicker in getting to grips with things like referencing and searching skills. I wasted a lot of time in the first few months.

📖 Our programme is unlike anything my friends are studying; they are studying academic subjects, like History. We were told this, but I don't think it is something I fully realised until I was in the middle of it.

📖 You are not told everything. Get used to independent reading, to top up what you are given in lectures.

📖 During the whole experience of the first nine months I felt like a fish out of water. I had forgotten a lot of my previous subject knowledge. Had I kept reading, even a little bit, during this time, I may have been more confident during lectures. Instead I am in a state of permanent catch-up and I don't like that feeling, it affects my confidence.

📖 Start pre-reading early. Do this before all modules start.

📖 Before you start your programme, ask for a reading list, prepare yourself by looking at these before you start your programme.

📖 I had a gap year, so I needed to refresh essay structure and get back to writing in an academic way again which took time.

📖 I am a mature student. Get to know everyone – you will be supporting each other through the duration of the programme. Age has no boundaries; everyone brings different things to the classroom.

📖 Be prepared to study independently and understand how you work best. Do you study best in the mornings or in the evenings? Plan your 'down time' so that you start studying independently early on, or you may get left behind and feel like you are always playing 'catch-up'.

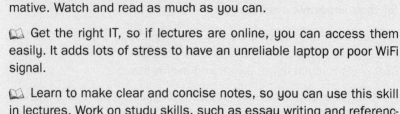

📖 Access student paramedic sites on social media, which are informative. Watch and read as much as you can.

📖 Get the right IT, so if lectures are online, you can access them easily. It adds lots of stress to have an unreliable laptop or poor WiFi signal.

📖 Learn to make clear and concise notes, so you can use this skill in lectures. Work on study skills, such as essay writing and referencing. This would have helped me feel more confident. Do the suggested reading.

📖 Try to research subjects, paramedic news, and new policies – all of this will help you. Pick topics that you find interesting and research them a bit – as you will need to do this once you start.

📖 Use a variety of available resources: YouTube videos, podcasts, quizzes, flash cards. It pays to know what sort of learner you are, for example whether you are a visual, auditory or verbal learner ... I love podcasts as I can hear how all the new medical terms are pronounced.

undertaken some preparatory reading before starting their studies. You may be surprised by the comments on the amount of information needed and the change of lifestyle, as illustrated by the students' comments.

Box 3.1 highlights the fact that there are some strategies students can employ before they commence their university programme. Greater preparation before commencing a programme of study may make the transition into academic studies easier. You will see that the comments in Box 3.1 also reflect the change in delivery of some aspects of programmes through the COVID-19 pandemic.

Delivery of the programme content

Throughout the COVID-19 period, most institutions continued with small group sessions for the practical elements of the programme, but used Microsoft Teams (or other online platforms) for larger sessions that would usually be delivered face to face via a lecture format. In many places these lectures have been recorded, so students can access them at any time; this has been extremely welcome. Other lectures have been pre-recorded for student access, whenever suits their personal circumstances, rather than at a set time or day. There is no doubt that higher education institutions and the NHS generally have learned to adapt, change and move most things online if required. Some have adopted a 'mixed-delivery approach' with some online sessions combined with face-to-face teaching. In reality, if a student wants to meet with a member of staff for a brief meeting on a day when the student does not need to be in university, then it makes perfect sense to do this online. The benefits are three-fold: students and members of staff save time by not travelling; it is cheaper (there are no travel costs); which in turn means there are fewer environmental considerations. Ask what the situation is with the institutions you are considering. Think about how you learn best; what suits your learning style? Once you have successfully navigated Year 1, the preparation before the next year of study is equally as important, as described in Box 3.2.

As the comments in Box 3.2 highlight, some students in Years 2 and 3 regret not making the most of their study periods or independent study time afforded to them in Year 1. The comments relate to the change in academic level, the commitment required and the fact that as the student progresses it all seems 'to come together' and makes more sense. Interestingly, the comments relating to simulation are both positive and negative.

From an academic and clinical perspective, simulation is something that you will need to practise. It is used extensively in both undergraduate and postgraduate studies and forms the basis of practical assessments within the academic environment. You may also find simulation being used by your mentors/PEds as an additional means of assessing your skills and knowledge when in practice. It can be an experience of personal growth as you respond to feedback given on your performance as you compare yourself to your colleagues, both in performance and knowledge. Preparing for simulation is very sensible and students who prepare for it will get the most from these experiences.

𝓔 Refer to Chapter 10 for more information about learning in simulation.

Academic challenges are not the only concerns for students; finances seem to be a theme for many. It can be difficult to manage your finances, juggling studies with paid employment. Sometimes students graduate with a debt to pay. Make sure you are fully informed before you embark on your studies (see Box 3.4), and make use of the student support available at your university.

Box 3.2 Comments from students in Years 2 and 3 on preparing for the next academic year and academic study generally

📖 Re-read the things you are not happy with over your holiday time. I did not make the most of my study time in Year 1 and I wish I had used it wisely. I have had to work hard to catch up.

📖 Year 1 was fun, but now it is getting more serious as we are being asked to do more at university and in practice. More is expected of us and I don't want to look a fool, so I am working really hard. I wish I hadn't wasted so much of my time in Year 1.

📖 As the modules/units pass it will make more sense; it all starts to come together and makes more sense in practice. You will have to work hard to be as good as you can be.

📖 There's a big jump in knowledge and learning, but in a good way.

📖 Study hard, you'll see the rewards.

📖 Go to the academic team if you are having any trouble, they will do all they can to help you or point you in the direction of someone who can.

📖 I could have been much more prepared, but I learned as I went along; that suited me, as I was open to everything that came with the programme.

📖 There is more focus on A&P, medications, how to research and find evidence; you will need to be much more organised.

📖 Do more research into job roles within the ambulance service.

📖 Do pre-reading/independent study before lectures; you will learn so much more as a result.

📖 Revise and go over notes regularly, not just for assessments. Everything that you will cover is needed every day in your eventual job; it's not just learning it for an assessment – this is the wrong approach to take.

📖 Paramedic courses require a lot of independent study, so you need to be very disciplined with yourself. Days when you don't have university or placements are so good for going over lectures and extra reading, so use them!

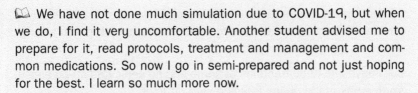 We have not done much simulation due to COVID-19, but when we do, I find it very uncomfortable. Another student advised me to prepare for it, read protocols, treatment and management and common medications. So now I go in semi-prepared and not just hoping for the best. I learn so much more now.

📖 Some people in my group hate learning in simulation, but I would rather make mistakes in this environment than on a real patient, when it could be really serious. It depends on your attitude; it isn't about the staff having a go at you, it is about you learning and making yourself a better student.

📖 I really don't like my practice being scrutinised in a simulated environment, it is not real and does not reflect who I am when I am with real patients.

Box 3.3 Students' comments about online learning

📖 Personally I find it hard to stay focused with online learning. If the WiFi is bad, it means I cannot engage with the learning as it takes forever to unmute or turn the camera on and then the laptop crashes out of the call. On a positive note, it is incredibly helpful to have lectures recorded or pre-recorded; it gives you the ability to look back over them and not just have to rely on lecture notes.

📖 I found online learning helpful with the theory elements of the programme, as you can re-watch complex lectures as many times as you need.

📖 I do not like the fact that even in Year 2 now, I do not know all the people in my cohort, as we missed out on being together in Year 1 (due to COVID-19 restrictions). Peer support is really important for well-being and we have missed out on that.

📖 I have enjoyed online learning. This year it has been more organised and planned into our timetables, so I know when I am studying from home. This is useful as a mature student with children in school.

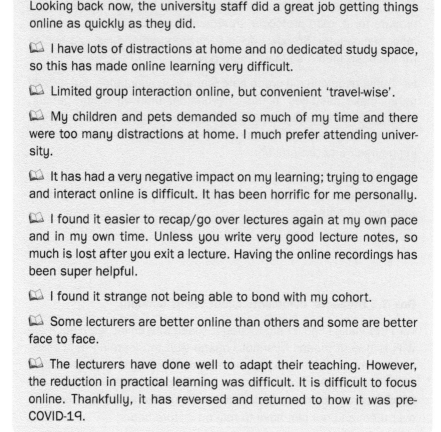

📖 Not great initially, but our whole world was turned upside down. Looking back now, the university staff did a great job getting things online as quickly as they did.

📖 I have lots of distractions at home and no dedicated study space, so this has made online learning very difficult.

📖 Limited group interaction online, but convenient 'travel-wise'.

📖 My children and pets demanded so much of my time and there were too many distractions at home. I much prefer attending university.

📖 It has had a very negative impact on my learning; trying to engage and interact online is difficult. It has been horrific for me personally.

📖 I found it easier to recap/go over lectures again at my own pace and in my own time. Unless you write very good lecture notes, so much is lost after you exit a lecture. Having the online recordings has been super helpful.

📖 I found it strange not being able to bond with my cohort.

📖 Some lecturers are better online than others and some are better face to face.

📖 The lecturers have done well to adapt their teaching. However, the reduction in practical learning was difficult. It is difficult to focus online. Thankfully, it has reversed and returned to how it was pre-COVID-19.

I would expect online learning to become more embedded in all programmes of study and for institutions to improve online learning.

Finances

As the comments in Box 3.4 from Year 1 students highlight, finance needs to be given careful consideration. Even though this has improved in the last few years (see Chapter 5 for more details). Finance is not the only factor in your decision-making process. As discussed in Chapter 2, there are many other important considerations when choosing a university programme.

Box 3.4 Comments of Year 1 students about the finances associated with paramedic study

📖 Had I known how financially difficult it would be, I would have learned how to save and budget better, before all my money had gone!

📖 Money disappears fast and that's without going out much, too.

📖 My friends on other paramedic programmes are worse off and some are better off, I should have looked more closely at this before starting. I was just so desperate to start my career, but I may have got better results had I taken a year out to work and save.

📖 Try not to take on too much additional work – university is busy and tiring.

🔗 Refer to Chapters 4, 5 and 6 for more information about making your decisions.

Clinical placement

Generally, all student paramedics cannot wait to have their first shift out in practice. The comments in Box 3.5 are a mixture of both generic and personal experiences, but they should give you an idea of the variety of feelings associated with the clinical environment. Be aware that programmes differ in the focus of placement. Some programmes will focus on the role and employment opportunities for the paramedic in other areas of the NHS, such as walk-in centres, general practitioner surgeries, and emergency departments. Therefore, students may spend much less time than they expect on ambulance vehicles and more in wider NHS placement areas to prepare them for the reality of paramedics working outside the ambulance service role. Programmes will reflect the diversity of the paramedic role in their particular locality and the partnerships developed between the institution, the NHS and ambulance service.

🔗 Refer to Chapters 8, 9 and 10 for more detail and explanation of the comments in Box 3.5.

Box 3.5 Comments of Year 1 students about the ambulance-focused practice environment

📖 The distance I have to drive to and from my placement is much more than I expected. It's expensive and we sometimes don't finish on time, so shifts are long.

📖 The job is quite physical. I wish I had worked on my basic strength before starting. It is difficult to eat well and healthily on shift and sometimes there is a lot of sitting about which doesn't help.

📖 It is not as busy on shift as I expected it to be.

📖 Shifts are great, but be prepared: sort your uniform out, get food ready, make sure you are on time and look smart and smile – that always helps and no-one wants to see a miserable face. Oh, and learn to like tea!

📖 Be open-minded and get to know your mentor or PEd. You will learn so much if you are enthusiastic and want to learn.

📖 I have been a lot more involved than I expected and the majority of people are friendly and helpful. As in any job there are some people who you may not get on with. You have to be an adult and try to sort this out, or agree to disagree.

📖 Bring a spare pen, and be prepared to give it away – people always lose pens! Buy a fob watch. Get your driving licence and a means of transport, so you can get to your placement safely at all times of the day and night. Invest in a stethoscope, but talk to your lecturers to make sure you get one that will be good enough for the rest of your career.

📖 Get to the gym! All the equipment is heavy and cardiopulmonary resuscitation is hard work.

📖 Moving and handling is not just about strength, it is also about technique.

📖 I have been surprised at the pace of work. I was expecting it to be much more of a rush all of the time. In reality, we spend a lot of time with each patient and have more waiting around than I expected.

📖 Placement is different to what I expected because of the different types of calls. There is more social care than I expected. The aim is to keep people at home as much as possible, which is not what I expected, but I should have done more research.

📖 I expected to feel like a 'spare part' but my mentor and colleagues make me feel included. It is really important to make sure you rest between shifts.

📖 Everyone has a 'first time', even for the most experienced paramedics. You are not expected to know everything.

📖 It's not all about saving lives and trauma; sometimes it can be chilled and relaxed. Enjoy those moments.

📖 It's not all about medical emergencies. Talking and building a rapport quickly is super-important.

📖 I wasn't expecting to be so involved so early on. I expected just to observe so it is lovely to get involved.

📖 Not all paramedics are easy to get along with, or that empathetic (as in any job, some people have more bad days than good ones). Some are stressed or worn down by having done the same job for years. Establish how much 'banter' you are prepared to listen to or tolerate – if it is aimed at you. Having said this, others have also come through similar 'student paramedic' routes and totally understand the right approach to get the best from students.

📖 Establish early on where your own limit is for humour and banter. Don't let people behave in ways that you are not comfortable with.

📖 Paramedics I have met so far are lovely and ensure you are supported at all times. They will answer any questions and you can have a laugh (at appropriate times).

📖 Have your own support network – you will need it as the work can be stressful. Talk about your worries. Be honest with yourself about your weaknesses and be open to the things you may struggle with.

📖 My expectations of how tiring placement can be were far too low. It is tiring just working with different people. Shifts can be influenced positively or negatively by the staff you are working with.

📖 Take travel sickness tablets with you, the back of an ambulance can be very bumpy.

📖 Consider getting a Healthcare Assistant job over the summer holidays. This broadens your horizons, if it is a hospital or primary-care environment, and keeps you in a medical environment. It enhances your patient care and you get paid.

📖 Be confident in what you have been taught but don't be afraid to say that you don't know how to do something. Ask lots of questions (when it is appropriate to do so), as that will help to boost your confidence.

📖 Placement can be stressful. You need to be in the right 'headspace' yourself in order to look after others.

📖 It is not just physically draining, it is emotionally and mentally exhausting at times. There will be people that come into your thoughts and you reflect on; you may never know if they survived or not. All you can hope is that you did your best. That is very tough.

📖 Don't expect it to be like TV shows, it is not. It is a lot less intense than the media make it out to be. There are lots of welfare and social calls and far fewer high-intensity situations and trauma.

📖 It is not like the TV. Some calls really are as simple as talking to your patient; they may have called as they are lonely.

📖 Some situations can be very emotional. It is good to know yourself and understand what might trigger your own emotional reaction. It is okay to have reactions – we are all human after all!

The aim is that you will develop from being a student to become an educated professional, and the comments from Year 2/3 students in Box 3.6 highlight aspects of this development. Not all students will achieve this progression and personal development over the course of their studies. However, it is the aim of paramedic higher education to produce graduates who employ critical thinking, are competent and skilled, and who provide high-quality care to their patients.

The development alluded to in Box 3.6 is made possible by commitment to academic study and learning in the clinical environment. This would be

Box 3.6 Comments of students in Years 2 and 3 about the practice environment

📖 I now keep an anonymised reflective journal of calls I go to that are quite out of the ordinary or are 'interesting' jobs, as they are things I am unlikely to see again. I don't have to do this as it is not something we have to do, but I learn better by reviewing things after they have happened and it helps me.

📖 Expectations of some ambulance staff who you thought were right in Year 1, you now may begin to question, as you know more. Think about how to manage this; it is a bit disappointing, but is the real world.

📖 Start attending calls as early as you and your mentor or PEd feel is appropriate. The more experience you can get doing this now, the less of a shock it will be when you are registered.

📖 Use the knowledge and skills you get taught in university, such as physical assessment, when you are with your mentor or PEd, otherwise you will forget them and this won't help your patient when you are the registered paramedic.

📖 Practice educators enjoy teaching. Don't worry about feeling like a 'spare part' or that you are in the way. Generally, people are happy for you to be there.

📖 I now expect so much more from myself. I don't feel supernumerary anymore, I feel like a crewmate.

📖 If you change base sites or placement areas, it may knock your confidence and you have to start getting to know people all over again. At the time this is a pain, but in the long term it helps develop your communication skills more quickly.

📖 It is great going to a new station or base site. Don't be anxious about being 'new' again. Different people teach differently and you may learn a lot more.

📖 It is okay to feel nervous before going to a placement; it means you care! Be honest with yourself and your practice educator about any worries that you may have or if you feel uncomfortable.

📖 A lot of healthcare staff are overworked and tired. So they may not always be in the best mood. It is okay and normal to feel tired and 'down' sometimes. But try to be positive as it makes yourself and others around you feel happier.

📖 Healthcare staff can have a dark sense of humour; it is often used as a coping mechanism and often brings some positivity and joy to a sad situation. It can be a shock at first though.

📖 There are lots of abbreviations and acronyms in healthcare. If you don't know what something is, then ask.

📖 In Year 1, I didn't think I'd ever be prepared for registration. It is all not so daunting now; I am more confident, but still apprehensive, which, as you are sometimes caring for people in life/death situations, is a good way to feel. Being blasé and thinking you know it all, is when you make mistakes and get things wrong.

📖 Take your time, work hard and be comfy with anatomy and physiology. It is the basis for most other things you will do from Year 2 onwards.

📖 Consider your capacity to succeed in university work, as well as in practice, they are different beasts. Look at other options. I found placement was a lot more relaxed and patient-focused than I expected. Of course, I expected patient care to be paramount, but I did not expect to be able to build such a rapport and connection with patients in a professional role. It is truly one of the best parts of the job and gives an insight that is unique to the paramedic profession.

📖 As you move through the years, more is expected of you. You will be 'attending' to the patient, at certain calls. This can be daunting and feel overwhelming. Remember you are still learning and your mentor is with you, it does not have to be perfect every time. Being 'in the deep end' is sometimes a good learning experience, but keep talking to your mentor.

📖 It is not all about ambulance service work. In Year 1, you may not appreciate the value of wider NHS placement. Placements are crucial to you understanding healthcare more widely. You may never get the chance to experience them again. Just as the ambulance service has its own culture, so do other healthcare areas. Go there with an open mind, smile and take it all in; ask questions. This has the chance to make you a more well-rounded clinician, who can provide more information to their patients about what to expect in various healthcare environments.

📖 The more you put into your placements, the more you will get out of them. Be proactive, take the initiative and ask questions. It is the best way to learn. Placements in the wider NHS are very useful to understand how patients are treated in different areas. It gives you an understanding that you can then pass onto your patients.

limited without a clear ability to manage your own time and an understanding of how you will progress towards achievements.

The comments made by Year 1 students in Boxes 3.1 and 3.5 demonstrate some of their honest regrets related to their choices, in respect of study, career and placement issues. These students have embarked on the journey of beginning to understand themselves.

The importance of self-awareness and self-management

You will see from Box 3.7 that some of the aspects of being a student paramedic did indeed come as a shock. For some individuals it is not an easy transition into the role of being a university student or being a student paramedic. As the comments in Box 3.6 illustrate, the transition issues continue into the later study years.

Box 3.7 highlights the fact that the journey to knowing yourself continues long into your studies and probably long into the period after registration. We can also see that career choices shape some people's personalities over time. Some of the comments in Box 3.7 relate to self-awareness and the concept of resilience. The following chapters will address in more detail the points made here.

Box 3.7 Comments of Year 1 students about time and self-management

📖 Maybe I should have looked into becoming an ambulance support worker first, so I would have known more about what to expect, but I didn't want to wait. University was the quickest way to get where I wanted to be.

📖 I have struggled being away from home. It gets better, but had I known how tough it would be I may have stayed nearer home.

📖 I wasted too much time socialising. I have some major studying to do in the holidays. I fought hard for my place so I have let myself down by not maximising my potential. My results this year have been disappointing and it won't happen next year.

📖 I thought I was worldly wise – until I went into practice . . . it was not at all what I expected. Some awful and some great moments. I have learned so, so, so much about myself and who I am. Maybe I could have been more use to patients had I known this before starting my studies.

📖 I have needed help to come to terms with some of the experiences I have had in practice, and my practice and academic team have been there for me. Stupidly, I thought by talking to them, it might affect my place on the programme – how wrong I was and I suffered on my own for too long before talking. Use the resources you have access to; there is so much help available, but no-one can read your mind – you have to open up.

📖 Get a diary/use a calendar for important dates to do with university, placement, rent and other bills.

📖 I wish I had known how much I would need to manage my time more effectively and efficiently.

The comments in Boxes 3.1 to 3.8 are *snippets* from a wide variety of students, and it is worth delving into these topics in more detail later in this text. Students' viewpoints will continue to be included throughout the chapters, to provide more detail in many areas and generally provide personal commentary.

Box 3.8 Comments of students in Years 2 and 3 relating to time and self-management

📖 Our lecturer told us that over time we would change; I thought that was rubbish. How right she was, I meet up with my old friends now and think I have nothing in common with them. Actually I think they are immature and have no insight into the real world. Even though I play along at the time, when I am with them, the gaps between us meeting up are getting longer. I guess part of that is about who I am now and part of it is the career I have chosen.

📖 Whether you like it or not this job will change your personality to an extent. This affects some people more than others.

📖 One of my colleagues didn't like the people she was working with in practice, didn't like the [ambulance] service culture and found there was not enough time to care for people as she wanted. She left – it wasn't for her. It took her a while to come to this conclusion, and it was a brave move. I respect her for making the decision. I guess it is not for everyone.

📖 If you are struggling in practice or university – *talk* to someone and don't suffer in silence. It is not good or healthy to keep things to yourself.

📖 If you are on a three-year programme, Year 2 may be a bit of a grind; bear with it, work hard and use your study time wisely. Be disciplined with your time, it will pay off.

📖 Learn how to manage your time well. You need to learn a lot in your own time, so do not use independent study days as a day off. Otherwise, you will struggle. You get back what you put in.

📖 Set aside at least one day per week for self-learning (independent study). There is a lot to know.

📖 Don't break the learning cycle over holiday breaks, keep reading. Books will be your friends, so read lots.

📖 As a Year 3 student, this is my advice: be yourself. Do not try to fit the mould of what you think a paramedic should be. Don't give up, everything is so new and overwhelming in Year 1, but you will be confident soon. Study hard in all years, but make sure you have a life; surround yourself with positive people.

📖 You will not be taught how to be a paramedic. Your lecturers and PEds will give you the foundation, but you must apply yourself independently in order to succeed.

📖 Most of the people in your cohort will probably work in the same geographical area as you after graduation. So, you would have known them for three years when you start work as a registered paramedic. They are a great source of support and you are going through the same doubts and questions as them. Your cohort is a safe place to talk and this will help you to look after yourself.

A few more detailed comments on the reality of the student role

I had been encouraged by people who knew me that I had the ability to handle the increasing levels of education the programme involved. In reality, as the programme progressed, I had to give more and more time to study if I was to stay on target; this meant that the outside paid work, socialising and down time which had been possible during Year 1 were increasingly squeezed in the subsequent years.

A major help came in talking to students who were in the year ahead. They gave me pointers as to what was coming which meant I spent some of the holidays reading up on subjects we would study when we returned to university. This proved invaluable as I would have struggled to keep up without it.

As far as placement experience went, I had little idea what to expect. I knew it wasn't going to be like the popular hospital dramas on TV but also, unlike other students, I had not come from a St John/British Red Cross background so had limited ambulance experience. In some ways this may have helped in that I had no preconceived ideas about how things should be done and this meant I asked lots of questions and learned things from scratch.

It might be hard sometimes to find your place within the crew. The student role is not always clearly defined. Speak with your practice educator, try to make yourself useful but also try not to get in the way. It's a fine balance but after a few shifts you will get a better understanding on how crews work.

As a more mature student I was happier in placement with older members of staff, but I needn't have been scared to mingle with my cohort. Make time to get to know everyone in your cohort – you have three years together. Older and younger students will be friends, and age has no boundaries.

The more detailed response above has been included to enable the reader to understand some of the points considered and strategies used by one student before and during their paramedic studies. Having an awareness of the potential issues you may encounter may help you prepare and plan for your future studies. The comments presented here do not just reflect the good parts about being a student paramedic, they provide a realistic picture.

The detail provided in the following chapters should help you develop a more detailed understanding of the student paramedic role and the idiosyncrasies of studying for a paramedic qualification. However, it would be unwise to examine only the student perspective; the academic, mentor and PEd viewpoints will enable you to appreciate a wider perspective than that of the student.

How to be successful as a student paramedic

The responses in Box 3.9 are from academics and paramedic practice educators PEds in response to the question: 'What makes a student paramedic successful?'.

This chapter's main focus has concentrated on using student comments to illustrate the wide variety of students' experiences. The inclusion of comments related to both academic study and clinical placement is intentional to help explain what to expect from study and practice perspectives.

Box 3.9 What makes a student paramedic successful?

Paramedic/PEd response: The most successful students I have mentored have been those that cared about their patients. Students can be taught academic and clinical skills but we can't teach them caring, empathy, common sense or life experience. If a student has these raw materials to begin with, the rest invariably follows. These qualities, together with a sense of humour, a pride in the profession and a willingness to learn will ensure success in both placement and at university.

Academic responses: The ethos of higher education is often somewhat of a shock to students. You are 'treated like a grown-up' and are expected to take a great deal of responsibility for your own learning. There is limited time in class in which to teach you, and modules specify a large number of hours you will need to commit to your own study. Pre-reading is invaluable and students that have taken time to increase their knowledge before the programme will be at an advantage. You don't need a specific reading list for this; generic anatomy and physiology textbooks are a good place to start.

Your module guides are the most valuable documents you will receive on your programme, as they highlight the content, learning outcomes and assessment criteria of the modules, and help you to study effectively.

Do not stay silent if you feel you are struggling or falling behind. Academic teams and mentors are there to help and will go out of their way to support you.

Paramedic/PEd response: I believe the key to being a successful student paramedic is to embrace your chosen career pathway and academic journey with true wholehearted commitment and dedication, with a passion to achieve your goal and with an informed and detailed understanding of the programme you will study. Being open and prepared to accept anything offered to you throughout your study enables you to build both varied and fulfilling experiences. Additionally, self-control is vital in managing time effectively. You will need to complete academic assignments while also attending shift-working placements and remembering to live a 'professional' student life, all of which is slightly different from students on other non-professional/clinical academic programmes.

Paramedic/PEd response: The best students are those who are motivated and happy to be on placement. We can't make them learn; it has to come from them. They need to have an open mind and be honest with their emotions. They also need to possess a professional attitude towards patients and other crew members. It is a hard learning curve at the beginning but when these points are appreciated, students can have a very good experience from their placements within the wider NHS and ambulance service.

Paramedic/PEd response: If you are clear on the role from the beginning you will not be disappointed; you need to have realistic expectations. As a junior student (Year 1) I found the best way to learn was to watch and assist ambulance staff, putting what the university taught me into practice. As long as you are aware that ambulance work is predominantly social care and chronic condition management, with major trauma and critically ill patients being a fraction of the care ambulance services provide to the public, you will know what you are getting into and what to expect.

Paramedic/PEd response: For both students and graduates, the most important thing to remember is having the right attitude. Having a positive attitude towards each call (no matter how minor it might seem) and a positive working relationship with your crewmate is essential. I have found that a good shift or a bad shift has much more to do with who I am working with and how we get on, than what patients or situations we encounter. Adopting a positive attitude will always benefit your working relationship. If this is good, it bodes well for patient care and things seem to work seamlessly well.

Further reading

College of Paramedics: *Become a Paramedic*. Available at: https://collegeof-paramedics.co.uk/COP/Become_a_Paramedic/COP/BecomeAParamedic/Become_a_Paramedic.aspx?hkey=f10838de-b67f-44a0-83b7-8140d8cdba83 (accessed 8 April 2022).

College of Paramedics website: https://www.collegeofparamedics.co.uk/ (accessed 12 April 2022).

NHS Careers: *Paramedic*. Available at: https://www.healthcareers.nhs.uk/ explore-roles/allied-health-professionals/roles-allied-health-professions/ roles-allied-health-professions/paramedic/paramedic (accessed 8 April 2022).

Step into the NHS: *Finding Work Experience in the NHS*. Available at: https://www.stepintothenhs.nhs.uk/work-experience (accessed 8 April 2022).

4 WHAT STYLE OF ACADEMIC PROGRAMME IS RIGHT FOR YOU? HAVE YOU CONSIDERED A DEGREE APPRENTICESHIP ROUTE?

Gemma Howlett

Do your research. This is an important decision.

The main route to becoming a Health and Care Professions Council (HCPC) registered paramedic in England is via a programme at a higher education institution (HEI). The degree apprenticeship route is discussed in this chapter, and the undergraduate degree route is discussed in Chapter 5.

Prior to the development of higher education (HE) programmes, many paramedics started their careers being employed by an ambulance service and working on patient transport vehicles (for this you had to be at least 21 years old). Then they would undertake ambulance service or in-house training to become technician grade staff, and then additional training to become a registered paramedic.

Many paramedics have gone on to combine working and studying to achieve certificates, diplomas, degrees, master's degrees and PhDs. Some clinical staff have years of practical clinical experience and a variety of academic qualifications, and will act as paramedic educators (PEds) for student paramedics. Additionally, many staff act as PEds after completing a short PEd module. Sometimes this forms the start of their journey to post-registration studies, though sometimes individuals wish to complete the PEd module and do not wish to undertake further academic study.

In the NHS it is very much up to the individual clinician how they choose to develop themselves and how their continuing professional development (CPD) will be used. The focus of their CPD will often depend on their specific interests and future career aspirations.

As the College of Paramedics (2022) explains, there are more ways to become a paramedic:

- Take a full-time approved qualification in paramedic science (for example, at a university) and then apply to an ambulance service for a job as a qualified paramedic.
- Apply for a role as a student paramedic with an ambulance service and study while you work (commonly referred to as an 'in-house' route).
- Apply for a degree standard apprenticeship in paramedic science with an ambulance service; these are 'linked' to a university.

However, it is also important to recognise that 'Not all Paramedics Wear Green' (College of Paramedics website 2022) and some people will choose not to work for an ambulance service. Students should take opportunities to work in the wider NHS and explore the variety of roles that are now available for registered paramedics.

What is a degree apprenticeship?

Degree apprenticeships are designed in partnership between employers, HEIs and, where needed, the relevant professional body. They combine work with study and may include a work-based, academic or combined qualification, or a professional qualification relevant to the industry (Institute for Apprenticeships and Technical Education (IFATE) 2022). A degree apprenticeship enables you to gain a full undergraduate degree while you work. In general, they take three to six years to complete (this can include time to obtain relevant experience in an initial employed role) depending on the course and qualification (UCAS 2022). You will spend most of your time in your work environment, and study is generally on a part-time basis (UCAS 2022). You may, for instance, study one day a week and work the rest of the week or study in short study blocks and work around the blocks (UCAS 2022). For paramedic degree apprenticeships this ratio will vary depending on the programme and the option the ambulance service has chosen.

Paramedics are subject to statutory regulation by the Health and Care Professions Council (HCPC). They set the standards of proficiency required for entry to the professional register. The paramedic apprenticeship standard (in order to lead to eligibility to apply for registration with the HCPC) must be aligned to all relevant HCPC standards, as with any other approved HCPC paramedic programmes, to ensure that apprentices are eligible for entry to the HCPC register on completion. In addition to obtaining the degree, an apprentice must be deemed to have passed the End Point Assessment. In the case of the paramedic degree apprenticeship this is integrated, so is generally aligned with a university's standard ratification of award processes. All gateway components need to have been completed by the learner as well as obtaining the degree qualification. In order to satisfy the End Point Assessment gateway, the apprentice must have met all the knowledge, skills and behaviours mapped out in the apprenticeship standard. The knowledge, skills and behaviours are part of the approved apprenticeship framework and are determined by the HCPC Standards of Proficiency and employer input (IFATE 2022). Apprentices must also achieve the Level 3 certificate in emergency response ambulance driving course, Level 2 English and Maths, all required modules considering any recognition of prior learning, and the practice assessment document (IFATE 2022).

Are there any differences in a qualification between an apprenticeship and a direct entry undergraduate degree programme?

Apprenticeships have traditionally been seen as a more vocational route than traditional study; in many ways this is true. They are designed to be vocational, a 'real job where you learn, gain experience and get paid. You're an employee with a contract of employment and holiday leave' (Gov.UK 2022). Within the ambulance sector a variety of apprenticeships are currently being used by ambulance services, such as apprentice facilities assistant, mechanic, emergency care assistant (ECA), associate ambulance practitioner (AAP), emergency medical technician (EMT), and emergency medical dispatcher. You will work for the organisation in which you have been recruited directly to an apprenticeship, or you will in some cases apply for a specific apprenticeship role. You will work while also studying for your apprenticeship qualification; the title and academic level of the apprenticeship will dictate what qualification you will be awarded once completed. For a degree level paramedic apprenticeship, you will be expected to obtain the full degree. Some higher education providers will deliver the same programme to its apprentices and direct entry undergraduate degree students; some have bespoke apprenticeship degrees with altered delivery models to better suit the employer and apprentice learner. Whichever route the employer has chosen, the need to complete a full BSc (Hons) degree is the minimum threshold standard expected by the HCPC for a Registered Paramedic. This will entail studying while working full time. Some of the study will be done on study days (known in apprenticeship terms as off-the-job training), and some will be done in your own time (as is the normal self-study requirement for a degree). This is a great challenge and one which surprised some current apprenticeship students.

Paramedic apprentice student comment: Be prepared to study in your own time. Apprenticeships are not easy. It is funded like other apprenticeships, so you get paid while studying but there is a lot to do and and a lot to learn. To get the most out of it and really understand the materials at the level you are happy with, it is likely that you need to do this in your own time as well as on the learning days.

Paramedic apprentice student comment: There is a lot of studying – more than I thought there would be. You get access to lots of resources, so it is all there for you, but you need to do a lot of reading around subjects in your own time to make sense of them.

Paramedic apprentice student comment: There is a lot of work to do but you get more used to things like writing essays and how to read around a subject. You just have to be prepared to put the work in.

Why would I choose an apprenticeship?

There are many reasons to choose an apprenticeship programme. You will get real-life experience working alongside your degree. Your degree is fully paid for by your employer using the apprenticeship levy fund, so there is no cost to you. You will get paid a salary while working and studying (UCAS 2022). Apprenticeship salaries vary and will be dependent on which role you have in the organisation and which organisation you work for, for instance the ECA salary and AAP salary are different. You do also have to be mindful of some of the potential negatives when weighing up your decision on which route is best for you. It is hard balancing working and studying at the same time, and this is even more difficult with families, care commitments or other responsibilities you have, so these need to be factored into your decision. You won't qualify for any student loans and as an apprentice you may not get the traditional *university experience* (UCAS 2022).

Accessibility and opportunity are some of the key reasons that apprenticeship learners have told us they chose the route. Many apprenticeship students are already working in the organisation, and this is one of the development opportunities that staff are given, in place of other *in-house development* that was offered previously. Many apprenticeship students are older than an average direct-entry student and will often have roots and commitments established in the area in which they live; they may also have financial commitments such as mortgages that make moving to a full-time direct-entry student programme more difficult, or not at all possible. Some learners intentionally wait for internal routes to become available as they feel that *on-the-job* experience would be a better route for them and would suit the way they learn better (see Box 4.1 for comments).

Box 4.1 Why did you choose a paramedic apprenticeship?

📖 **Paramedic apprentice student comment:** I already had a degree and had therefore accessed undergraduate student loans previously so would not have qualified for any more student finance. As well as this, the thought of going to university at my age was terrifying. The apprenticeship felt different; it was supported by my employer, there were other people like me in my situation on the programme and I could do the course alongside my work. It was a win–win situation for me.

📖 **Paramedic apprentice student comment:** I like the fact that the apprenticeship is employer-led and learning is supported while you are working, so there is lots of relevant on-the-job training. The fact that the course is subsidised by the government apprenticeship levy was an added bonus for me but not the number one factor in the decision.

📖 **Paramedic apprentice student comment:** I chose the apprenticeship route for a few reasons; it was fully funded, lifting a financial burden; I could work full time while studying, helping financially and practically; my previous experience as an ECA was incorporated into the delivery of the course.

What will I be studying?

You will complete a full BSc (Hons) degree on a HCPC-approved programme in order to reach the stage where you can apply to the paramedic register. You will study a variety of modules, the learning outcomes of which will be linked to the standards of proficiency. Depending on the course, this will include a dissertation for the final year project and the achievement of the full tariff of academic credits of 360 (120 for each year of study). Some programmes permit a process of APEL (Accreditation of Prior Experiential Learning) or APL (Accreditation of Prior Learning) to allow you to enter at Level 5 (Year 2 of a standard undergraduate degree). Most programmes recognise your ambulance service experience towards all or some of Level 4 (Year 1 of a traditional degree programme). You may find this challenging if you have had no formal higher education experience previously. Trusts and universities will help with this by providing access to resources that help prepare you for academic writing. For those of you with Level 3 qualifications such as emergency care assistant qualifications, then you may be required to complete a bridging programme or some Level 4 modules. Or you may be required to study the whole three-year degree programme. This will depend on which service you work for, or aim to work for, and which apprenticeship provider they work with.

Paramedic apprentice student comment: I most definitely would have studied degree-level essay writing somehow and tried to prepare for it a bit more. As the first year for us was practical, it felt as if we did not have enough experience in formal essay writing and we were expected to just get on with it.

How will I be studying?

The course design of apprenticeship programmes will normally reflect the apprenticeship learners and the circumstances of their role and study. Many will offer a blended approach with learning delivered using a mix of online learning and face-to-face learning. Some lectures, seminars and group tasks will be delivered online and will then be complemented where needed with face-to-face sessions including activities such as simulation, practice sessions for clinical skills, scenario days and practical assessments. This blended approach enables access to courses even if there is a significant distance from your base location and your learning location. Many trusts also offer payments for expenses and overnight accommodation in line with their policies on learning travel expenses, to enable travel to a specific learning location when required. It is good to find all of this out before you commit to an apprenticeship course to understand the full terms and what you might or might not have to pay for yourself. This will help you to make the decision if it is the right path for you. Trusts and their partner universities will have information available on Trust intranet sites and will often hold recruitment events where you can find out about their programmes.

Paramedic apprenticeship student comment: I found the online sessions difficult to start with as I wasn't comfortable with all the software and programmes we used. But with help and practice I got used to them a bit more. There were some people in our group that picked them up quicker than others, so they helped loads with people like me that took a bit longer. I like them now and it is much better than travelling in for all sessions.

Paramedic apprentice student comment: Being treated as an adult learner has really helped me and inspired me to work hard on this course. I enjoy the mix of online learning and face-to-face learning with our tutors so I think it is the best route for me.

Work and study: what are the challenges and how do I deal with them?

There are many challenges on an apprenticeship programme, some are the same as any programme of study, and some are unique to the apprenticeship. What is important is that you consider how these challenges may differ in order to weigh up the best option for you. Are they challenges of a standard undergraduate programme or are they challenges only if you are doing an apprenticeship? Working full time and studying a full degree is tough (see the student apprenticeship comments in Box 4.2). Your position in the organisation will change and therefore your relationship with

Box 4.2 What are the challenges you have faced on the apprenticeship?

📖 **Paramedic apprentice student comment:** Combining family time and study time has been difficult. My partner and I didn't realise how much work it would be and I think it surprised us both. We have eventually worked out a system of who does what and when, and that helps fit everything in.

📖 **Paramedic apprentice student comment:** It has been a steep learning curve for me, the only learning I had done in the last few years was my Emergency Care Assistance (ECA) course and then mandatory training and things, and they give you all that you need really. Finding your own information, knowing what to do with it, how to take it in and use it, was really new to me.

colleagues will change; this will be explored in more detail shortly. You will have a lot of studying to do while working in a very pressured work arena as ambulance services continue to operate under significant strain. Time management is vitally important; you need to designate study time along with life and personal commitments and work. Working on your time management skills and how to prioritise work and commitments is something you can start working on before you start the programme. This will help you to start developing skills in this area if you do not already have them, or to make improvements. Once you are on the programme, university study support departments can also give you help and guidance on time management strategies or point you in the direction of resources that may help with this.

Transition from staff to student in the same organisation, what are the key considerations?

A big difference with the apprenticeship programme is the shift from staff member to learner which most direct-entry students do not need to deal with as they enter the organisation as a learner (there are of course exceptions to this but generally these are not a frequent occurrence). As an apprentice, even if you join specifically onto an apprenticeship or student paramedic pathway, you will spend time in the organisation working in the role you are first given such as ECA or Associate Ambulance Practitioner (AAP) and will then move to the paramedic apprenticeship programme. You will be part of the workforce and build working relationships with colleagues some of whom may become friends. Navigating the change in relationship to learner and colleagues and having critical conversations with colleagues around performance and professionalism can be challenging. However, you must navigate this and invite colleagues that you may not have invited previously to critique and review your management of patients, your communication, your knowledge and understanding. Hearing a critique on these elements from colleagues who you may have worked with for many years can be difficult, but an openness to professional challenge and a willingness to learn will help. As well as them critiquing you, you may at times need to challenge them in turn on areas of practice or something else that you do not agree with.

While working in an ambulance trust you are held to account for your behaviour. You are expected to adhere to the trust's values, and their general employment policies. However, as a student paramedic and, of course, a registered paramedic you must also consider regulator expectations. The HCPC issues guidance of conduct and ethics for students (HCPC 2016) which are all elements you need to adhere to. You may need to consider, for instance, your social media communications, WhatsApp conversation threads that you are involved or included in. They may or may not have been a cause for concern or consideration previously, or you may not have been aware that your communication on all platforms both in and out of work needs to be considered professional and in line with professional body standards of behaviour. You must consider your behaviour, values, ethics and professionalism both in and outside of work. In your learning context, colleagues and practice educators will be asked to make comments on your behaviour and communication as a student paramedic apprentice. This may be through your practice assessment document or electronic platform.

Another consideration (and potential challenge) is moving from being a competent clinician back to being in the knowledge deficit stage and being a novice again, i.e. from being a clinician to being a learner. This can be a big change and a difficult one, but acceptance of this and seeing yourself as a learner will help you get the most out of the development. When you started out you would not have been competent in your role, but instead the expectations change and you learn new skills. As a student paramedic working towards professional regulation, you will need to have a more in-depth (or different) view of areas of practice in which you would have previously felt comfortable and confident. The level of knowledge expected is higher on many elements of practice that you will have been familiar with previously, such as clinical assessment strategies, illness and injury or skills. It is not a reflection on your previous ability or intended to highlight poor practice in the context of your previous role; instead, it is reflective of the progression and the higher standard needed of you to become a fully autonomous clinician. Acknowledging and accepting a knowledge deficit and the need to build on your existing knowledge early in the journey will help you combat this and put you in a productive learning space. Apprentice learners who have worked with paramedic colleagues previously, comment on how easy some of them made patient assessment, communication and treatment look. A lot of their critical thinking and decision-making takes place as an inner dialogue, so someone that may be a novice or not at the same grade may not appreciate how much work goes into making it look that easy. As a learner, the early realisation of how much work and knowledge is required to make safe, effective and considered clinical assessment and treatment is vast, and you will need to put considerable effort in to reach the same level of knowledge and understanding.

Challenging poor practice or unprofessional behaviour may also be something that you have to contend with as a prospective registrant. Throughout your course, in addition to learning the clinical elements of the role, you will also learn about professionalism, expectations, codes of conduct and behaviour. You may not have been aware of these before, or you may have been aware of them but understood them to be wrong; or you may not have been aware of how to report or raise concerns or have the confidence to report those concerns and understand the responsibility you have to do so. This is a very challenging situation but one that needs to be addressed, as illustrated by the comments in Box 4.3. In recent years there have been reports by various organisations of concerning behaviour within some ambulance services – behaviour people have not had the courage to report before. Understanding the expectations on you and being willing to challenge things that you observe to be wrong is incredibly difficult, but incredibly important. It is difficult for any learner to raise a concern, particularly those learners on apprenticeships who have worked with the clinician or staff member previously and who are now working with them as part of their new learner role.

Box 4.3 How have you found the transition from staff to student?

📖 **Paramedic apprentice student comment:** It has been a difficult transition; the more you learn, the more difficult it is to observe some practice that you have seen previously and assumed was okay, but is actually not best practice. Trying to have those critical conversations is really difficult with some people. I have thought about patients I had been to before that I probably would have treated differently if I went to them now, and I think I would have advocated for them better than I did when I saw them.

📖 **Paramedic apprentice student comment:** It is a bit strange really, you are having to work out your own learning styles, and for me I hadn't thought about that ever really. I don't remember thinking about it even at school, and then you are trying to work out how that fits with the different supervision and mentoring styles that you come across. It is difficult working out whether they want you to be hands on and happy for you to be involved or whether they want you to be a bit more in the background to start with. Before I had a clear role, I knew what I could and couldn't do. It is different now.

📖 **Paramedic apprentice student comment:** I was allocated to a practice educator that I was friends with, and it was difficult to start with. It was difficult to take critique from them and I took it really personally to start with. We had a really honest conversation with each other and set out expectations and how we would manage and approach feedback. This worked well and we have a good and professional relationship now. We have clear boundaries when on shift and I am not sure what would have happened if we had not had the conversation.

The relationship with your general colleagues will change, and you will have a practice educator and practice educator team that will be allocated to you as a student apprentice learner. This may be the first time in your clinical journey that you will have had a nominated practice educator or a team of practice educators that need to review your performance and practice formally. To move from colleague to student learner and practice educator is a significant change in relationship and one that needs to be considered. There will be a shift in power dynamic from your position working with colleagues to your position as a student learner. A colleague now plays a pivotal role in your development and progression. Both parties need to have an awareness of this and understand the significant shift in relationship. It can be difficult for both parties to handle the change; awareness and discussion of this shift can help, and it is important that you have that conversation. The conversation should be about expectations, how to have critical conversations, and where and when these should ideally take place; these would all be good elements to set out as you start this phase of your progression. It is helpful to have an open dialogue about things that you consistently need to improve on, and things that you need to be aware of within boundaries that you have each set out and agreed, as you go through the programme. Raising issues early is also important for both parties.

Are practice placements different?

As an apprentice learner you will work in the organisation, so you do not have traditional placements the same way as direct-entry undergraduate students do, in that some of your time in the organisation is spent working in your existing role. This is known as *on-the-job training*. You will then have a portion of your time off the job and under supervision from a practice educator, where you can practise your clinical decision-making, clinical assessment skills and treatment pathways and options. Depending on which trust and course you use, this *off-the-job* learning under supervision might be as part of a double-crewed ambulance or as a supernumerary learner. Programmes will either work on a minimum hours expectation for their supervised or supernumerary practice element or base their practice requirements on competencies and practice experience against the designated learning outcomes to the relevant practice modules. This is different from a more traditional apprenticeship where you work in the actual role that you are an apprentice in. You will have both roles, one as a student (apprentice) paramedic and the original role or the last role you had in the service before starting the apprenticeship. Alternative placements are variable in apprenticeship programmes and, again, will depend on which programme and employer you carry out your apprenticeship with. Some offer alternative placements within their organisation, so you may work with teams such as clinical support desks, despatch, Hazardous Area Response Team (HART), virtual reality simulation placements, advance clinical teams and others, depending on the trust. Some programmes will send their paramedic apprentices to alternative placements outside their organisation in different areas of the NHS.

How do I get a place on an apprenticeship programme?

All apprenticeships are funded by the Education and Skills Funding Agency (ESFA). Government funding rules require that you must have the right to live and work in the UK, must be in employment, paid at least the legal minimum wage, and have a written and signed agreement for the apprenticeship with your employer. A full-time apprenticeship programme will require you to work a minimum of 30 hours per week. Therefore, seeking employment with a service that offers an apprenticeship programme is essential if you do not already work for a trust that offers a programme. Some trusts recruit directly to their paramedic development pathway and some trusts have the apprenticeship available in the organisation for existing staff but do not recruit specifically for it; you would be required to apply when in employment with that service. There will also potentially be either a final separate or combined recruitment process for the education provider as per their requirements. Trusts will often provide support and guidance for staff who wish to develop professionally and are not already on a defined development pathway. There are several ways that you can prepare for the recruitment process, once you have decided which service you are going to apply to. Find out all you can about the service, about the development opportunities it offers including their paramedic apprenticeship provision. Find out about the university or universities that the organisation partners with to deliver the apprenticeships. Make sure you read the pre-interview and pre-recruitment documents that are sent to you to be clear on what the organisation and university expect from you.

Do all trusts offer apprenticeships?

The ESFA is an executive agency sponsored by the Department for Education (DfE) which has its focus on English education providers and organisations. The devolved nations have their own departments which regulate and set policy and strategy for education. All English ambulance services currently have a progression route for their internal clinical staff to get to paramedic level; many of these offer this via apprenticeship programmes. At the time of writing, in England eight (of the ten) ambulance trusts currently offer paramedic degree apprenticeship programmes with a variety of different education providers; check the websites of the ambulance trusts for more details.

What qualifications do I need?

Qualifications required as a minimum are Level 3 English and maths, Level 2 English language GCSE or Level 2 English Functional Skills and Level 2 maths GCSE or Level 2 maths Functional Skills. (Equivalent qualifications can be considered on an individual basis by the ambulance service and the higher education provider.) You will also need to be employed by the service. In some services you can be employed from the outset on an apprenticeship pathway where you move through the pathways and relevant roles in often the quickest time possible (within university course regulations and depending on the job role requirements of your grade/employer).

What do I need to do to prepare, and what students wish they had known before they started?

As discussed throughout this chapter, an apprenticeship route is not easy. There are challenges around workload management, studying alongside working, and the transition and mixing of student and staff roles. However, it is a route that may enable you to access higher education if you were restricted from doing so previously. It provides a route where you are constantly able to consolidate your learning in a practice environment, working and studying alongside clinicians throughout your programme. You are paid a salary while you study on a programme. Apprenticeships create accessible staff development routes and enable trusts to place more of their internal staff on paramedic education routes.

When speaking to apprentices they often discuss the things they wish they had done before the programme that would have made things feel a little easier or made them feel more confident when they started. One of the key things that many of the apprentice learners say is that they could have started their development sooner and made the most of being surrounded by clinicians and students who have gone through, or are going through, what they will eventually go through. They say that getting into the habit of studying early is beneficial. If you know that you want to be a paramedic and want to develop onto a paramedic apprenticeship, then start engaging with students, ask them what they are learning about, and what journals they are reading. You will be able to access journals through an NHS Athens account if you do not have a university account yet. You could join or start a study group with other peers, students, clinicians and pick a subject each week. Start having critical conversations about clinical decision-making, get into the silent dialogue that is often going on in your paramedic colleague's head. Try and understand their decisions, the treatment pathway that they used; all of this will give you a good head start and an understanding of what you are moving into. Make the most of the access you have as a developing clinician to fellow clinicians and learners; they are an invaluable resource as you progress through your journey to becoming a paramedic. More *hints and tips* can be found in Box 4.4.

Box 4.4 What advice do you want to pass on?

📖 **Paramedic apprentice student comment:** Speak to your colleagues if you have a question – both before and during your course. There is no such thing as a stupid question. Your colleagues on the road will be your lifeline, so use them.

📖 **Paramedic apprentice student comment:** Discuss any issues early on; the university in my experience is excellent at providing adapted learning and items to help you in your studies. Be honest and open, and speak out when you are struggling.

📖 **Paramedic apprentice student comment:** I wish I had studied or had more Anatomy and Physiology knowledge before I started. I think it would have made a lot of the content a lot easier for me to understand, like illnesses and injury, and assessment. I would urge anyone that knows they have a place on a programme to start studying this before – don't wait until you start.

📖 **Paramedic apprentice student comment:** Be ready to read around subjects. Start this reading before you start. You can speak to other students about subjects they are looking at, journals they are reading, and then start there.

📖 **Paramedic apprentice student comment:** Have strategies for time management, learn how to plan an essay and understand what you are doing before you start writing.

As can been seen by the comments, some research, careful decision-making and weighing up of the pros and cons should be done before you make a decision. This decision will be as individual as you. Take your time and make the best decision for yourself, the way you learn and your individual circumstances. Chapter 5 will explore the direct-entry undergraduate degree route in more detail.

References

Health and Care Professions Council (2016) *Guidance on Conduct and Ethics for Students.* Available at: https://www.hcpc-uk.org/globalassets/ resources/guidance/guidance-on-conduct-and-ethics-for-students.pdf (accessed 8 April 2022).

Institute for Apprenticeships and Technical Education (2022) *End-Point assessment plan for Paramedic fully integrated degree apprenticeship standard.* Available at: https://www.instituteforapprenticeships.org/ apprenticeship-standards/paramedic-integrated-degree-v1-2 (accessed 12 July 2022).

Universities and Colleges Admissions Service (UCAS) (2022) *What are degree apprenticeships?* Available at: https://www.ucas.com/apprenticeships/ what-you-need-know-about-apprenticeships/degree-apprenticeships-0 (accessed 12 July 2022).

5   WHAT STYLE OF ACADEMIC PROGRAMME IS RIGHT FOR YOU? HAVE YOU CONSIDERED A DIRECT-ENTRY UNDERGRADUATE DEGREE?

Amanda Blaber

The focus of this chapter will be on the higher education route, where HEIs work in partnership with their local NHS ambulance trust. It will use similar chapter sub-headings to Chapter 4, for the reader to be able to draw direct comparisons. Please read both chapters.

What is a direct-entry undergraduate degree?

The direct-entry undergraduate degree is usually a three-year full-time programme of academic study based at a university for academic and simulation study. It includes time in placement with the local ambulance trust and potentially a variety of wider interprofessional placements at acute hospitals, community or primary care services, which may be NHS or voluntary sector. Candidates apply to the universities of their choice via the Universities and Colleges Admissions Service, widely referred to as UCAS. Generally (but please check with the individual university you are considering applying for) there is no contract of employment with an employer. If you wish to undertake part-time work (or work in the holidays) you secure this for yourself and manage work alongside your studies. But as you will be on a full-time programme of study, you must be available for university study and placements – your study comes first.

It may be worth taking a few sentences to explain academic levels of study and the variety of qualifications available. As Table 5.1 shows, the academic level is indicative of the qualification obtained after the programme of study. The variety of titles given to the programmes indicates the academic level of study achieved. One of the most common misconceptions is the title *degree*.

Table 5.1 Various levels of undergraduate study

Undergraduate year	Academic level of study	Certificate	Diploma	Degree
1	4	✓	✓	✓
2	5		✓	✓
3	6			✓

The government coined the phrase 'foundation degrees' during their inception in the 1990s. Generally foundation degrees (FDs) are of two years' duration and students complete academic Levels 4 and 5 only. Bachelor of Science (BSc) or Bachelor of Arts (BA) degrees will usually be of three years' duration (or longer) including a research component and generally a lengthy piece of research-focused work called a *dissertation*.

> **Important point:** In 2018 the HCPC raised the level of qualification for paramedics' registration. Currently they need to achieve a Bachelor degree with honours. Education and training courses that are below this threshold have been withdrawn since 1 September 2021 (HCPC 2018).

In consultation with the professional body, the HCPC made the change to the threshold for paramedic registration on the basis that a higher level of academic level was needed to deliver the standards of proficiency to the depth required in contemporary paramedic practice. But it is wise to be aware of the various academic levels, to ensure you understand the academic demands of the programme you are applying for.

Are there any differences in qualification between an apprenticeship and direct-entry undergraduate programme?

Both programmes award a degree-level qualification (academic Level 6). The difference is mainly in respect of being a full-time student or being an employee during your study period.

It may be worth explaining what the (Hons) at the end of a degree title may mean. When distinguishing between BSc and BSc (Hons) programmes, the 'Hons' part of the award may or may not be linked to the dissertation. For example, in some institutions students can exit the institution with a BSc if they fail to submit/choose not to complete their dissertation. In other institutions the dissertation is part of the overall award and failure to complete the dissertation will mean the student cannot be awarded their degree at all. This is not usual. As the important point above demonstrates, the student requires a Bachelor degree with honours, in order to be eligible to register as a paramedic with the HCPC. To be clear, with all pieces of work, students are generally allowed a second and possibly a third attempt, should they refer (fail) at the first attempt.

Why would I choose a direct-entry undergraduate programme?

There are many reasons why people choose programmes at different academic levels. These reasons may not always be so obvious and in many cases are personal (see Case studies 5.1 and 5.2).

CASE STUDY 5.1

Tim has a BSc (Hons) in Sports Science and as a result has a substantial student loan. He has explored a degree apprenticeship route with his local ambulance trust but has been advised that he needs to be an employee for a minimum of one year before even being considered. Tim is keen to start a career as soon as possible. Even though he has debt, he has calculated it will be quicker for him to complete the full-time undergraduate degree and then get a higher paid job as a paramedic in three years' time, than wait for an opportunity to do a degree apprenticeship. Tim has secured a job as a healthcare assistant in his local hospital, which is a flexible contract (zero hours). He can work during his holiday periods and maybe manage a few hours' paid employment on his days off.

Tim in Case study 5.1 cannot easily access a place on a degree apprenticeship, so even with debt, he has decided the most suitable route for him is to have the security of a place at university with a definite start and completion point. As Case study 5.2 highlights, sometimes candidates apply to university courses without considering the potential issues they may face.

CASE STUDY 5.2

Sally is considering applying for university paramedic study. Sally has a strong support network with her friends and family. She is finding her access course hard work but wants to be a paramedic. She enjoys learning more practically, all her friends have paid jobs and she is missing the money she used to have before she started studying again. Sally does not want to move away from home, she wants to study nearby. The local ambulance trust is not offering places to non-employees at this time and there is a waiting list for the degree apprenticeship route. So Sally has decided to apply for the direct-entry undergraduate degree option at universities local to her home. She is only applying to one or two universities. In conversations with her friends and family, Sally says she may find study at BSc (Hons) level too challenging, but is applying anyway.

Sally may not gain entry to a BSc programme. If she is struggling with her access course, she may not meet the entry criteria for BSc (Hons) study. Sally is narrowing her options by potentially only applying to one or two universities, but of course she also needs to consider her social and support networks, moving away from home is not for everyone. Case studies 5.1 and 5.2 help to explain that sometimes students apply for, and end up on, programmes for a variety of reasons. Decision-making is not straightforward or without external influences. This misunderstanding around levels of study, together with the complex financial situation surrounding paramedic study, can lead to extremely varied educational standards of students within a cohort of student paramedics. Hopefully the case studies have highlighted that each student has their own personal circumstances, competing demands and situations to take into account when choosing their type of study.

Candidates need to be clear what they are applying for, the differences between programmes of study at various universities and to be honest about their own expectations and abilities.

What will I be studying?

Chapters 8 and 9 deal with this is more detail. Broadly, there are two considerations for universities to address when planning a paramedic-focused undergraduate university programme: the HCPC Standards of Proficiency for Paramedics (the governing body) and the College of Paramedic Curriculum Guidance (the professional body).

How will I be studying?

Again, this will be detailed in Chapters 8 and 9. There will be a mixture of lectures, seminars, discussion groups, and workshops. There will also be some simulation activities and online study. You will be required to work on your own, researching and reading for assessments/assignments and also to work in smaller or larger groups with other students (from your cohort or from other programmes). In addition to this, you will have time on placement working with other healthcare clinicians, where you will have competencies (skills) in which to demonstrate competence and to be able to explain your knowledge of the subject/skill.

Work and study: the challenges and how to deal with them

As an undergraduate student paramedic you have to manage your time well. Some programmes with have blocks of time on placement, others will have placement each week. Again, think about which approach will suit you best, as an individual. You will have to talk to members of staff, get to know them, work with them and also talk to patients, even from day one. The same applies to your teaching team and members of your cohort.

You will not have the demands of being employed by an ambulance trust, but you will have to demonstrate professionalism and commitment. There are more details in Chapters 8 and 11.

Practice placements

Placements on a direct-entry undergraduate degree may be slightly more diverse than on a degree apprenticeship. Universities will liaise with their placement partners (acute and community trusts) to provide short placement experiences within areas recommended by the College of Paramedics Curriculum Guidance document. These are just as important as ambulance-specific placements and enable student paramedics to gain experience and an understanding of wider NHS areas, such as mental health, midwifery, children's care and so on. This also helps to promote interprofessional working and learning. There are more details about placements in Chapters 15, 16 and 17.

How do I get a place? What qualifications will I need?

Explore the UCAS website for direct-entry undergraduate paramedic degrees. These are mostly degrees in Paramedic Science. UCAS and the College of Paramedics websites contain useful information on career choice in addition to specific university courses and their content/structure. The entry criteria and course structure for each university is clearly visible on the UCAS website. If you are unsure, then use the contact details for the university concerned and ask your questions.

Visit open days at the universities you are interested in, whether that is face to face or online initially. Ensure you are studying subjects/level to meet the entry criteria for the universities you wish to apply for. There is more useful advice on this in Chapters 4, 5, 6 and 7.

Summary

It is hoped this chapter (and Chapter 4) have provided you with clear comparisons and differences between the degree apprenticeship and the direct-entry undergraduate degree route options. The world of education can be a confusing one, with its own language, so ask your questions, and make sure you understand and read the rest of this book to give you a more thorough understanding of the choices you need to make and the knowledge you need in order to make the right choice for you.

The following chapters use the word *student paramedic* generically to mean degree apprentices or direct-entry undergraduate students. Where there may be differences, this is highlighted.

References

College of Paramedics (2019) *Paramedic Curriculum Guidance.* Available at: https://collegeofparamedics.co.uk/COP/ProfessionalDevelopment/Paramedic_Curriculum_Guidance.aspx (accessed 12 July 2022).

Health and Care Professions Council (2018) *Standards of Proficiency for Paramedics.* Available at: https://www.hcpc-uk.org/resources/standards/standards-of-proficiency-paramedics/ (accessed 12 July 2022).

Universities and Colleges Admissions Service website (careers advice): https://www.ucas.com/careers-advice/employment/how-to-become-a/paramedic (accessed 12 July 2022).

Universities and Colleges Admissions Service website (course searching): https://www.ucas.com/explore/subjects/paramedic-science (accessed 12 July 2022).

6 PRACTICAL CONSIDERATIONS

Helen Abrahams, Kim Tolley and Amanda Blaber

Having considered the more academic aspects of choosing the right programme for you in the previous two chapters, it is equally important to consider the more practical aspects. This chapter has used the topics mentioned by students in the questionnaire responses to gauge what topics to include.

Location – near home or further away?

This is obviously a personal decision. Some students will be restricted by their personal circumstances. Other students will want to move away from their family and friends and want to experience university life. Some applicants will take up employment and then commence study, or undertake study that involves paid employment.

Increasingly, students are choosing to live nearer to where they call home (whether that be near friends/family or not) and attend the nearest paramedic programme to them. They are, however, generally not living with their parent(s), instead choosing to stay close to home but living independently. There may be many reasons for this but support networks, rental costs, the cost of living, bills and subsequent debt on leaving university are certainly considerations for many students. See Box 6.1 for details.

Box 6.1 Students' views on location of academic study

📖 **Student paramedic comment:** I got my place during Clearing, so I did not have much time at all to think about it. Now, I wish I had taken my time to research different places and maybe have a year out, and to get some healthcare experience – I think that would have made Year 1 much easier. A year seems a long time to wait, but in hindsight it really was too much of a rush for me from Clearing to the start of the term.

📖 **Student paramedic comment:** This is my second degree, so I guess I am a mature student now. I have done the 'uni life' bit, so I have chosen to come home, live with friends and study hard this time round! Deciding whether to live away or stay closer to home for university is a big decision. I have been used to working and having money to spend, now I have to tighten my belt, which is hard, but I am doing what I want to have as a career. If I had not rushed to university the first time, I may have come to this conclusion earlier.

📖 **Student paramedic comment:** There are so many more universities that run paramedic degree courses now, so there will be one near where you live. Choose carefully, the subjects within the degree are all similar, but the way the programmes are structured can vary quite considerably. So make sure you know yourself and what you want. Moving away was part of growing up and becoming independent for me. Looking back, the distance from home, in miles, was less of a problem than I thought, and only made a difference when travelling home for holidays.

📖 **Student paramedic comment:** The programme itself and placements are often busy, emotionally draining and strenuous. On top of this, each year I have to find and move house, meet new work colleagues and make new friends. It is tough and someone with less resilience may find it too much to cope with. At times it has been challenging being so far away from home, away from people who would help you out cooking you a meal, doing some washing and so on. But I have made a strong circle of close friends and there is lots of help from university support services and my university tutors have proved invaluable when I have needed them. I would recommend anyone thinking of moving away to give it lots of thought and be realistic. But it is more than possible and for me it was a great decision.

📖 **Student paramedic comment:** I wish I could move out; I have a partner and family! Running a house, school runs, family commitments and so on, makes me busy without starting on a student paramedic programme. I have to plan my weeks very carefully, so I have quiet time in the house to study. Sometimes shifts/study days change, which mess up my plans, but this will happen when I get my paramedic job, so the family just have to get on with it. But it is not easy for them either, it's a tough programme, but it will be worth it.

The comments in Box 6.1 provide insight into some of the factors that influence decision-making for students. As they demonstrate, support networks are an important consideration.

Support networks

Think about who provides you with support when you need it. Do you think you can manage with these important people being quite a distance away, or would you prefer to keep them nearby? Any healthcare role involves personal investment in your patients and clients. This can be extremely rewarding, but not always a happy experience and without distress for the patient, their family and perhaps yourself. You may need the support of your established network, in addition to the new friends you will be making and the colleagues and staff you will get to know as your studies progress.

ℰ Refer to Chapters 1 and 18 for more on support and resilience.

As you can see from the students' comments in Box 6.2, support networks are extremely important to student paramedics, in whatever guise.

As mentioned by the students in the comments in Box 6.2, support networks come in all shapes and sizes, and each student will have an individual approach to establishing and maintaining these networks. It is important not to overlook the importance and value of thinking about your existing support networks and being realistic about your individual requirements.

Reflection: Points to consider

Having read the comments from students about the importance of choosing a university, the 'home or away' decision and the importance of your support networks, write a list of the pros and cons of your university choices. This may help you think more deeply about what is involved and may highlight issues that you had not previously considered.

Box 6.2 Students' views on support networks

📖 **Student paramedic comment:** I had a good support network in my family (being married, with a grown-up son); they were always encouraging of what I was doing. I found, though, that as my clinical experience developed and the number of 'difficult' call-outs I went to increased, I became more and more selective about what I would tell my family. This was partly as I did not want to upset them with some of the things I'd seen, but also because as you progress in your paramedic experience you realise that relatives and friends can't always understand or appreciate some aspects of the job – you have to be in it to fully understand it. As a result you keep some things to yourself. This can be difficult in terms of ensuring you don't let things get on top of you, especially if you've been to a traumatic call-out where you encountered something upsetting. That's where I began to rely more and more on my fellow student paramedics (who were also encountering some things for the first time). We were a very close-knit cohort and strongly supported each other. Also, my paramedic mentor and programme tutors were brilliant in supporting me/us. I guess you develop different levels of support from different people as you progress through the programme. It ties in a lot with developing your personal resilience.

📖 **Student paramedic comment:** Losing my support network has had a big impact on deciding whether living so far from friends and family is worth it. Travelling back home every month or so takes a big toll on you, not only financially but also physically, which can make keeping up with studies and placements hard work.

📖 **Student paramedic comment:** A support network is important while on a programme like this, as it can be quite intense and emotionally challenging at times. I am quite a distance from home and it is impossible to keep travelling home. Of course I keep in contact with people, but I need to become independent too. My advice would be to make sure you find someone who you are comfortable talking to, and don't be afraid to ask for help or support from university; they've dealt with it all before and really do help. Good luck!

Visiting universities

Visit the UCAS website for a list of programmes offered and then explore the specific university websites that are relevant to your choices. Also visit the College of Paramedics website for information pertaining to students.

Think about your current studies and what level of study best suits you. Do internet research about the various programmes on offer and make a shortlist of HEIs that you wish to consider. Look at the wider website for the HEI and look at things that are important to you, such as sports facilities, social clubs, or student events. Although programmes are competitive, it is really important for you to be happy during your period of study in an institution.

Attend open days where at all possible. Since the COVID-19 pandemic, many HEIs are offering online open days, in addition to ones held on campuses. Attending online events may help you to 'shortlist' universities, with a view to attending campus open days for the universities you have 'shortlisted'. Here you usually have the opportunity to hear from the lecturers running the programmes and from the current students, and you can ask questions that may be generic or specific to the programme. You will get a sense of the academic environment, location and whether the programme is what you expected or not, as the student comments in Box 6.3 illustrate.

Let's talk about money

Embarking on a university programme is a big decision and one really important factor to consider is the financial commitment.

Fee status of the programme

University programme fees are something you need to research for yourself. At the time of writing, the picture is extremely varied across England for paramedic programmes. The same cannot be said of other health professional courses. For example, student nurses have to pay tuition fees. But they are eligible for a Tuition Fee Loan from the Student Loan Company (SLC) to cover the cost of fees, even if they already have an equivalent qualification. This loan has to be repaid, when they start earning over the threshold for loan repayment. This is not the case with paramedic

Box 6.3 Students' views on visiting universities

📖 **Student paramedic comment:** Open days are a must. You get a better feel for a place by going there than by just reading a prospectus. You also meet fellow 'wannabe' paramedic students who you keep bumping into at different university open days! This is especially good if some of you make it to the same cohort at the same university – meaning you already have a couple of friends on the first day!

The chance to talk to the programme leaders/current students/past students is often part of the open day experience. At my university we got the chance to speak to current students on their own without the tutors. This meant we could ask whatever we liked and get a true idea of what the programme involved. I thought this was a very good idea and made me want to attend this university more than the others I'd seen.

📖 **Student paramedic comment:** I attended several online open days. You can listen, make notes and listen to the questions others are asking or typing. Once you gain confidence, you can do the same. I found it helpful to write a series of questions that I wanted answers to, whether that was online or in person. Comparing and contrasting is really important. It is very individual though; what suits one person will not suit another. The worst thing you can do is choose a place because your friend is going there.

education, although the professional body, the College of Paramedics, has made representations to the Department of Health and Social Care (DHSC) to address the anomalies. At the time of writing, the College has successfully achieved more parity. For the 2022 to 2023 academic year, students studying paramedicine can also have their eligibility assessed on a case-by-case basis if they are ineligible for tuition fees and maintenance support because they have an equivalent or lower qualification. Students will be eligible for NHS Learning Support Fund provisions from the start of their 2022–23 academic year. The College of Paramedics has worked with the DHSC alongside key stakeholders, including colleagues in Health Education England (HEE) to bring parity with other AHP professions for pre-registration paramedic students who already hold an undergraduate degree. As you can see from the examples in Table 6.1, the situation is

Table 6.1 Examples of the potential variation in fee status

Student	University fees	Any funding provided to the student by the local clinical commissioning group (CCG)	Travel expenses	Uniform (check with the university)
1	£9000	None	None	Not provided
2	£9000	None	Paid	Provided
3	£9000	Monthly amount paid direct to student	Paid	Provided
4	Paid by CCG to university	None	None	Provided
5	Paid by CCG to university	Monthly amount paid direct to student	Paid	Provided

hugely variable and you need to establish the situation at each university and their partner ambulance trust to whom you wish to apply.

As you will notice, Student 5 in Table 6.1 is financially better off than Student 1. Unfortunately these financial irregularities are a reality and may well affect your decision-making. These differences are something that you need to be aware of and should be explored during your research and visits to the universities. In addition to the programme costs, you will need to factor in the cost of living for your chosen location of study.

Accommodation costs

At the risk of stating the obvious, parts of England vary considerably in terms of the cost of accommodation and the cost of living – rent, buying food and socialising. Research this carefully and be realistic. You will need time away from your studies to relax, so try to factor this in.

Travel costs

As with other healthcare professions, paramedic programmes will involve working with paramedics on ambulances and other vehicles. You will need to get to your placement area. Research the areas that you may be expected to travel to for clinical placement, and look at the worst-case scenario in terms of distances that you may need to travel. Also consider how often you are expected to do this and over how long a period, as the costs involved will add up over time.

> **Student paramedic comment:** I would say you definitely need your own car. You can use public transport for a lot of things, but if you finish a shift after an overrun at 2am you'll be waiting a long time at the bus stop (possibly in the freezing rain!). I can't think of a student in our cohort who didn't have their own transport – it's a necessity.

How will you get to the clinical placement: using your own car or by public transport? When considering shifts, it may not be possible to get public transport to some areas, or after the end of shifts. Your own personal safety is also a huge consideration – you may be finishing a shift in the early hours and need to get home safely.

Ask about reimbursement of travel costs. As with funding, some programmes may offer this, some may not. If travel costs are reimbursed, be realistic that you will have to pay for the travel up front and then claim costs back. There will be a delay in receiving the money you will have paid out.

Working while studying

Ideally, your studies should be a priority so that you can achieve your potential. However, HEIs are mindful of the financial situation of their students and understand that many students need to supplement their income by undertaking paid work throughout the duration of their studies. Many HEIs will provide guidance on this with regard to an appropriate balance between paid work and study. In discussion with colleagues in other universities, they usually recommend no more than 15–20 hours of paid work per week. However, this will not be suitable for all students, as the student comment below indicates.

Student paramedic comment: Managing your money through your studies is something you definitely need to keep on top of if you don't want to find yourself struggling more than a student normally has to struggle. I would say it is possible to have a job outside of study in the first year; however, in the second (and if you have a third year) it becomes increasingly difficult. It's not impossible, I know other students managed it but I couldn't have. I saved as much money as I could prior to starting my studies and worked hard to earn money beforehand so that I didn't have to get a paying job during the programme and could concentrate on my studies. I've still come out with a student debt, but at least it's not as big as students who had to pay fees on top of living costs.

You will come out with a student debt, it's unavoidable. However, just how big that debt is can be up to you in your choice of university, your financial preparation before starting, and in how closely you manage your money during the programme.

As a student on a paramedic programme, you are likely to be expected to undertake some shift work. If you have never worked shifts previously, you may find your sleep becomes disturbed and you struggle to balance shifts on placement with study and outside work commitments. You also need to consider what type of paid work may fit into your programme, as the student's comment above highlights. For instance, if you have regular work each Saturday, is it possible to keep your Saturday job if you have to undertake placement hours on some Saturdays? This is another aspect to consider carefully.

℘ Refer to Chapter 8 and the section on shift work for more detail.

Can you afford it?

Unfortunately, the reality of the situation is that a lack of money may impact upon your studies. It is therefore really important that you take into consideration all of the points raised in this chapter. It may be that you postpone your decision to study for a year, while you gather some healthcare experience and accumulate some funds, so you can concentrate solely on your programme. This is not the end of the world. Be realistic about the demands of the study, placement, shifts, and potential lack of money, and make your decision accordingly. At least you know what you are letting yourself in for! Unfortunately, the drain on finances is not just related to your accommodation and living expenses – there is potentially driving instruction to consider.

Health, well-being and good character

Applicants would be wise to read the HCPC booklet entitled 'Guidance on Health and Character' last updated in 2017 – the full reference/web address is given at the end of this chapter. This document covers all health professionals that are registered with the HCPC, not just paramedics. It also provides explanations for prospective applicants about the importance of such issues.

The main purpose is to ensure that applicants to the register can practise safely and effectively. The safety of the public is a key aspect of this too; this must be protected. If a concern is raised about an applicant's health or character with the HCPC, they are able to take action in order to protect the public.

Trust, confidence and professionalism are cornerstones of healthcare work and central to the relationship between a registrant and the service user, no matter the professional title, for example paramedic or social worker. It is the HCPC's role to check registrants'/applicants' health and character, in order to reduce the potential risk of harm to the public and uphold the trust the public have in any healthcare profession/professional.

The notion of *good character* is central to what the HCPC examine. They look for any evidence of past actions which may imply the person is not of good character. Any evidence of untrustworthiness or dishonesty, actions that may have harmed a service user or member of the public are key aspects that are examined. These may all affect the public's confidence in the registered professional. Obviously, this is equally important for recruitment to paramedic programmes, and will be investigated using the universities' usual processes.

Health can mean different things to different people. In this context the HCPC are clear that *health* means medical conditions which may affect an applicant's or registrant's fitness to practise. A person may have a medical condition or be unwell, but they are managing their condition and are able to practise safely in their profession. Health conditions and disabilities do not routinely need to be declared, unless the condition or disability affects a person's *fitness to practise*. The HCPC in their documentation are clear that it is rare that declarations of this kind affect registration, but it is important that applicants/registrants tell the HCPC any information that may be used to make decisions about whether that individual should be granted registration.

To drive or not to drive?

The picture is varied in respect of driving. The reasons why this is the case requires some explanation. Currently there is no requirement to hold a full UK manual driving licence to register with the HCPC as a paramedic (HCPC 2022).

Yes, there are other paramedic roles that do not involve driving, such as cyclist paramedics and paramedics working on oil rigs. Other than the ambulance service, the more usual paramedic roles are working in primary care in GP surgeries and walk-in centres, and sometimes in emergency departments in hospitals. However, the more unusual posts (cyclist and oil-rig paramedics) usually require experience as a paramedic in order to be shortlisted for interview. So at some point, if you want to work for an ambulance service, you will probably need to hold a full manual UK driving licence. However, there are restrictions on people driving emergency vehicles with certain medical conditions (see DVLA 2022), so check also with the Human Resources department of the ambulance trust you may want to work for after registration.

The picture is further muddled by what is known as category C1. The weight of ambulances becomes an issue here; generally they weigh in excess of 3500 kg. After 1997, changes outlined by the DVLA (see https://www.gov.uk/old-driving-licence-categories) meant that passing a full UK manual test no longer entitled you to drive vehicles in excess of 3500 kg, as it had previously.

Many applicants to paramedic programmes will also need to take an additional theory and practical test to have category C1 on their existing full UK manual driving licence. The point at which students are required/need to do this will depend on the programme of study and their age. Some programmes involve part employment with ambulance trusts, so for these programmes students need to have C1 on their licence before starting their studies. Other programmes require just the full manual UK driving licence and, if you do not have C1, it may be suggested that you plan this into your vacation periods so you possess it before completion.

Some programmes may not require you to drive at all. It may be strongly suggested to you that you have some means of getting yourself safely to and from clinical placements. It is important that you consider your shift start and end times and the location of placements; think about whether you can get to placements by public transport at all times of day and night. Do you really want to be waiting for public transport at 2am in the rain? It is generally not the case that you can sleep on site as you are required to leave the premises once your shift is over. Sometimes, you may be required to stay on after the end of your official end time, so you need a reliable means of transport home.

Before you jump in and enrol to take your C1 theory and practical, please consider the financial implication to obtaining this category. You should enquire about the costs involved from driving schools with experience of preparing student paramedics for the C1 tests. Also explore the DVLA weblink in the suggested reading/websites at the end of this chapter to learn more.

Student paramedic comment: You are going to need a C1 on your driving licence if you didn't pass your test before 1997. The cost of getting this is significant, so you need to factor it in. Even if you already have a C1 category on your licence (as I did) it's worth getting a couple of lessons in an ambulance equivalent vehicle if you've not driven one before, just so you know what it's like. You don't want the first time you get behind the wheel of something bigger than a car to be on the first day of your blue-light driving course.

Student paramedic comment: I found I was struggling to get to placement sites (ambulance and some wider NHS sites) on time for early starts, and getting home late at night, especially in winter, was stressful. It is all much easier now I can drive and have my own transport.

Once you possess category C1 on your driving licence you will need to complete a *blue-light* driving course. This is usually managed by the partner ambulance trust or the paramedic's first employer (if they choose employment by an ambulance trust). If you are studying via a degree apprenticeship, this will be managed by your ambulance trust employer.

However, it is likely that most registrants' first employed post as a paramedic will be with an NHS ambulance trust, mostly working on an ambulance, perhaps occasionally on a solo responder vehicle. Therefore, it is commonplace for NHS ambulance trusts to stipulate that applicants also have category C1 on their full manual UK driving licence. Some universities may have a partnership approach to this issue with their local NHS ambulance trust, such as the trust lending students the money for the C1 tests and the student paying this back once they are employed.

This chapter has addressed many aspects that require the undergraduate applicant to be self-aware, to address the potential difficulties realistically, and to be honest about the realities of undertaking a paramedic programme.

References

College of Paramedics (2019) *Paramedic Curriculum Guidance* (5th edn). Bridgwater: College of Paramedics. Available at: https://collegeofparamedics. co.uk/COP/ProfessionalDevelopment/Paramedic_Curriculum_Guidance. aspx (accessed 19 April 2022)

College of Paramedics (2022) *Become a Paramedic.* Available at: https://collegeofparamedics.co.uk/COP/Become_a_Paramedic/COP/ BecomeAParamedic/Become_a_Paramedic.aspx?hkey=f10838de-b67f-44a0- 83b7-8140d8cdba83 (accessed 19 April 2022).

Department of Health and Social Care (2022) *NHS Financial Support for Health Students* (6th edn). NHS Learning Support Fund. Information for the academic authorities and students for the 2022 to 2023 academic year. Available at: https://assets.publishing.service.gov.uk/government/ uploads/system/uploads/attachment_data/file/1101894/NHS_learning_ support_fund_6th_edition_2022_to_2023.pdf (accessed 8 September 2022).

DVLA (2022) *Compare old and new driving licence categories.* Available at: https://www.gov.uk/old-driving-licence-categories (accessed 19 April 2022).

DVLA (2022) *Current Medical Guidelines: DVLA Guidance for Professionals.* Available at: https://www.gov.uk/guidance/assessing-fitness-to-drive-a-guide-for-medical-professionals (accessed 19 April 2022).

DVLA (2022) *Driving License Categories.* Available at: https://www.gov.uk/driving-licence-categories (accessed 19 April 2022).

DVLA (2022) *Adding categories to your driving license.* Available at: https://www.gov.uk/adding-higher-categories-to-your-driving-licence (accessed 19 April 2022).

Health and Care Professions Council (2017) *Guidance on Health and Character.* Available at: https://www.hcpc-uk.org/globalassets/resources/guidance/guidance-on-health-and-character.pdf (accessed 19 April 2022).

Health and Care Professions Council (2018) *New Threshold for Paramedic Registration.* Available at: https://www.hcpc-uk.org/news-and-events/blog/2018/new-threshold-for-paramedic-registration/ (accessed 19 April 2022).

Health and Care Professions Council (2022) *Standards of Proficiency for Paramedics.* Available at: https://www.hcpc-uk.org/resources/standards/standards-of-proficiency-paramedics/ (accessed 19 April 2022).

Universities and Colleges Admissions Service. Available at: http://www.ucas.com/.

PART 3
Making the most of your academic study

7 WHAT IS A 'PROFESSIONAL' PROGRAMME?

Kim Tolley and Amanda Blaber

Chapter 2 briefly mentioned the fact that paramedic studies incorporate both an academic and professional qualification. This means that you will leave your university with an academic qualification – either a BSc (Hons) or MSc degree – and the eligibility to register with the Health and Care Professions Council (HCPC) at the point of successfully completing the period of study.

It has already been stated that healthcare students are different from other university students, and the role of regulatory bodies such as the Health and Care Professions Council (HCPC), and professional bodies such as the College of Paramedics (CoP), and the impact they have on student paramedics, will be discussed further in this chapter. You will also have a chance to explore what constitutes professional behaviour as a paramedic – an important area that will impact on your final reference from your university to the HCPC.

What is the Health and Care Professions Council (HCPC)?

The HCPC is a multi-professional regulator in the UK. Paramedics, as allied health professionals, are one of the health and care professions that are regulated by the HCPC. The main objective of the HCPC is to protect the public and uphold confidence in the professions it regulates. To meet this obligation, it recognises that it needs to support you both as a student and registrant.

To be able to practise as a paramedic in the UK you must be registered with the HCPC. The 'paramedic' title is a designated title, one that is protected by law. This helps to ensure that the level of care delivered by any UK paramedic meets the relevant HCPC standards. This is the same for many other healthcare professionals, such as nurses, who are regulated by the Nursing and Midwifery Council (NMC), and doctors, who are regulated by the General Medical Council (GMC).

So, what does the HCPC do?

Standards

The HCPC sets the Standards of Proficiency for Paramedics (HCPC 2023), Standards of Conduct, Performance and Ethics (HCPC 2016a), Standards of Education and Training (2017), and the Standards of Continuing Professional Development (HCPC 2018). These standards help ensure that health and care professionals are properly educated, keep their knowledge and skills up to date, and continue to meet the standards for professional conduct and professional practice when re-registering.

Your education and training will enable you to understand and meet the HCPC standards. To support your learning, the HCPC Guidance on Conduct and Ethics for Students (HCPC 2016b) provides learning materials (CPD advice for students) in the student hub section of its website. You should read and refer to these materials throughout your learning.

To be able to register with the HCPC, an applicant must be able to demonstrate that they meet the standards of proficiency for their profession. Successfully completing an HCPC approved programme of education should ensure that you meet these standards of proficiency.

Registration

The HCPC maintains the register of paramedics and only people whose names are on the register can be employed and use the title 'Paramedic'. This is what is meant by a protected title. It is a criminal offence to use the title if your name does not appear on the HCPC register. The register is accessible online (https://www.hcpc-uk.org/check-the-register/) and anyone can cross-check a name or registration number. So, patients and employers could look your name up on the register and check that you are a registered paramedic. Near the end of your programme, you will be guided on how and when to complete the process of registration. This is an exciting step and marks the start of your career in healthcare as a fully qualified registrant. All your experiences, both at university and in practice, work towards this goal to ensure that you are ready for the challenge.

Approved programmes of education

The HCPC checks the quality of the education programmes that student paramedics undertake, so that when you complete your programme you have met all the standards required and can then apply to go onto the register of paramedics. This ensures that only individuals who meet the HCPC standards are allowed to practise as a paramedic. The HCPC will meet with your university to do this and may also ask you about your experiences.

Continuing Professional Development (CPD)

You might think that once you are qualified as a paramedic that all your studying is over; in fact, the opposite is true.

Once on the register, paramedics must be able to demonstrate their professional development by undertaking educational and professional study, often called Continuing Professional Development (CPD), maintain a portfolio of learning, and adhere to the HCPC Standards of Continuing Professional Development (HCPC 2018). Some of your CPD may be organised by your employer. Additionally, you may wish to attend CPD organised by other organisations, such as the CoP. As a paramedic, like all the other professional groups regulated by the HCPC, you will be required to renew your registration every two years and you will find out more about this as you go through your course. Other health professionals have a similar system, with nurses and doctors having to revalidate every three years and five years respectively. Each of these systems has their own specific requirements, but they are focused around CPD and reflection. All these systems aim to ensure, in part, that the registered health professionals confirm they are 'fit to practise'.

These are the standards that the public will measure any paramedic against and what they expect. If any paramedic does not meet these professional standards this may result in a complaint from a member of the public or their employer. This can have serious implications and may result in a fitness to practise investigation by the Health and Care Professions Tribunal Service (HCPTS). The HCPTS is the fitness to practise adjudication service of the HCPC. This is the same for all healthcare regulators, which also deal with complaints through their tribunal services.

These differences make a paramedic programme very different from any other programme, for example in engineering or maths. The difference is mainly linked to being a registered health professional and in Chapter 13 we will consider the trust that the public places in all healthcare professionals, including paramedics. This is linked to the registration, which comes with responsibilities to ensure that you meet the standards required of paramedics each day.

Fitness to practise

We have already stated that all registrants must have the skills, knowledge, character, and health to practise their profession safely and effectively. This means that you must be 'fit to practise'.

The HCPC operates a process where concerns about its registrants' conduct, competence, health, or character can be raised with the HCPC. It is obliged to consider all concerns raised with it and decide whether this means that the registrant's fitness to practise is impaired. Impaired fitness to practise means more than a suggestion that the registrant has done something wrong. It means a concern about their conduct, competence, health or character that is serious enough to suggest that they are unfit or unsafe to practise their profession without restriction, or at all.

One important thing to remember is that fitness to practise concerns may include concerns about events that involve issues outside of professional or clinical performance. The conduct of a paramedic outside of their working environment may involve fitness to practise where it could affect the protection of the public or undermine public confidence in the profession. These are very important parts of the trust that people who we care for expect from us. There is a lot more information on the HCPC website about this function and also the HCPTS that we mentioned earlier, which makes independent decisions about fitness to practise.

Box 7.1 refers to the role of the HCPC and provides guidance for students to undertake more investigation. The CoP is also mentioned, and more detail is provided about this organisation in the section below.

What is the College of Paramedics (CoP) and what is its role?

The College of Paramedics (CoP) is the recognised professional body for paramedics in the UK. The CoP represents its members in all matters affecting their clinical practice and supports them to achieve the highest standards of patient care. Its main role is to 'represent paramedics' in all matters affecting their clinical practice. It also provides support and advice to candidates, students, associate and full members of the CoP.

Box 7.1 Comments about the role of the HCPC and CoP

🎓 **Academic response:** The HCPC is there to protect the public and ensure that its registrants maintain high personal and professional standards.

The HCPC is there to protect the public and uphold confidence in the professions it regulates. It does this by ensuring that its registrants maintain high professional standards. Understanding these standards and being able to embed them into your practice will help you to achieve them every day. The HCPC publishes a range of resources and delivers learning events to help you understand and keep up to date with the standards.

The CoP is influential in forming the future of paramedic education. It runs CPD events and produces several curriculum frameworks that shape paramedic education across the UK. As the professional body for paramedics in the UK, it does have influence.

🚨 **Practice educator (PEd) response:** It is worth joining the CoP in order to keep abreast of developments in your profession. It runs excellent CPD days and offers guidance and support to paramedics, both qualified and those still a student.

📖 **Student paramedic response:** I know there are some countries where just about anybody can call themselves a paramedic after having had hardly any training or education. The fact that we have to register with a regulatory body which will only let us be called 'paramedics' once we have achieved a whole raft of criteria gives a value to the title 'paramedic' which is greater than anywhere else in the world – we're not just medics, we're HCPC paramedics! That means we have met standards that the public can have confidence in and that we ourselves can have confidence in – the people who decide who can practise as paramedics have decided we are fit to practise, and that gives me a confidence I wouldn't have if I'd only done a first-aid course and put on a green jumpsuit.

🚨 **Practice educator (PEd) response:** It is important to understand your roles and responsibilities from day one. Take time to explore the HCPC website – look through documents that it provides and understand how you will function individually. There are many supportive documents on the HCPC website, explaining how they help students and registrants alike. You will also find examples of fitness to practise cases. Familiarise yourself with the CPD guidance and learn how the HCPC functions in the development of the paramedic profession and educational programmes. Having an understanding and awareness of this will assist in your development from a general student to a professional student, and then into a healthcare professional who takes great pride in obtaining and maintaining their registration and being part of a professional regulatory body. I would massively suggest becoming a member of the CoP early on; yes, there is a cost – but it is worth it! Lots of work goes into developing study days that are specifically aimed at the paramedic profession and delivered by specialists. Additionally, once you are registered there are CPD activities and guidance notes to help you continue your learning and development.

As with any professional body there is a membership cost, but this is significantly reduced for student paramedics, and with this membership comes access to numerous local CPD and educational events. Full CoP members and students are covered for medical malpractice and liability insurance as part of their membership. Full-time students practise under supernumerary status and work under the close supervision of their practice educators or clinical supervisors at all times. Students would not be liable for any errors or mistakes during their full-time student status; this is different with degree apprentices, who need to clarify the situation with their employer.

Another aspect of the CoP's work is to support HEIs in the development of programmes of study. All programmes on the UCAS website have undergone internal scrutiny by the individual university's quality processes and external scrutiny from the HCPC before finally gaining approval of their programme by the HCPC. This process can take up to a year or more to achieve from inception to successful approval. *Paramedic Curriculum Guidance* from the CoP (CoP 2019) details the approval and endorsement of programmes:

> To achieve endorsement requires programmes to produce graduates at a minimum of BSc (Hons) throughout England, Wales and

Northern Ireland, and SHE Level 3 (SCQF9) in Scotland. This aligns with the Quality Assurance Agency for Higher Education Subject Benchmark Statement – Paramedics (QAA 2019).

So you may also see the CoP logo on university presentations/paperwork. This denotes that the programme you are investigating has undergone the CoP endorsement process, in addition to the HCPC and internal university validation.

Having discussed some aspects of academic study in Chapter 3, it is appropriate to examine what is meant by the term *professional behaviour*.

Professional behaviour

The HCPC *Guidance on Conduct and Ethics for Students* (HCPC 2016b) makes clear that any concern relating to conduct or, more accurately, misconduct, outside your programme of study is important and that there are certain professional responsibilities. It is clear that conduct outside of study is scrutinised and in serious circumstances may affect the student's ability to complete their studies, gain the final qualification or register with the HCPC. Some definitions of professional behaviour are given in Box 7.2.

The HCPC lists 10 main points within the guidance document (HCPC 2016b), with further detail provided on each point. Take time to read through Table 7.1 carefully and refer to the HCPC document itself for more detail.

Table 7.1 Guidance on conduct and ethics for students

Promote and protect the interests of service users and carers
Communicate appropriately and effectively
Work within the limits of their knowledge and skills
Delegate appropriately
Respect confidentiality
Manage risk
Report concerns about safety
Be open when things go wrong
Be honest and trustworthy
Keep records of your work with service users and carers

Some of the terminology used in Table 7.1 may not be familiar to you and will require further reading. Do not worry too much about this, as your programme of study will address these concepts in more detail and relate them to the work of a paramedic.

Box 7.2 How would you define the term 'professional behaviour'?

🎓 **Academic response:** Professional behaviour can be defined as conforming to the technical or ethical standards of one's profession. For many health professionals, including paramedics, these standards are explicitly set out by the HCPC. Some are generic and some profession-specific. These standards should be adhered to at all times and do not become of less value just because you may be having a bad shift.

🚨 **Practice educator (PEd) response:** It is important to understand that professional behaviour applies not only to when you are at work, but also in your personal life. Take care when using social media. Many students and qualified paramedics have posted 'inappropriate' information which may be indefensible if questioned.

🚨 **Practice educator (PEd) response:** For me this is quite simply the most important thing. I view professional behaviour as a multitude of actions and not just the way that you conduct yourself at work. You wear a uniform, so wearing this smartly and with pride to represent your profession, the language you choose to use daily, the actions you choose to take outside of work that impact on the public's perception of you (you never know when that person may just be your patient), and the way you conduct yourself in work, with colleagues and patients alike – all go towards developing your professional behaviour. How you behave at university and in your private life is equally important because, speaking from experience, you get noticed there as well. Social media – well, all I would say, is use it appropriately. Professional behaviour overall, for me, is who you are. We have all chosen a profession that makes us hugely recognisable in the public eye, and we will be noticed. Remembering that, both inside and outside of work, doesn't stop you from having fun and enjoying your journey, but it does stop you from simply getting into a whole world of problems.

📖 **Student paramedic response:** The public often don't know you are a student. We wear the uniform of our university and/or ambulance trust. So, you are dressed in a uniform of some description. It may or may not be the same as a paramedic's uniform. Sometimes, it's only your epaulettes/name badge which mark out the difference. You are representing a lot of other people when you put that uniform on, not just yourself. The public see the ambulance service as a whole and other paramedics get an impression of your university when they look at you and the way you behave. Act like a professional even before you become one.

Being professional, in my opinion, means being the best paramedic you can be and doing the best you can do for your patient. It's treating every patient like they are a relative of yours. If your mum needed a paramedic today, how would you want her to be treated? The elderly lady you get called out to is someone's mum or gran. Treat them like your own.

🚨 **Practice educator (PEd) response:** Attitude is also about interaction with the ambulance crew you are on placement with. Your mentor maybe crewed with a member of staff who is also learning and who will also need to improve their skills. A shift is not just about you learning, but about working all together to look after patients and to develop each other's skills set. There are other sorts of students working with the ambulance service, not just ones from universities, so remembering this is important for good working relationships with all staff.

Health and character

The HCPC *Guidance on Health and Character* (2021b) is another important document to read at the beginning of the programme and to refer to during the programme.

There are two elements to this: *health* and *character*, but they can be intertwined.

On successfully completing an educational programme of study the student paramedic will be asked for information as part of a declaration of *good character* and this forms one part of the application process to join the HCPC register as a paramedic. The following refers to the relevant part of the HCPC guidance on character and health respectively.

Your character

When it comes to character declarations, the information you must provide as an applicant and a registrant is slightly different.

As an applicant

We ask you to make a declaration about your character as part of your application. In this declaration you need to tell us if you have ever:

- been convicted of a criminal offence or received a police caution or conditional discharge for a criminal offence other than a protected caution or protected conviction (these are cautions and convictions that you do not need to tell us about) in any part of the United Kingdom; or
- received cautions or convictions in countries outside the United Kingdom, if the offence is one that could have resulted in a caution or conviction in England or Wales.

Source: https://www.hcpc-uk.org/registration/health-and-character-declarations/what-is-a-health-and-character-declaration/character-issues-that-need-to-be-declared/

Your health

When we talk about 'health', we mean any health conditions which may affect either an applicant or a registrant's fitness to practise; that is, their ability to practise safely and effectively.

We expect registrants to monitor their health and ensure they maintain their fitness to practise. Standard 6.3 of your Standards of Conduct, Performance and Ethics (HCPC 2016a) states:

> *You must make changes to how you practise, or stop practising, if your physical or mental health may affect your performance or judgement, or put others at risk for any other reason.*

If you are worried about any of these during the course, it is always best to speak to someone at the university. Do not leave it until you are about to finish the programme to check.

The HCPC guidance also gives you lots of advice if you are worried about health issues. Before you commence any healthcare-related programme of study or employment, you will need to complete an occupational health questionnaire and potentially attend an appointment with an occupational health professional. Any issues will have been discussed with you at the start of the course by a member of the occupational health department at your chosen university who undertook your appropriate health screening and vaccinations. If you are on a degree apprenticeship route, you will have had occupational health screening as part of your contract of employment. During your programme the university will be your point of contact for anything related to your health or character. In addition to this, as part of admission or employment, you will also have to be screened by the national Disclosure and Barring Service (DBS) for cautions or criminal convictions. This is to protect the public. Forms will be sent to you prior to starting an academic course or employment. You will need to disclose any changes to your university or employer throughout the time on your programme. Failure to do so may have some serious ramifications – remember you are in a public position of trust and, as such, you need to demonstrate trustworthiness and honesty.

When you are about to register or during your career as a paramedic, you may worry about having to tell the HCPC about health concerns. Their guidance makes it clear that:

> *You should tell us about your health condition if it affects your ability to practise safely and effectively. You should also tell us if you are not sure whether your health condition affects (or could affect) your ability to practise, or what steps you need to take to stay safe and effective.*

> *You do not need to tell us if your health condition does not affect your practice or you are sure you can adapt, limit, or stop your practice as needed to remain safe and effective. In other words, you do not need to tell us so long as you can meet Standard 6.3.*

While each registrant is responsible for ensuring their own fitness to practise and to manage risk, the HCPC expects registrants to seek appropriate healthcare advice when they have health concerns and to follow the advice of medical professionals. This applies to conditions that affect your physical health as well as your mental health.

The guidance has useful flow charts that you can use to ask yourself these questions on character and health. However, the best people to talk to are your university as they will be able to help guide you.

Any misconduct outside (or as part of) the programme of study is a serious matter and may affect your long-term career aspirations. In this sense, you should not see your behaviour and conduct inside and outside the university/placement area as being separate. Your conduct at all times needs to be of a high standard and appropriate to a professional eligible to apply for the protected title of 'paramedic'.

The following subsections are intended to draw your attention to areas where there are high expectations for student paramedics.

Attitude

Conduct includes one's attitude to colleagues, service users, families, and academic/practice staff. The HCPC expects the student to be polite and to communicate appropriately and effectively with service users, colleagues, academic and placement teams. Inappropriate attitudes to any parties can potentially be construed as misconduct. Some advice is given in Box 7.3.

⌀ Refer to Chapters 1 and 2 and the discussion about communication and its importance in healthcare environments.

It is clear from the comments in Box 7.2 that attitude encompasses both practice and academic areas of your life and will affect your relationships.

Timekeeping and appearance

Part of professional behaviour is your timekeeping and appearance. Many students are under the misapprehension that timekeeping when in university is less important than when reporting for shifts with their

Box 7.3 What is your advice to students about their attitude?

👆 **Academic response:** Your attitude can have a massive effect on the effectiveness of your interactions with patients, carers, fellow students, and tutors alike. A negative attitude can easily be detected in your body language. At best, this will impede your communication, and at worst it may result in complaints or escalate potentially violent situations.

🎓 **Practice educator (PEd) response:** Attitude is so important. Remember that people who call for an ambulance are often frightened and in pain. What may seem minor to you may be the end of the world to them. We are not in a position to judge our patients – we do not know the road that led them to where they are now. Treat all patients with respect and dignity. Putting a patient at ease will often change an obstructive attitude to one of cooperation. It is very rare that I have been unable to talk round even the most aggressive patient by maintaining a non-judgemental and friendly attitude.

👆 **Academic response:** The HCPC provides advice to students in its *Guidance on Conduct and Ethics for Students*. Students are required to conduct themselves in line with this guidance and can find themselves in serious trouble if they do not, which can lead to fitness to practise processes within their HEI being initiated.

📖 **Student response:** When you think about it, we are a service industry aiming to give 'customer satisfaction'. OK, we don't call our service users 'customers', but the principle is there. We want people who use the service to have a positive experience of it even when, sadly, the outcome of their call is not a happy one. A caring and professional attitude goes without saying, but I learned that you can never underestimate the way in which having this attitude can help calm people or benefit a situation.

People who have had to call an ambulance often say, 'the paramedics were brilliant'. You then find out that they are referring to an event from years ago – people never forget what you have done for them or how you acted; even if it was just another job to you, it could well have been a defining moment for them. Our attitude at work can generate letters from the public, both good and bad. I prefer the good ones!

> 🎓 **Academic response:** It is important to remember that attitude extends to your time in university and the various placements you will undertake as well as your time on shift. Being polite and treating others with respect is imperative. The adage 'manners cost nothing' is very true. You can 'ace' your academic work and still be marked down on your conduct and attitude. This subjective area is probably one of the most important in paramedic practice. Ask yourself often, 'how do you come across to others?'

practice educator or clinical supervisor. Both practice and academic staff note lateness; in some institutions, registers are taken, and lateness officially recorded in both arenas. Any academic asked to write a reference for a student at the end of their studies may be asked by the employer to record episodes of lateness/sickness and absence. It is their professional duty (your lecturers are also professionals with registrations to professional regulatory bodies) to report this as accurately and honestly as possible. Therefore, your personal and professional conduct and performance is under scrutiny in both the academic and practice environment.

When in the practice environment students are required to adhere to the uniform policy for their respective partner ambulance trust or, if not provided with a uniform, the clothes policy for the programme provided by the university (for the purposes of this chapter the term 'uniform' will be used). Some university study may require students to wear their uniforms in the classroom or simulation environment. Students need to be aware that on such occasions full uniform should be worn and appearance should be as smart as when on placement.

You are invited into people's homes, and you are the first point of contact many of your patients will have with the NHS. Your attitude and appearance are what people will use to make their first judgement. It is important to make an excellent first impression, as the comments in Box 7.4 highlight. If you needed a paramedic, who would you rather have care for you: a smart, friendly, helpful paramedic, or one who looks dishevelled, wearing a non-ironed uniform and dirty boots, who looks unenthusiastic and is unfriendly?

Box 7.4 What do you believe is the value (or not) of your uniform?

Student paramedic response: When you first get your uniform it is tempting to be seen wearing it. We were warned about not going 'clubbing' in it or wearing it down the high street when popping out for some milk! Sometimes, though, when you're on your way to the start of your shift and have to stop to get petrol or nip into the supermarket to get your meal deal for lunch, you may be in uniform. I always put a coat over my uniform in that situation so all people can see are my trousers. I don't want to stroll into a supermarket looking like a paramedic when I wasn't yet one. Supposing someone collapsed in the store – everyone would expect me to leap in and do something! Being in uniform (even if it is not the regulation ambulance uniform, a polo shirt with Student Paramedic on it somewhere is enough) outside of your shift is false advertising! Why put yourself in that situation?

Practice educator (PEd) response: Appearance is important! Be proud of the uniform you wear. It may be Christmas, but will the family of the patient in cardiac arrest really be filled with optimism when they see the flashing Santa badge pinned to your lapel or the tinsel taking the place of your bootlaces?

Practice educator (PEd) response: I think uniform has high regard and value with the job we do and serves a purpose. First and foremost, it encourages a professional attitude, as we display the crest and badge of the service for whom we work. Secondly, it sends the message that everyone is equal within the organisation; the lay person we are all in the same uniform. We wear epaulettes that provide distinction of grade.

Practically, it is tough, can be washed over and over, and is designed to minimise injury to you through its simple ergonomic design. Although I am not sure it is designed with women in mind; this could and should be addressed.

Academic response: First impressions count! Patients will be far more willing to trust and cooperate with a smart, friendly paramedic than with one who slouches into the job with shirt tails hanging out, and upset at being called out in the early hours.

Sickness and absence

Students should make sure they are aware of the procedures to report in sick to both academic institutions and practice placement areas. This information is usually available from programme handbooks.

The number of hours accrued in the practice placement environment is specific to individual programmes. Most students will be required to keep a note of the number of hours accrued in both theory and practice. Students should also keep their own record of sickness and absence; official university and practice records can sometimes not reflect what either party believe to be accurate. This is important information and will be requested by potential employers when you are applying for jobs.

Consent

The term *consent* means obtaining the person's permission. For paramedics it usually refers to permission to do something to the patient, such as taking blood pressure. In healthcare, the term *informed consent* is often used. and can be summarised as a person having enough information, in a format they understand, so they can make an 'informed decision' about whether or not they consent to a procedure/treatment and so on. We would also suggest that it could also be about the person's decision *not to* receive care or services. Box 7.5 contains some examples of situations where consent may be difficult to obtain. There are other types of consent that are discussed in the HCPC consent and confidentiality document.

Reflection: Points to consider

Think about the potential issues with gaining consent for someone who is unconscious. What do you think are the issues here?

Consent is a concept that needs to be continually in your mind, and you may need to adapt your practice accordingly. You will meet various situations, as described in Box 7.4, and many will require discussion with your practice educator or clinical supervisor. You are learning – when in doubt, ask, and do some investigation for yourself.

Box 7.5 When informed consent may be difficult to obtain

Practice educator (PEd) response: Wherever possible, gain consent from your patient and explain to them what is happening. In some cases, this may be impossible, for example, unconscious patients or those with lowered levels of consciousness. This should not be a problem as long as you are working in the best interests of the patient at *all* times.

Practice educator (PEd) response: Obtaining informed consent is difficult when there are significant language barriers, especially when there is no-one available to translate. While there is the option to utilise language lines (which I recommend), where translation can happen over the phone, in this situation you could initiate a process by physically demonstrating what is required and sending and receiving communication gestures.

Academic response: Consent need not be explicit. Implied consent is just as valid as that which is explicitly given. An example of this is, if you ask a patient permission to cannulate and they offer you their arm. Keep your patients informed of what is happening at all times. They have a right to know in order that they can make an informed judgement. Talking and reassurance pay dividends.

Student paramedic response: Consent is not just a one-off thing you ask for at the start of your assessment; it can be situation-specific at times. For example, just because I have been given permission to take my patient's blood pressure, I don't assume they have given consent for me to start unbuttoning their top and attach the 12 lead stickers! I will tell the patient what assessment observations I need to take and what the procedure involves in a way they can appreciate and ask 'is that OK?' before proceeding. Often they will pre-empt me and offer their arm for the blood pressure cuff or their finger to take a sample of blood to measure their blood sugar, which is implied consent. Even if they say, 'do whatever you need to do', I will still inform them before doing anything, just in case they meant 'do whatever you need to do – except the procedure you're about to'.

CASE STUDY 7.1

Attending patients who are under the influence of alcohol can provide a multitude of issues in relation to obtaining informed consent – assuming that the patient is conscious, behaviour will vary individually. Some people will find the situation they are in highly amusing, others will be sad, some aggressive, and it is vital to ensure that you have their attention and that any information you give them is appropriately understood and that you are able to get a reply that you believe shows their understanding. This is easier said than done. The difficulty is that the longer you take trying to get this consent, the longer it takes to perform interventions. It is important to remember that you are working in the best interest of the patient.

Case study 7.1 highlights the potential difficulty and volatility when caring for patients under the influence of alcohol. The value of excellent communication skills cannot be emphasised enough.

⌀ Refer to Chapter 2 for more about the importance of good communication skills.

Consent is complex and is an integral part of any student paramedic programme, so the legal and ethical issues surrounding informed consent will be addressed during your studies.

Confidentiality

Confidentiality refers to both practice and academic work. Information about service users that was given to you in the line of your work as a student paramedic is confidential. As a student, you should not pass on any details about a service user without the permission of your practice educator or clinical supervisor. When in doubt, check, or err on the side of caution. The HCPC also provides specific *Guidance on Confidentiality* (HCPC 2021a). The guidance states that it is important that you get the service user's permission, or 'consent', before you share or disclose their information or use it for reasons which are not related to the care or services you provide for them.

You must only disclose confidential information if:

- you have permission
- the law allows this
- it is in the service user's best interests
- it is in the public interest, such as if it is necessary to protect public safety or prevent harm to other people.

(*Source*: Standards of Conduct, Performance and Ethics, Standard 5.2 (HCPC 2016a))

See Case studies 7.2 and 7.3 for more on confidentiality.

Student paramedic comment: Patients trust us with information about themselves and their health which they may not want shared with other people. It's obvious that we would never deliberately break this confidentiality, but I have heard of occasions where paramedics have been in situations where confidentiality could be compromised. You never know whether the member of the public who is in earshot of your conversation about a patient with another paramedic is not actually a relative of that patient – you could unknowingly let out some information the relative didn't know which significantly alters their relationship to the patient. Think carefully.

It is important to note that confidentiality is not always broken maliciously. Case studies 7.2 and 7.3 outline examples of confidentiality in differing circumstances.

CASE STUDY 7.2

A paramedic was working on a rapid response vehicle and was using paper patient report forms. After finishing a call, they would place the patient report form on the 'dash' of the vehicle. These had been placed face up with patient information visible. On returning to the station for a break an officer saw the patient records and was able to read confidential information.

It appears that the paramedic imagined that the physical barrier of the windscreen would keep the patient information safe and that others would not make a point of reading information from the clipboard. A simple mistake and lack of appreciation of the wider meaning of confidentiality led to a breach of patient confidentiality and quite serious consequences for the paramedic, in the form of disciplinary action.

The paramedic in Case study 7.3 fully understands their professional responsibilities both during and outside of work situations. A less experienced or less well-informed paramedic may have experienced difficulties in a similar situation. It is important to understand confidentiality in all its guises and in a variety of situations in order to appreciate the complexity of situations that you may find yourself in.

CASE STUDY 7.3

A paramedic (Sally) was asked for advice by a friend (Bob). Bob's partner had problems and needed to speak to someone. Sally did not know Bob's partner but agreed to speak to her on the telephone to see if she could advise her. It must be stressed here that this was in Sally's own time and not in work time. When Sally spoke to Bob's partner it became apparent from her medication that she had a history of severe mental health problems and psychotic episodes. It was obvious that Bob was not aware of this. When Bob asked Sally what the matter was and if she had been able to help, Sally could not comment. To do so would have been a blatant breach of confidentiality. Remember that confidentiality issues do not go away just because you are out of work and not on shift.

It is important that you clearly understand your institution's policies regarding confidentiality when writing assignments and examinations.

Read and clarify the policy with your lecturers, as this may vary from institution to institution.

Confidentiality and social networking sites are inextricably linked, yet many students need the link to be made clear to them.

Social media networking sites

Reflection: Points to consider

- Think about the last five things you posted on Facebook or any other social networking forum?
- Do you think you would be happy for your university lecturers to see what you posted?
- What does the content of your page say about you?
- What impressions might an outsider form of you, without meeting you, from looking at your posts?
- Remember some institutions and employers look at individuals' social media accounts.

The use of social media is an area that many registrants and students find lacks clarity. The first point is that information placed on these sites is in the public domain and can therefore be viewed by other people. Even if it is on a private group/page, it is classified as being viewable by anyone, and you do not know who is accessing other computers.

The HCPC document *Guidance on the Use of Social Media* (HCPC 2020), which you should read in full, contains several sections relating to the main points to consider when posting on social media.

When you post information on social networking sites, think about whether it is appropriate to share that information. If the information is confidential and is about your service user, patient, client or colleague, you should not put it on a site. This could include information about their personal life, health or circumstances. It can be easy to add together information in a post to identify something about an individual even if you don't have their picture in the shot. You can see where the accident happened for example if it is a picture of the roadside. Try to think before you post that someone, or their loved ones, that you have cared for might see the post and put yourself in their shoes to imagine how they might feel.

You do not need to include their name in order to break confidentiality. The guidance (HCPC 2020) warns: *'We might need to take action if the comments posted were offensive, for example if they were racist or sexually explicit.'*

In short, do not enter into any social networking discussion that involves patient care or comments relating to anyone you have cared for, colleagues, academics, or friends for that matter. The HCPC document also balances these warnings with the positives of engaging professionally with social media and the ability to network in a responsible and professional manner.

The advice given in Box 7.6 reiterates the importance of understanding the potential consequences of your actions when engaged with social media.

What about you personally posting photographs of yourself in uniform, for instance? The HCPC Standards of Conduct, Performance and Ethics (HCPC 2016a) currently states: *'You must make sure that your conduct justifies the public's trust and confidence in you and your profession.'*

It could be argued that a photograph of you standing in your uniform is innocuous enough, but who is to say that the photograph will not be used by someone else, altered and then appear elsewhere as an inappropriate and unprofessional image? Ultimately, it is your responsibility for posting it initially. Please check your individual university and practice area policies on social media usage for specific details relating to your localities.

It is hoped that this chapter has raised your awareness of some important issues related to becoming a professional. Sometimes students can make innocent mistakes, but the key is to be honest, act with integrity and learn from your mistakes (and those of others) during the course of your studies and experiences in clinical practice.

Box 7.6 Advice on social media use for student paramedics

🎓 **Academic response:** Go to the HCPC website, click the 'complaints' tab and then take a look at the 'hearings' section to see reasons why registrants (not necessarily just paramedics) have been disciplined or struck off. Too many of them are related to inappropriate use of social media. Such a waste of a career!

🚨 **Practice educator (PEd) response:** Be very, very careful how you use social media. What will your trust think about photographs of you in uniform? Think twice about the posts you share, the language you use and the opinions you voice. Many staff have ended up in serious trouble because of the thoughtless use of social media.

🚨 **Paramedic response:** A moment's madness on a social networking site could cause a lifetime of sadness if it costs you your career.

📖 **Student paramedic response:** We were warned that photos on Facebook of us in uniform and/or in a compromising situation were an absolute no-no. Also, putting up things about jobs we'd been to which could potentially breach confidentiality were an obvious thing to avoid. I guess the rule is: don't put up anything you wouldn't be happy for your programme leader, practice educator or work colleagues to see.

🎓 **Academic response:** Many more employers are implementing social media searches of prospective employees, to judge professionalism and suitability for employment. Carry on using social media in an unprofessional way and you may not even get to this point. HEIs and ambulance partners will not tolerate inappropriate use by student paramedics.

References

Clarke, V., Harris, G. and Cowland, S. (2019) Ethics and law for the paramedic. In A.Y. Blaber (ed.) *Blaber's Foundations for Paramedic Practice: A Theoretical Perspective* (3rd edn). Maidenhead: Open University Press.

College of Paramedics (2019) *Paramedic Curriculum Guidance* (5th edn). Available from: https://collegeofparamedics.co.uk/COP/ProfessionalDevelopment/Paramedic_Curriculum_Guidance.aspx (accessed 19 July 2022).

College of Paramedics. Available at: https://collegeofparamedics.co.uk/

Harris, G. and Fellows, R. (2019) Continuing professional development (CPD): pre and post registration. In A.Y. Blaber (ed.) *Blaber's Foundations for Paramedic Practice: A Theoretical Perspective* (3rd edn). Maidenhead: Open University Press.

HCPC Student Hub. Available at: https://www.hcpc-uk.org/students/

HCPC Getting on the Register: Available at: https://www.hcpc-uk.org/registration/getting-on-the-register/

Health and Care Professions Council (2016a) *Standards of Conduct, Performance and Ethics.* Available at: https://www.hcpc-uk.org/standards/standards-of-conduct-performance-and-ethics/ (accessed 19 July 2022).

Health and Care Professions Council (2016b) *Guidance on Conduct and Ethics for Students.* Available at: https://www.hcpc-uk.org/resources/guidance/guidance-on-conduct-and-ethics-for-students/ (accessed 19 July 2022).

Health and Care Professions Council (2017) *Standards of Education and Training.* Available at: https://www.hcpc-uk.org/resources/standards/standards-of-education-and-training/ (accessed 19 July 2022).

Health and Care Professions Council (2018) *Standards of Continuing Professional Development.* Available at: https://www.hcpc-uk.org/standards/standards-of-continuing-professional-development/ (accessed 19 July 2022).

Health and Care Professions Council (2020) *Guidance on the Use of Social Media.* Available at: https://www.hcpc-uk.org/standards/meeting-our-standards/communication-and-using-social-media/guidance-on-use-of-social-media/ (accessed 19 July 2022).

Health and Care Professions Council (2021a) *Guidance on Confidentiality.* Available at: https://www.hcpc-uk.org/standards/meeting-our-standards/confidentiality/guidance-on-confidentiality/consent-and-confidentiality/ (accessed 19 July 2022).

Health and Care Professions Council (2021b) *Guidance on Health and Character.* Available at: https://www.hcpc-uk.org/resources/guidance/guidance-on-health-and-character/ (accessed 19 July 2022).

Health and Care Professions Council (2023) *Standards of Proficiency for Paramedics*. Available at: https://www.hcpc-uk.org/resources/standards/standards-of-proficiency-paramedics/ (accessed 19 July 2022).

Quality Assurance Agency for Higher Education (QAA) in partnership with the College of Paramedics (2019) *Subject Benchmark Statement – Paramedics*. Gloucester: The Quality Assurance Agency for Higher Education.

8 HOW IS STUDYING A PARAMEDIC PROGRAMME DIFFERENT FROM STUDYING OTHER SUBJECTS?

Amanda Blaber

You may have friends who have studied other subjects at university and who talk about their experiences, or you might have studied at university before yourself. It is important to bear in mind that generally students who are studying healthcare subjects, such as physiotherapy, midwifery, nursing and operating department practice, have a different university experience from students who study subjects where there is no clinical practice component, such as geography, English literature, social sciences and history. This chapter is more representative for students on full-time undergraduate paramedic programmes of study, although some elements of the chapter will be generic to any student studying for a paramedic degree.

Generally, students on healthcare programmes have a longer academic year than other programmes, usually lasting 40–45 weeks. Healthcare students also have to study while spending time in the clinical environment and have exposure to shift work. This chapter will relate specifically to how your study experience may be different and address some of the issues that may arise. Topics the chapter will cover include the different types of programme structure, how to manage your time and independent learning (including considering different learning styles), and, finally, hints and tips on how to look after your physical and mental well-being as you study, including how to cope with night shifts.

As stated at the beginning of the text in the *How to use this book* section, this text will not cover study skills, as these are textbooks in their own right and a chapter on such issues is not sufficient. There are numerous texts available on study skills, should you require them. These should be used if you have concerns about assignment writing, referencing and accessing literature, for example. This chapter specifically addresses the issues that a student paramedic may encounter and does not give more generic study skills advice.

Levels of study

Chapter 5 briefly introduced the importance of understanding the right level of study for you. You need to appraise your academic capability and enjoyment of study honestly. The fact is that you cannot pass a paramedic programme without passing both theoretical and practical elements. They are equally important, so it is sensible to make sure that you are applying for the right type of study for you, whether it be a degree apprenticeship or full-time BSc (Hons). The other routes to become a paramedic (such as Diploma) are no longer an option, due to the profession recognising that a Bachelor's degree with honours is the most appropriate qualification for an undergraduate paramedic, in order to equip them for contemporary practice and enhance the quality of patient treatment and care.

𝒫 Refer to Part 2, Chapters 4 and 5 for more detail on course options.

This creates a dilemma for people who do not possess the academic qualifications for entry to a HEI degree-level programme. Or who are not academically able to achieve the HEI entry requirements. In this situation, there are numerous clinical patient-facing roles that are available, both in the ambulance service and wider NHS. Explore these and get a job in the NHS, it may be that a work-based apprenticeship may be more suitable for you (mixing employment and academic work) and your employer will be able to assist you with such decision-making. If you pursue a Bachelor's honours-level route and you do not really enjoy academic study, this can potentially lead to a miserable experience. If you choose an academic level that is too challenging for you, it may be that as your studies progress to a higher academic level you are constantly disappointed with your results, frustrated by your lack of progress and ultimately lose motivation and confidence. These feelings may also affect your experience and progress in the clinical environment.

It may be that you thrive in the higher education environment after not enjoying school or college. You find you become very focused on your goal and you are able to work hard and achieve very good results, the outcome all your lecturers would be aiming for. It is good to see students who initially struggle to achieve their potential.

On the other hand, if you choose an apprenticeship route, you may end up wishing you had chosen a full-time Bachelor's degree route, with potentially more university-based time. This may result in you feeling frustrated, not academically stretched and wishing you had studied on a full-time basis.

These varied scenarios have been included to encourage you to think a little more deeply about exactly what you want from your paramedic studies. Much of the time, especially when subjects are popular, the university process seems to be about the university choosing you, not about you choosing your university programme carefully. 'I just want a place anywhere on a paramedic programme' is not always the best approach and it may be wiser to wait, refocus, gain experience and reapply until you are totally satisfied with your choices and decision-making, as the comments in Box 8.1 show.

As alluded to in the various comments in Box 8.1 there are numerous and wide-ranging decisions for the student to make. Paramedic studies are not *one size fits all*. The variety of programmes, in respect of structure, academic focus and location, is huge and demands investigation so that you make the right choice for you. The following sections of this chapter aim to help inform your decision-making by providing some generic information on which you can build.

Credits

Any programme is made up of a number of academic credits. Table 8.1 explains the credit system and your route to a Bachelor's degree. As the study of subjects aligned to paramedic work are mostly science based, you will find most, if not all, paramedic programmes will be Bachelor of Science and have the title of BSc (Hons) Paramedic Science or similar.

Across the course of an academic year a student will study a number of modules/units that each carry a small number of credits, usually between 10 and 60. When each of these is passed, they are added together at the end of the academic year.

Generally, students are required to pass 120 credits at their level of study before progressing into the next year of study. In some circumstances, students will be able to carry over some credits into the next academic year (for example, if they are waiting to resubmit a piece of work or re-sit an examination), but this is at the discretion of the examination board.

Box 8.1 How important is it for students to choose the right level of academic study for them?

📖 **Student paramedic response:** The first year was relatively familiar in terms of the level of study. I had just finished an access course (in order to get to university) which was set at the same Level 4 as the first year of university. As a result, I knew what amount of input I needed to give to achieve the results I was after. The jump from Level 4 to 5 was a lot bigger than I expected though; in the second year the work really ramped up. It was a good learning curve though, because I learned how much more work was needed to achieve the same results as the year before. It also gave me an idea of how much more I would need to put into my essays/dissertation in the final year when the work was at Level 6.

Essays in the first year only needed one or two references per paragraph, whereas in Year 3 it was closer to one per sentence! It was good though, as by Year 3 I was reading around a topic so much, I was developing a much broader and deeper knowledge of it. Even though a lot of what I'd discovered didn't end up in an essay, it meant that what did get put in was really relevant. You learn how to pack a lot of quality information into a small number of words . . . which has some relevance to practice too; being able to inform hospital staff about your patient with a short, succinct, but detailed handover is a skill worth developing – Year 3 essays taught me how to do that!

🎓 **Academic response:** It is important for students to choose the correct style of academic study for them. However, remember that whether studying via a degree apprenticeship or full-time HEI degree route, studies will all begin at the same level – Level 4. Each year builds upon the last, giving you solid foundations to progress from level to level, so that by the time you reach Levels 5 and 6 you will be prepared. Studying hard and getting a solid grasp of the basics in the early years of a programme will pay dividends as the level of study becomes more challenging. Remember that if you have been successful in getting on to the programme in the first place the team will have deemed you to be at a good standard. Some students will find academic work more challenging than others, but remember that academic skills can be taught if the student is prepared to listen and take the advice given to learn, improve and progress.

> ⚑ **Paramedic/PEd response:** One of the main elements to para-
> medic practice is that it is a continuous challenge; therefore, I feel
> that it is only right to also challenge your academic ability. However,
> I also acknowledge that people are different and learn in different
> ways and are ready for study at different times in their lives. If you
> find the level too challenging there are usually step-off points in pro-
> grammes which will enable you to leave with academic credits, but
> you will not be eligible to apply to become a paramedic without suc-
> cessfully completing the Bachelor's honours degree.

Table 8.1 The academic credit system

Year	Academic level	Total credits per year	Academic award/qualification
1	4	120	Certificate
2	5	120 (240 total)	Diploma/Foundation degree
3	6	120 (360 total)	Bachelors degree, usually a BSc (Hons) (in arts subjects this will be a Bachelor of Arts or BA)

Generally, you will receive a letter/email from your institution after the
formal examination board meeting has taken place, detailing your credits for the academic year and if you are required to resubmit/re-sit any of
the modules/units and when. Again, refer to the handbook relating to
your chosen programme of study for more specific detail. The programme structure will provide more specific detail about the way the
programme is organised.

Clinical practice aspects of programme structure

Research the programme structure thoroughly online for the universities/
employers to which you are interested in applying. You should have the
opportunity to get more detail if you are able to attend the specific university open day/evening, whether that is online or face to face. Paramedic
and other healthcare programmes have both theoretical and practice components. These can be organised in very different ways, depending on the

institution. Generally, the time that you spend in clinical practice with paramedics and paramedic PEds is woven into the programme in one of three ways:

1   Supernumerary block placements (ambulance or mix of wider NHS placements)
2   A few supernumerary clinical shifts on most weeks
3   Supernumerary and employed status

Each of these approaches will be discussed below. A word that may require some explanation is *supernumerary*; see the definition below that explains the term in relation to paramedic studies.

Definition: Supernumerary

When an ambulance crew has a student with them, there will be three of them in the vehicle. The student is additional to the clinical staff, does not form part of the crew, and is thus *supernumerary*. The student paramedic is there to observe, learn and take part in the patient's care under the direct supervision of the paramedic PEd.

Supernumerary block placements

The term *block placement* refers to a system where students spend a period of time in university studying the theoretical and possibly some skills/simulation content; this may range between 6 and 12 weeks (the time may be ambulance-specific or a mixture of ambulance and other wider NHS placements, depending on your programme structure). After this period in university, the student will attend the clinical area, in this case an ambulance station, to work with their paramedic PEd and other appropriately qualified staff. At this point, the student is usually expected to mirror the shifts of their PEd, when realistically possible, and may spend up to 37 hours per seven-day week in the working environment. Some programmes may have an expectation of fewer hours per week, others may require a *full-time* commitment. If the student works fewer hours, there may be an independent study day per week.

During the course of these block placement weeks the student will also have university work to do, such as essays or examination revision, that will require submission/sitting when they attend the university for the university theory block.

Supernumerary clinical shifts on most weeks

Programmes that take this approach generally start each academic year with a few weeks in university, five days per week. After this period, the student attends university one day per week and agrees two or three clinical shifts (depending on how many hours in each shift) with their PEd for the remainder of the week. This generally leaves the student with one day for independent study and two days off each week. Each week in university the student will be focusing on specific subjects, discussing what has been observed in practice during the week and working towards their end-of-module/unit assessment.

⌀ Refer to Chapters 8 and 9 for more information on subjects to be studied on paramedic programmes.

Supernumerary and employed status

Some programmes have arrangements with their partner ambulance trust where student paramedics can be employed (starting in a support-worker role, not as a paramedic – note that ambulance trusts use different names for this grade of staff) after reaching a certain level of competence on the programme.

This approach generally also includes a block placement approach. Some weeks the student will be in university for up to five days per week. For some practice weeks the student will be working as a student paramedic and will have supernumerary status when on ambulance shifts. This usually means being the third person in a crew, when working in an ambulance, or the second person, if working in a car. For other weeks, the student will fulfil their role of employee for the ambulance trust, and will work, within their scope of practice, as part of a crew and not in a student paramedic role. There may be the opportunity to work in a support-worker role at other times during the year, such as holiday periods. Some of these programmes have shorter holiday periods, as the student is accumulating supernumerary practice hours and also needs to work as an employee for the trust for a contracted number of hours per year.

⬠ Refer to 'the degree apprenticeship route', which is discussed in Chapter 4.

It is important that you understand the differences and implications of each of the three structures explained above. Box 8.2 explores some thoughts about each of the approaches from the student, academic and paramedic/PEd perspective.

The comments in Box 8.2 demonstrate the flexibility of programme structures. The variety of approaches towards placement experience demonstrates the individuality that HEIs can develop in respect of their programmes. HEIs need to include the necessary subject specificity and cover the content recommended by the College of Paramedics (2019) and ensure students are prepared to meet the Standards of Proficiency for Paramedics (HCPC 2023). All paramedic programmes are externally validated by the HCPC, which measures such programmes against the Standards of Education and Training (HCPC 2017).

The following sections refer to study skills and aspects of self-care that are particularly pertinent to the student paramedic enrolled on any style of paramedic programme. They should be read in conjunction with a general study skills text.

Managing and planning your studies

As you can imagine, the programme structure is likely to have a big impact on the way you manage and plan your studies. Your experience of working independently may also have an impact on your success, or lack thereof, at planning and managing your studies. To understand the amount of self-directed study that is required for any programme, look at the amount of learning hours allocated for each module. You will not be taught everything you need to know in class, and you will see that taught sessions make up only a small percentage of the allocated learning hours. It is important that you develop as an independent learner as well as an independent practitioner. Do not underestimate how much work is involved! The student comment on page 136 demonstrates how organised, disciplined and structured it is possible to be.

Box 8.2 In your opinion what are the things a prospective student needs to consider about these approaches to paramedic study?

🎓 **Academic response:** It is important to remember that the number of supernumerary hours a student must accrue may be specified in their programme documents; attendance both in theory and practice may be monitored. While it is of value for students to experience working for their trust as an employee early in the programme, they often struggle to fit in the required number of supernumerary hours when the programme follows this route. Supernumerary block placements are of value as they allow the student to put into practice the skills and information they have acquired while in university. Students can concentrate on their academic studies and placement and not have to worry about fitting in 'employed' shifts.

📖 **Student paramedic response:** I worked with the system of supernumerary clinical shifts on most weeks. We were encouraged to fit two 12-hour shifts into each week alongside our university work. In Year 1, this was tough as we were getting to know the booking systems, staff and how it all worked. So on quite a few weeks I only managed to book one shift, leaving me short of practice experience. This all worked out fine in Years 2 and 3, as I knew what to expect and was more motivated and organised myself much earlier.

🚨 **Paramedic PEd response:** While placement/supernumerary hours are focused around working actual shifts with a mentor, this does not mean there won't be ample opportunity for students to work on coursework, exam revision, etc. I have always explained to students that this is not an either/or situation. Being on placement quite often gives an excellent opportunity for mentors to help students with their university work and it is particularly useful to link theory with practice. While it is not feasible for a student to write an assignment while on shift, it is possible to advance the theoretical aspects of the job by exposure to and discussion around the different conditions encountered.

🎓 **Academic response:** Supernumerary placements are of great benefit to students, allowing them maximum contact with their mentors and opportunity to practise their skills under direct supervision.

This is not always the case where students make up part of an operational crew, for example some foundation degree programmes. As part of an operational crew, students will often end up driving the patient to hospital, when challenging cases are being treated in the back of the vehicle, thus missing valuable opportunities to manage these cases under direct supervision.

Paramedic PEd response: There are positives and negatives to both types of clinical practice facilitation; however, the main points to consider are continuity, exposure and time management. In paramedic practice each patient varies considerably from the last, making it impossible to plan for what you will see and how frequently you will see things. By having continual exposure (two or three clinical shifts per week) you are more 'available', and this reduces the feeling of being pressured into seeing as much as possible in the short space of time; this is a potential negative of block placement. I think it depends on what you are used to; whatever the system used by your university, you will get used to it. Additionally, with continual placements you are developing your time-management ability, as you need to plan academic study into your working week, while maintaining a healthy work–life balance.

Academic response: I have taught on programmes where students are required to undertake supernumerary block placements; these are parts of employment and programmes where students do supernumerary shifts each week alongside university work. Each approach has positives and negatives. Some students struggle to separate their employed ambulance service role from their role of being a student, others struggle with completing university work while on a block clinical placement, and others struggle with managing shift patterns and university days. For all of these struggles, many students just enjoy being in the clinical area, whatever form that takes. Prospective students need to be aware that these variations exist and think about which approach will best suit their learning approach and personal needs.

Note: All programmes are different, in respect of the amount of practice hours that students are expected to accumulate across the duration of their programme.

Student paramedic comment: I thought of my study days in terms of three blocks of time – morning, afternoon, evening. I would then study during two of those blocks and take the third one off. I found I studied best either in the morning or evening, so I would take afternoons out and do something to recharge the batteries. You might study better during morning and afternoon, or afternoon and evening – whatever suits you. If you take two blocks for study and one for yourself you'll get the work done and keep yourself refreshed.

Let us now explore some of the realities of each of the placement systems explained above.

Supernumerary block placement

Prior to your block placement, the university staff will deliver much of the material required for you to complete whatever module/unit you are studying and the associated assessment. Now, however, you will need to undertake additional reading and research the resources that are introduced at university. As a student you may have competing demands when you are at university full time for a period of weeks, such as peer pressure to socialise and/or having to work in the evenings/at weekends. Before going to clinical placement it would be wise to borrow library texts (if they are not available as e-books or online articles) and have a clear idea of what is required in terms of the assessment for this part of the programme. While you are on clinical placement it may be difficult to coordinate shifts with the commitments of your lecturers, if additional appointments are required. With this type of programme structure you need to be extremely disciplined with independent study and keep working towards both your academic work and clinical assessment, which will be assessed by your paramedic mentor/PEd.

Supernumerary clinical shifts on most weeks

This approach usually incorporates an independent study day on most weeks, in addition to university attendance and generally two (12-hour) or three (8-hour) supernumerary clinical shifts per week. The student will generally have weekly contact with their university lecturers and paramedic PEds. This should enable the student to discuss and clarify any issues that occur while on placement with university staff quite easily, and also to continuously focus what has happened on the road with the theory discussed in lectures. Theoretically this should make planning and managing your studies easier. However, in reality some students are not disciplined enough to utilise the independent study time successfully. Some students struggle with the concept of working independently, deciding what it is they need to study. This may be your first experience of not being told exactly what to study and focus upon. University lecturers should be able to provide guidance on this, but only if you report you are having difficulty planning and managing your studies.

Supernumerary and employed status

As with supernumerary block placement, this approach will potentially entail several weeks away from the university campus, so diligence and a disciplined approach to study is essential. Accessing resources from university is generally not an issue, with remote access and many texts now available as e-books. It can become quite complex for the student in respect of assessment in practice when mixing supernumerary and employment status. The nature of the paramedic role is one of unplanned and often unexpected experiences, so practice assessment can rarely be planned. It can be quite frustrating for many students if, during the course of their employed time, they experience an episode of patient care that requires assessment in their student role. If the student is part of a crew, being paid and not in a supernumerary role, no assessment is generally allowed, as the student will not be working with their PEd or being supervised. Generally this assessment should only take place when they are working with their PEd; this is generally not the case when they are working shifts during employed weeks.

No matter what the type of placement arrangement, it is important that you ensure that placement assessment documentation is completed in a timely manner, as it may not always be possible to obtain signatures or feedback after the event.

You would be wise to research and read a study-skills book that makes sense to you and that you find informative. Studying at an HEI will be different from school or college; it is much more about personal responsibility and commitment to your studies. In addition to taught lectures, other forms of teaching and learning will be used, such as group work, presentations and simulation.

Learning outcomes

Each module or unit will have a set of learning outcomes. Each student must meet these specific learning outcomes. The assessment task, whether it be coursework, an assignment or an examination, will be designed to test the student's competence in meeting the learning outcomes. The lectures, seminars, workshops, skills sessions and guided study will be focused on delivering and discussing material that is specific to the learning outcomes. Students will also be provided with information about the assessment task and deadlines for submission of work (or examination date) and the subsequent planning and management of work is the students' responsibility. Any materials given to the cohort while at university are generally introductory, and the students will be expected to undertake additional reading and expand their knowledge sufficiently in order to excel at the assessment task.

Time management

Students on healthcare courses often have lots of *balls in the air* that they need to juggle. Many students will have family commitments, the pressure of working part-time hours in addition to meeting the demands of shift work as a student paramedic. It is easy for studying and independent study to take a back seat in favour of prioritising what needs to be done now. The inevitable consequence is that a submission date looms and you are trying to study at times when you are not productive, not reading sufficiently and rushing your work in order to meet the deadline. By knowing your learning style and study habits (both good and bad) you may be able to make a positive impact. Managing your time more efficiently may help.

Reflection: Points to consider

- At what time of day do you most enjoy studying?
- At what time of day are you at your most productive?
- Do you plan your studies to coincide with the answers you have given to the questions above?

With so many aspects to consider, the student paramedic may benefit from planning their studies on a weekly basis. No two students are the same, so each should plan their studies to suit their needs and make the most of times in the day when they work efficiently and are at their most productive. It is also important to plan in leisure time, socialising and relaxing activities. Many students find this approach works for them and their planner becomes their support network, telling them what to do and when to do it. A planner generally enables you to be more disciplined, not leave your work until the last minute and, gradually each week, work towards your final goal of a completed piece of work that is of the standard you wish to submit, or fully prepare for an examination. In Box 8.3 students, academics and mentors/PEds give a variety of opinions on time management.

Planning your study is one aspect of learning; it is also important to understand that your learning style may affect your approach to learning.

Learning styles: what type of learner are you?

As individuals we learn in different ways, that is, we have different learning styles. Your learning style is an important aspect of understanding more about yourself, and it is important to appreciate that the way subjects are taught may not always appeal to your preferred learning style. As a student, it is easy to *switch off* when you encounter a teaching style that you find uncomfortable or not to your taste. As an adult learner it is important to recognise the reasons why this may be the case and work on a strategy to enable you to get the most from all teaching strategies.

This is not a new concept, and the work of Kolb (1974) and subsequently Honey and Mumford (1986) is seminal in the discussion of learning styles.

Box 8.3 What advice would you give to student paramedics about time management?

Year 1 students:

📖 Try to start assignments early, to get the most out of lectures.

📖 Make sure you plan your study time. Don't be tempted to schedule placement/other work when you should be reading/studying.

Year 2/3 students:

📖 At times when you don't have assignments, don't stop reading. Do preparation for the next term in your holidays, not tons, just a little, so you know what is coming when you return to university.

📖 In Year 1, I wasted so much time, I could have used my independent study time much more to reduce the pressure that is on me now. I always feel like I am playing catch up. If I had used my time wisely, I would not feel like this, I would be in control and getting better marks.

📖 Get into the habit of additional reading early. Things like anatomy and physiology are essential to placement and understanding what is happening to your patients, so you can always read that and learn something you didn't know. And you will be asked questions on it by your mentor/PEd.

📖 Start studying topics you know will be covered in the next year, this makes the workload more manageable.

🎓 **Academic response:** Start your assignment early and (if you are permitted to do so) make sure you send an assignment plan to your tutor. This will ensure you are thinking along the right lines and haven't wasted valuable time writing about the wrong things or tackling things in the wrong way.

When it comes to studying for tests and exams, ask your tutor in which areas you should direct your revision. Again, this will save valuable time which may have been spent revising the wrong things.

If you feel you may be falling behind, do not leave things to get out of hand. Speak to your tutors and to your student learning support tutor who will be able to help.

🚨 **Paramedic PEd response:** Just because you are out on placement does not mean you cannot continue your academic studies. Not all shifts are busy, and a lot of time can be spent on standby. I have always used this time to work with my students on their academic studies. This has always proven invaluable to the student and in a way gives bonus study time that has not necessarily been timetabled in. Over the years in this bonus time I have been able to clarify areas students did not fully understand, research specific conditions we may have encountered, and work through question and answer sessions.

🎓 **Academic response:** Don't forget that your module handbook/ guide should clearly explain what the assessment criteria are. Read all module material carefully to ensure that you are fully aware of what is required. Also be especially aware that there may be considerable amounts of reflection, etc. hidden in practice portfolios.

🚨 **Paramedic PEd response:** Time management is vital; pre-planning to ensure you have sufficient time to complete academic assignments is a priority, and continuing your own development with critical reading, reflection and independent study is a must. In respect of practice, time management is also important to ensure you arrive at work clean, punctual and with the resources required to carry out your shifts. You also need to make sure that you have eaten, that you sleep well and that you maintain a healthy body and mind by ensuring you manage time to ensure days of rest and relaxation too. Getting into a habit of effective time management at the beginning of study can only be of benefit and helps to ease the pressure of the demands of your programme.

There are many derivatives of their original work and some free online tools to assist you in self-assessment of your learning style. An understanding of what Kolb (1974) and Honey and Mumford (1986) proposed is important for the student to begin any self-assessment.

Kolb (1974) suggested that we all learn through a sequence of activities which are related. He suggested there are four stages to the activities:

1   An experience
2   Observations and reflections about the experience
3   A theoretical proposition about the event
4   Active experimentation and testing – by further action and testing the accuracy of the theoretical view of what has happened; the person will then circle the spiral of learning again from Stage 1

Kolb's (1974) learning theory has specific pertinence to student paramedics and their related practice experiences. Many paramedic programmes also encompass the use of reflection in trying to make sense of students' practice experiences.

The evidence-based clinician will also understand the theoretical information related to the practice experience and will reflect on their handling or performance of the event. They will also have an action plan should they encounter a similar event in the future. This is not exactly Stage 4 of Kolb's (1974) model, as encounters with patients cannot be 'staged' and are generally not exactly the same. Nonetheless, the model is relevant to the world of the student paramedic.

Kolb's (1974) model has been critiqued by Honey and Mumford (1986) as being simplistic and not taking into account the learning styles of the student. They proposed that individuals will spend different amounts of time at each of the four stages of Kolb's model, depending on the way in which they learn. For example, some individuals will reflect more than others (Stage 2), some will spend an inordinate amount of time reading and investigating the theory around the experience (Stage 3) but not think much about their own actions, and others will carry on to the next experience without spending much time at all on Stages 2 and 3.

Honey and Mumford (1986) proposed that there are four types of learners:

1   Activist
2   Reflector
3   Theorist
4   Pragmatist

Tables 8.2–8.5 outline the characteristics and teaching styles/activities that each type of learner will learn most from, as proposed by Honey and Mumford (1986).

Table 8.2 Activist characteristics and teaching activities

Characteristics	Teaching activities
People who learn by doing	Problem-solving
Need to get their hands dirty	Group discussion
Dive in with both feet first	Puzzles
Open-minded approach to learning	Competitions
Involve themselves fully and without bias in new experiences	Role play
	Explore lots of ideas all at once to come up with one or two that help solve a problem

Source: adapted from Honey and Mumford (1986)

Table 8.3 Reflector characteristics and teaching activities

Characteristics	Teaching activities
Learn by observing and thinking about what has happened	Paired discussion
May avoid leaping in and prefers to watch from the sidelines	Self-analysis questionnaires
Prefer to stand back and view new experiences from a number of perspectives	Personality questionnaires
Collect data and take time to work towards an appropriate conclusion	Time out
	Observing activities
	Feedback from others
	Interviews
	Coaching

Source: adapted from Honey and Mumford (1986)

Activist

The activist is generally enthusiastic about anything new and will try anything once. Activists have a tendency to act first and consider the consequences later. In terms of completing projects, they enjoy the ideas stage and new challenges, but once an action plan is in place to complete

Table 8.4 Theorist characteristics and teaching activities

Characteristics	Teaching activities
Like to understand the theory behind the actions	Models
Need models, concepts and facts in order to engage in learning	Statistics
Prefer to analyse and synthesise	Stories
Develop new information into a systematic and logical theory	Quotes
	Background information
	Applying theories

Source: adapted from Honey and Mumford (1986)

Table 8.5 Pragmatist characteristics and teaching activities

Characteristics	Teaching activities
Need to be able to see how to put learning into practice in the real world	Time to think about how to apply learning to reality
Abstract concepts are of limited use	Case studies
Need to see a way of putting ideas into action in their lives	Problem-solving
Experimenters, trying out new ideas, theories and techniques to see if they work	Discussion

Source: adapted from Honey and Mumford (1986)

the project the activist will become bored and lose interest in the implementation and completion of the task. If you recognise these characteristics in yourself and are well prepared, you may be able to find additional ways to maintain your interest. A student paramedic who is naturally an activist needs to be aware of the tendency to rush in, especially when patients are involved, as this may not always be the correct or most appropriate action. If you know this is your natural tendency you should force yourself to think before diving in. The activist is someone who needs to be busy all the time (this can be quite tiring for others) and may need to be controlled in a practice situation to prevent mistakes being made.

Reflector

Student paramedics who are natural reflectors may find practice experience or learning in simulation initially quite challenging and in some situations quite stressful. If your natural tendency is to observe and analyse information, you may need to make a conscious effort to push yourself to get involved. It is also important to be aware of how you may appear to others (family members, colleagues, mentors). Natural reflectors would not want to be thought of as unenthusiastic and disinterested.

Theorist

A natural theorist will enjoy the academic aspects of study and probably find independent study quite enjoyable. Theorists need to be mindful, when in practice, about the most appropriate time and place to be asking questions. If you are a natural theorist, you may find the practice environment quite constraining – you may have to wait to go and investigate a subject area, such as a certain medical condition, as you will not necessarily have the resources available to do all the reading and investigation that you wish to do at the time. A student paramedic with this natural tendency may have to work on the person-to-person skills of the paramedic role, such as communication and skills development.

Pragmatist

A student with a pragmatist natural tendency may find it difficult to relate the theory being taught in the classroom to the clinical area. If you have strong pragmatist traits you may find practice more interesting, as you will witness your mentors/PEds take action, but you may need your mentor to explain the theory behind the care being given to a patient in order for you to understand the link between theory and practice.

Remember that the learning styles described in Tables 8.2–8.5 are generally not exclusive; you may identify with several characteristics from all four tables. Most of us fall naturally into one of the four categories, but we will also possess characteristics from the other learning styles. Having an understanding of predominant learning styles may enable you to work on and develop what you may perceive as other useful attributes. This should also help you to develop a sense of who you are, which should be useful to your overall development as a student paramedic, in both an academic and practice environment, as reinforced by the comments in Box 8.4.

Box 8.4 What are the benefits of knowing your learning style?

🎓 **Academic response:** The different subjects you will study will naturally lend themselves to certain learning styles. For example, anatomy and physiology is an academic subject usually taught in lecture format, particularly if the cohort is large. While the lecturer may like to take a different approach to this subject, it is sometimes simply impossible due to logistics, for example room size and time available.

This form of teaching would appeal to the natural theorist, while the pragmatist may not enjoy it. Knowing your own personal learning style will help you to understand that it may not be the subject matter you do not engage with but the style of delivery. If this is the case you will be able to work out ways in which to undertake self-study of the subject that will make it more enjoyable. For example, a lecture on the pathophysiology of myocardial infarction could be built upon by discussing this with your mentor after attending such an incident and seeing it in reality. In this way you can see how this has relevance to practice and relate it to the underpinning theory. This approach would appeal to those with a different learning style.

Most programmes have a range of study and activities that will appeal, at some stage, to all learning styles.

📖 **Student paramedic response:** Early in the programme we did an exercise to discover what learning styles we most related to. This was useful in that it helped make us more aware of how we could tailor our personal study in such a way as to get the most out of it. As a visual/kinaesthetic learner, I found watching my mentor carrying out clinical procedures then copying what he did was far easier than reading about how to do them and then trying myself. As a result I made sure I was in a position to see how things were done by the different paramedics I worked with on shifts. I would then check with my mentor that I was doing these skills correctly and get his input too. I still read up on skills, etc., it just meant I learned them in a way that worked for me.

📖 **Student paramedic response:** I know I am a kinaesthetic learner so I really learn from and enjoy demonstrations and practice sessions. But I also know I need to focus and learn in other ways. Just having this awareness of learning styles has helped me.

Another learning preference that is worth exploring is the visual, auditory, reading (and writing), kinaesthetic (VARK) model of learning styles, which Fleming (2001) developed. He developed his four styles from the area of neurolinguistic programming, where the previous VAK model was used. Fleming (2001) added a further approach, that of reading and writing (R). This approach has been designed around the concept that learners use four ways to receive and learn new information, one or two of the approaches being dominant for each individual:

1   V = Visual
2   A = Auditory
3   R = Reading and writing
4   K = Kinaesthetic (movement)

For the purposes of this text only three approaches (VAK) will be discussed, as reading and writing approaches are more appropriately discussed in respect of school-age children, not adult learners. Understanding which approach you prefer will enable you to use the suggestions included in Tables 8.6–8.8 when studying in the academic arena or working independently.

Table 8.6 highlights the main points for consideration by students who prefer learning visually. Visual learning can be divided into two subsections, linguistic and spatial. If you prefer the visual approach to learning you may benefit from taking notes during lectures, using drawings to supplement your notes and then re-reading them afterwards for clarification. Think about the value of converting your lecture notes into a more visual reminder, such as concept maps, charts and illustrations.

Auditory learners have characteristics like those listed in Table 8.7. If you tend to learn more when an auditory style of learning is used you will benefit from lecturers or mentors summarising what has happened. You can help yourself by writing questions about the subject content from your notes and will find this an easier way to learn. Mentors/PEds and lecturers find that auditory learners enjoy being questioned and need longer to debrief.

Table 8.6 Characteristics of visual learners

Visual (linguistic)	Visual (spatial)
Learn through written language, e.g. reading and writing	Have difficulty with the written language
Remember what has been written down	Do better with charts, demonstrations, videos and other visual materials
Like to write down directions	Easily visualise faces and places by using their imagination
Pay better attention to lectures if they watch them	Seldom get lost in new surroundings

Table 8.7 Characteristics of auditory learners

Often talk to themselves
May move their lips and read out loud
May have difficulty with reading and writing tasks
Often do better talking to a colleague
May benefit from using a tape recorder, in order to hear what was said in lectures

Table 8.8 Characteristics of kinaesthetic learners

Kinaesthetic (movement)	Tactile (touch)
Will lose concentration without movement around them	May take notes for no other reason than being able to touch external surfaces, e.g. the pen, paper
Take notes by drawing pictures, doodling, diagrams	Use colour highlighters
When reading, will scan the material first and then focus in on the details, so need a while to read	When reading, will scan the material first and then focus in on the details, so need a while to read

Kinaesthetic learners often learn more if they are able to move and touch objects while learning. The characteristics are therefore divided into kinaesthetic (movement) and tactile (touch) in Table 8.8. If you are this type of learner you will relish the practical elements of paramedic study as it enables you to keep on the move and use your hands. A kinaesthetic learner will enjoy and learn best when lectures are more practical in nature and involve moving around the classroom. Many student paramedics will categorise themselves as kinaesthetic learners, but students must also be aware of, and use, strategies to help them apply themselves in different learning situations.

A large variety of approaches to learning are used on paramedic programmes, but not all strategies will suit all students. It is important that you do what you can to learn about yourself and develop learning and study strategies to make the most of all the information presented to you.

If you have a good understanding of your learning style you will be in a better position to look out for yourself.

Looking after yourself

The career you have chosen is one of unpredictability, varied stress, shift work, and is often physically and mentally demanding. In order to achieve any longevity in a career as a paramedic (which could be 30–40 years in length), it is of the utmost importance to look after yourself. This section considers physical and mental well-being separately, but they are inextricably linked.

⟲ Refer to Chapters 1 and 18 for more on looking after yourself both mentally and physically.

Student paramedic comment: Our programme was hard work. Really hard work! Dealing with night shifts and unpleasant or disturbing call-outs, while swotting for exams and trying to work out where Harvard referencing wanted you to put a comma or a full stop in your essay references, took its toll on all of us. It's important to look after yourself. You need rest time as much as study time. In fact, you won't learn as well if you don't rest well. It's all about having the right balance. Whatever equals rest and relaxation for you, make sure you schedule it into your week. I'd suggest getting out of the house and away from the computer and doing something which has nothing to do with 'work'.

I found early morning runs were great for keeping physically and mentally healthy. If I was under pressure from an essay deadline or after a difficult shift, going for a run cleared my head and refreshed me.

Physical well-being

Will I get ill?

As the comments in Box 8.5 clearly articulate, as a student paramedic you will be exposed to people who are ill and you will also be expected to undertake shift work, which may be a new experience. Both of these will be challenging to your immune system. Minor illnesses are usually more prevalent in the first year of a programme, as your immune system takes time to protect itself from the range and variety of bacteria, viruses and diseases you are exposed to. This has obviously become a more important question since the COVID-19 pandemic. Wherever you are, university or on placement, both areas will comply with government guidance. You cannot account for your colleagues, friends and patients/clients. As with any infectious disease, if you follow protocols and guidance you will help to minimise the risk to yourself.

To sleep or not too sleep?

Shift work is a unique experience, and though most shifts are manageable, the struggles some people face with night shifts can be difficult to explain to anyone who has never experienced them. Many healthcare workers struggle with sleeping when on night work, as the comments in Box 8.6 illustrate, and this is something that student paramedics often worry about when they first commence a programme of study.

As you will note from the range of comments in Box 8.6, each individual develops their own coping strategy. The most important thing is to be open-minded and try several strategies until you find a way that suits you.

Box 8.5 What would your advice be for minimising the potential for illness?

📖 **Senior student response:** Obviously don't make illness more likely. Use infection control procedures – gloves, hand washing, etc. – but try not to walk in with an anti-radioactive suit on! There is self-protection, then there's overreaction. Keeping your immune system strong and healthy will lower your chances of catching bugs.

🎓 **Academic response:** I would recommend eating foods rich in vitamin C or adding a supplement, prior to placement exposure. You will be ill, certainly in Year 1; don't worry, once you are a registered paramedic you will have an immune system to be proud of!

🔥 **Paramedic PEd response:** Expect to catch every bug going in your first year of placement. This is normal until your immune system develops, and shift work doesn't help. Disruption of sleep patterns can lower the immune system, as can stress. This will get better as your immune system adapts and you get used to shift work. Eat well and sleep well when you can. Make sure you leave time for yourself. Nothing lowers the immune system and affects health as much as stress.

🔥 **Paramedic PEd response:** Firstly and most importantly, personal hygiene needs to take priority: short nails, showering, clean uniform, hair tied up; however, this needs to be done in conjunction with effective clinical hygiene, the appropriate use of personal protective equipment and strict hand hygiene. Likewise, it is important to ensure vaccinations are kept up to date and you adhere to standard precautions, such as the safe handling of the disposal of sharps, segregating linen and cleaning equipment. Eating a healthy balanced diet, drinking plenty of fluids and ensuring a regular and healthy sleep pattern is important. Inadvertently, exposure to illness and catching the occasional one will assist in developing an immune system that rejects illnesses that you come across most often!

Box 8.6 What would your advice be for coping with shift work and sleeping?

📖 **Student paramedic response:** Everyone is different. I personally find sleeping for three hours in the afternoon helpful before a night shift. Then, after a shift, sleep from 09.00 or 10.00 until two hours before your shift starts. You need to learn about your body.

🎓 **Academic response:** Contrary to popular belief, all your lecturers will have experienced shift work at some point in their careers – so we do understand and we may have some helpful suggestions if you are finding it hard, but you need to talk to us. Some people hate it, some tolerate it, some love it – you need to make up your own mind. One thing is for sure, you cannot do this job without having to do shifts and night work. I only ever slept for five hours after any night shift, usually from 08.00 to 13.00, and that is a long time to be awake – until 08.00 the following morning. During waking hours I felt like a bit of a zombie; although I was capable of functioning, sometimes it felt like I wasn't really there, a feeling difficult to explain. Sleep when your body tells you it wants to (but generally not during your night shift!) even if it is only for an hour. Sleeping in the heat of the summer is worse, due to the light, noise and having to sleep with a window open – generally student paramedics do not experience this as they are on leave for most of the hot summer weather. But that will come soon enough once you are registered!

🚨 **Paramedic PEd response:** Shift work initially is a shock to the system. My best advice would be to get to know your own body clock well! You will soon learn what your body needs to function. Some helpful hints would be having a lie-in the morning before a night shift or getting some sleep in the afternoon leading up to a night shift, then ensuring you eat accordingly either overnight or when you return home and getting sleep the following day. Get some sleep after your final night but allow yourself time to tire throughout the day so you can still sleep that night, so your body returns to a normal pattern. Blackout curtains, showering before bed, not drinking caffeine near the end of your shift could all help with the process.

⚡ **Paramedic PEd response:** Adapting to night shifts is always a challenge for those who haven't experienced this before. Changes of shift patterns due to the rota you are working is particularly difficult. Changing from days to nights or vice versa was one of the things I found most difficult. I would just get used to working nights and find it was time to change over onto days. Most people get used to shift work over time. If your body tells you it is time to sleep take notice of it, even if this may be at an unconventional time. 'Power snoozing' is of immense value, and even 20 minutes can revitalise you. After many years in the job I always joke that I can fall asleep to order – immediately and anywhere!

Food – what to eat

Some student paramedics may not be used to preparing and cooking their own meals. Learn the basics of eating healthily before you start your programme, if you have to prepare your own meals and have not done so before. Eating healthily is important in maintaining physical fitness, so that everyday aspects of the paramedic role can be carried out safely, without danger to yourself or the patient, such as moving and handling. It also plays a part in maintaining mental health. Box 8.7 provides some ideas.

Mental well-being

You will face some extremely taxing (both physically and mentally) encounters with patients and families during the course of your studies and long afterwards. It is commonly accepted that it is impossible to prepare for every eventuality, but there are some things that may help you to develop an awareness of your own mental health and well-being and manage the various situations in positive ways. As individuals we have many aspects to our personalities, and what will affect one person may not affect their friend in the same way. Appreciating each other's differences and being able to recognise stress, firstly in yourself and then in others, is one major starting point. Conversely, it may be that what other people think is a major issue does not bother you. As the student comment on page 155 highlights, the patient encounters that you think will bother you are often the conditions you see more often.

Box 8.7 Is eating healthily important for student paramedics? What advice would you give?

📖 **Student response:** There is no excuse for not eating healthily during the times you are at university. On placement it is sometimes difficult. Often you only get one meal break and not a lot of time to think healthily; we often snack. I have no problem with snacking. The problem I have is with what we choose to snack. I find myself, having not eaten for a long period of time, just eating something sweet – to get my blood sugar up – and things like crisps. Not the best for long-term health. The food we can nibble on throughout the day and stay fit varies hugely. I would suggest nuts, fruit, malt loaf, sesame snacks, fruit bars, for example. I worked in fitness before this career choice and know that nothing makes me feel as good as being healthy and not hungry.

📖 **Student response:** It is so easy to reach for snacks that are not healthy. It's a bit like independent study, plan your food and be prepared.

🎓 **Academic response:** Eating healthily should not be a problem when in university but can become a challenge when on placement, particularly on night shifts when your body cannot work out whether it is breakfast or dinner time. Taking your own healthy packed lunch to work can be of benefit and will mean you do not miss a meal if you cannot return to base.

🚑 **Paramedic PEd response:** The pressures of being a student and living alone for possibly the first time, being responsible for your own shopping, cooking and being restricted with time can all lead to eating a very different diet. Getting into a routine to plan meals and eat healthily isn't that difficult once you start, and although many people will say it is hard to plan meals when working shift work, I disagree! You can still find time to prepare healthy foods, and there are plenty of healthy snacks that don't need to be put in a fridge that will see you through the day! As for sugar rushes, there are still healthy options available, and chocolate isn't that bad once in a while! If you start a routine, it soon becomes the norm, so start healthy eating at the beginning and you won't look back! I find cooking a large batch of food prior to nightshifts useful, so I don't have to think about it and for me cooking is also a stress reliever.

🚨 Paramedic PEd response: Beware the 4am chocolate attack! Without fail I would always crave something sweet at this time on night shifts. I would always take a pack up to work, so even if I did not manage to get back to base I could eat. This is far better than relying on getting back to base to microwave what you have brought or grabbing fast food. By taking my own pack up I have always been able to find time to eat on shift when I have been hungry. The only downside with this way of working is that the speed at which you eat will change. It is a standing joke in my family that my plate is always cleared first – years of working with the 'grab it while you have time' outlook!

Student paramedic comment: Sometimes you may go to a job which affects you more than others. For me it wasn't the trauma jobs (not that we go to that many!), it was some of the jobs where people were struggling with huge social or mental health issues which got to me most. At other times the academic workload may start to feel unmanageable, or it could be a life event that happens to a relative or friend outside of university that has an effect on you.

Lots of things can conspire together to put you under a lot of pressure. If this starts to affect your day-to-day life it is best to go and talk to someone. As students our first line of defence was talking with each other – a problem shared and all that. For bigger things, talking with our programme leader and lecturers was always beneficial. Our university also gave us access to free professional counselling services if we had issues which we needed help with. These could be accessed anonymously via student services, with appointments fitting in with students' schedules. I know that some students used this service and found it very helpful. The important thing is that if you find things getting on top of you, you needn't suffer in silence, go and talk to someone you trust. The help is there if you need it. Support your cohort and they will support you.

⫘ Refer to Chapter 14 for more on difficult cases and Chapter 18 for more on resilience.

Reflection

The importance of reflecting on issues should not be underestimated. Reflection happens naturally as part of the day. Within programmes it may be addressed specifically as a subject, part of an assignment, portfolio or other academic work. This section focuses on reflection as a means of maintaining positive mental health. Some people find it difficult to reflect; the process can be quite challenging, but generally becomes easier the more you begin to understand yourself and the role that you are entering as a paramedic. This chapter does not attempt to explore reflection in any depth, but there are some suggested texts listed at the end of the chapter. In fact there are numerous texts to choose from. Take some time to explore the subject and start to understand more about reflection.

Part of the learning process is reviewing things that have happened to you, whether it be in the classroom, in practice, with your PEd or when caring for a patient. Making sense of whatever is bothering you (or deciding that it does not and never will make sense) is the key to mental well-being, as Case study 8.1 demonstrates. As healthcare professionals we constantly discuss the importance of communication. This applies to us, not just patients and families. We need to recognise the value of talking to each other, our loved ones, professional

CASE STUDY 8.1

Andy was four months into Year 1 of his paramedic studies. While on shift with his mentor they attended a road traffic accident, involving the death (on scene) of a middle-aged man. Andy talked to his mentor about what had happened and the fact this was the first traumatic incident he had been to and first dead person he had seen. Andy thought about all that had happened and was personally reflecting on his experiences. He experienced no adverse reactions, such as insomnia, nightmares or loss of appetite. He was managing well at this point. Three days later he received a call from his home town, some miles away from university, to tell him that one of his best friends was dead, having been involved in a road traffic accident (he died at the scene). As more details emerged, it soon became apparent that Andy's friend's accident was within an hour of the one he had attended, albeit hundreds of miles away. Andy tried to learn more of the detail and began comparing the two incidents. He recalled minute details of his patient; this served to make his patient real and Andy obsessed about the same thing happening to his friend. On lengthy discussion, debriefing and reflection, Andy realised that he required time away from his studies to make sense of what had happened, to be with his family and friends, and to reflect. Andy used writing as one means of helping him cope. His account was personal to him, but enabled him to think about and explore more detail than he says he achieved by talking. Andy slowly came to terms with the ordeal, but never did understand why this had happened. Andy returned to be successful at his studies.

counsellors if that is what we require, without experiencing reproach or stigma.

Case study 8.1 demonstrates the vulnerability in each of us, and our ability to cope with extreme situations will be different for each of us. What is important is that we recognise that what we are feeling is unusual and becoming an issue, talk to someone and take action to improve our well-being. Andy's experience is clearly disturbing, but reflection and other coping mechanisms helped him manage his bereavement. Box 8.8 describes the use of reflection more generally and recalls some occasions where reflection has helped practitioners.

It may be that you encounter something during or after your studies that you are not able to understand or manage successfully on your own or with family support. Sometimes individuals need specialist help, in exactly the same way we may need specialist physical care. In such situations students need to access appropriate services.

⟲ Refer to Chapter 18 for more detail on resilience and coping strategies.

Box 8.8 Can you give an example of a situation where reflection was a useful tool for you to use? Did you appreciate the value of reflection when you were a student?

📖 **Student response:** I went to a job in the first year which involved a homeless street drinker from eastern Europe who was fitting. The patient was very difficult and abusive. The crew I was with were sure he was not truly having a seizure but was simply trying to get out of the cold. However, they explained that just because they were suspicious of this, and had seen people do this many times, they could be wrong in their opinion and had an overriding duty of care to take him into the Emergency Department (ED) for further assessment and treatment. At ED the man continued to be difficult. Afterwards we all felt quite annoyed that the man had appeared to be manipulating the situation by using the ED as a place to keep warm and sleep.

I went home and did a reflective study into this job and ended up changing my attitude towards the homeless man as I found out more about the situation he was in and the likely events which led to it. I also examined my own attitude and feelings about the job and why I had felt that way. By the end of the reflective process I felt I had a greater perspective on the job and came to the honest conclusion that had I been in the same situation as the homeless man I probably would have done the same thing as he did – there but for the grace of God and all that.

Consequently, while I may have developed a healthy scepticism in relation to some jobs we go to, I would now say that that scepticism is accompanied by a greater degree of understanding, empathy and appreciation of why people sometimes see the ambulance service as a short-term answer to some of their social problems.

🎓 **Academic response:** My first introduction to structured reflection was as a student myself, and I was initially not enamoured. Topics for reflection were specified in advance, and I was forced to reflect on some situations that were better left alone. This should never be the case and students should not have to 'dig up' disturbing instances that they have dealt with in their own way and moved on from. It is up to you what you choose to reflect on, and in many cases you will find yourself doing this naturally. It is second nature for us to talk through the jobs that didn't run so smoothly and discuss what we could have done to improve things. Structured reflection is the next step up from this and is an invaluable tool to improve practice, discover ourselves and find out more about certain presenting complaints. The frameworks used should not be viewed as rigid but should rather be used as a prompt for pointing out in what areas and in what way it may be useful to direct our reflection.

🎓 **Academic response:** It is true that sometimes students do not know what to reflect on, when asked to do so in a classroom situation or for an assignment. Be guided by knowing yourself. Is there something that is keeping you awake at night, a nagging feeling that you could have done more on a job, wondering what happened to that patient? I would say all of these are indicators that things are bothering you. Why not try using a reflective model to help prompt you to think about each event in an ordered and less chaotic way than your brain may do at inappropriate times of the day, such as 4am Just try it, it may well help you.

🚨 **Paramedic PEd response:** I used a reflective model too but I also used PowerPoint to reflect, still following a model of reflection but using slides to demonstrate my thoughts, feelings and abilities which I could then talk through and present to my peers. This way, I felt I got more out of it. After attending a cardiac arrest of a young person, writing it all down was fine and it demonstrated what I had done, but having the ability to reflect through discussion via a presentation allowed for others to share their views and opinions with me. This helped me to understand and explore my thoughts and feelings in more detail, as I had an understanding of how others would have processed this incident as well. Reflection was extremely beneficial to me throughout my study and I still use it frequently. I strongly believe reflection is the key to developing myself and improving my abilities. I also advocate the importance of reflection to students, and how it is useful for self-development, but also important in being able to maintain a healthy state of mind, as you can use it to reflect on your feelings.

> 🚨 **Paramedic PEd response:** It is vitally important to recognise that reflection does not necessarily have to take a formal, structured form. Some of the most valuable reflections throughout the course of my career have been informal and have taken place with my colleagues/crew in the crew room. This 'work family' are in the unique position of understanding exactly where you are coming from. This informal form of reflection has as much validity as structured 'academic' reflection, and its power should not be underestimated. The important thing is that you are beginning to develop a reflective personality, something that will stand you in good stead in the future.

Accessing services

Most programmes have a handbook where there is considerable information – read it! It will probably include a section on the roles of people within the programme team at your university. This brief section highlights some useful roles within university teams that may be able to help.

Personal tutor/lecturer

Usually programme teams will allocate students to individual lecturers in the team to act as personal tutors for the duration of the student's studies. This role is usually classified as pastoral, meaning this should be the person you go to if you want to discuss anything that may not be specifically related to programme content or subject-specific information. Your personal tutor will be able to signpost specific, specialised assistance, should it be required. A personal tutor is a role created to help students navigate their way through university systems, procedures and policies and to provide help and assistance. This role is invaluable, if students feel able to talk to their personal tutor. Most universities will provide a role description – find this and read about the role and responsibilities of personal tutors, as this may vary from university to university.

University services – student support and guidance

Outside of the student paramedics programme there will usually be a system of student support that has a university-wide focus. Services such as counselling, financial advice and student housing are commonly provided. Most universities have many more services; again, read the specific handbooks for your institution and you will find services and guidance that may be useful to you in the future. HEIs usually have strong support networks for their students and clear structures for accessing services.

Ambulance service support

During your periods of practice experience you will generally be supported by a registered paramedic who has additional experience and education to act as a mentor/PEd. If student paramedics are employed by the ambulance trust they may also be able to access the services offered for employed staff of the ambulance service. Again, more detailed information may be contained within the handbook that is specifically related to your institution and programme of study.

∂ Refer to Chapter 15 for more detail on these roles.

This chapter has highlighted some of the ways in which studying for a paramedic qualification may be different from studying other subjects.

References

Blaber, A.Y. and Harris, G. (2014) *Clinical Leadership for Paramedics.* Maidenhead: Open University Press.

Bolton, G.E.J. (2018) *Reflective Practice: Writing and Professional Development* (5th edn). London: Sage.

College of Paramedics (2019) *Paramedic Curriculum Guidance* (5th edn). Bridgwater: College of Paramedics. Available at: Paramedic Curriculum Guidance (collegeofparamedics.co.uk) (accessed 20 April 2022).

Fleming, N.D. (2001) *Teaching and Learning Styles: VARK Strategies.* Christchurch, New Zealand: Neil Fleming.

Health and Care Professions Council (2017) *Standards of Education and Training.* London: HCPC. Available at: https://www.hcpc-uk.org/resources/standards/standards-of-education-and-training/ (accessed 20 April 2022).

Honey, P. and Mumford, A. (1986) *Using your Learning Styles.* Maidenhead: Peter Honey.

Kolb, D. (1974) On management and the learning process. In D. Kolb, I. Rubin and J. McIntyre (eds) *Organizational Psychology* (2nd edn). Englewood Cliffs, NJ: Prentice Hall.

Richardson, M. (2019) Reflective practice in relation to pre-hospital care. In A.Y. Blaber (ed.) *Foundations for Paramedic Practice: A Theoretical Perspective* (2nd edn). Maidenhead: Open University Press.

Taylor, B.J. (2010) *Reflective Practice for Healthcare Professionals: A Practical Guide* (3rd edn). Maidenhead: Open University Press.

Thompson, S. and Thompson, N. (2018) *The Critically Reflective Practitioner* (2nd edn). Basingstoke: Palgrave Macmillan.

9 WHAT WILL YOU BE STUDYING?

Kim Tolley and Amanda Blaber

Your studies to become a paramedic will be as complex as the needs of your patients. You need to understand the whole patient in order to be able to care for them safely and effectively. This concept is known as *holistic* care. The subjects you will be learning about are diverse in order to prepare you to care for your patients in a holistic way.

Reflection: Points to consider

1   List the academic subjects you think will help you to understand most things about your patient.
2   List the academic subjects you do not think will be useful to you and your patients.

The HCPC (2017) Standards of Education and Training (SETs) set out the duties of the education provider. This is one aspect that the HCPC measures any programme against before an institution can offer a paramedic programme to students. We mentioned these in Chapter 7. The SETs cover six broad areas, as shown in Table 9.1.

In addition to the very broad SETs described in Table 9.1, the education provider uses the Standards of Proficiency for Paramedics (HCPC 2023) and the College of Paramedics (CoP) (2019) Curriculum Guidance document to develop a programme that meets the governing and professional bodies' exacting standards and will provide the student with eligibility to register on successful completion. It is these documents that provide clear direction on the subjects that require inclusion in any paramedic programme.

What subjects will I be studying?

The curriculum content recommended by the CoP is listed in Table 9.2, and the proficiencies required by the registrant (HCPC 2023) are listed in Table 9.3. Bear in mind that Table 9.2 only lists the broad categories of the topics of study; the full guidance document provides much more detail.

Any paramedic programme is much more than a skills-based qualification, something that comes as a surprise to many students. You may be familiar with some of the categories. Or you may be surprised by some of the subjects that are included, such as leadership and research. It is important to mention that your teaching team do not expect you to have studied all of these subjects before commencing the programme. There is a wide range of subjects to be studied and some subject areas may be completely new to you.

Table 9.1 Areas covered by the HCPC Standards of Education and Training (SETs)

1. Level of qualification for entry to the register
2. Programme admissions
3. Programme governance, management and leadership
4. Programme design and delivery
5. Practice-based learning
6. Assessment

Table 9.2 College of Paramedics curriculum content categories

Physical life and clinical sciences

Social, health and behavioural sciences

Patient assessment and management

Ethics and law

Public health and well-being

Personal and professional attributes

Leadership and management

Evidence-based practice and research

Table 9.3 HCPC Standards of Proficiency for Paramedics

Registrant paramedics must:

1. be able to practise safely and effectively within their scope of practice
2. be able to practise within the legal and ethical boundaries of their profession
3. be able to maintain fitness to practise
4. be able to practise as an autonomous professional, exercising their own professional judgement
5. be aware of the impact of culture, equality and diversity on practice
6. be able to practise in a non-discriminatory manner
7. understand the importance of, and be able to, maintain confidentiality
8. be able to communicate effectively
9. be able to work appropriately with others
10. be able to maintain records appropriately
11. be able to reflect on and review practice
12. be able to assure the quality of their practice
13. understand the key concepts of the knowledge base relevant to their profession
14. be able to draw on appropriate knowledge and skills to inform practice
15. understand the need to establish and maintain a safe practice environment

In your cohort you will have a mixture of colleagues, some with more of a science background, others who prefer the social sciences – this is usual! Diversity in your cohort is healthy, and it also generally means you are able to learn from each other, not only in respect of academic subject content but also your own experiences.

As with the CoP document, the HCPC Standards of Proficiency listed in Table 9.3 also have explanatory notes if you look at the whole document.

You can see that the two documents referred to in Tables 9.2 and 9.3 interact and complement one another.

Table 9.3 shows that, in addition to clearly defined subjects on the course, such as anatomy and physiology, there are other professional aspects that are equally as important, for example non-discriminatory practice and maintaining records.

Do all programmes cover similar content?

The general answer to this is yes. Institutions will have developed their paramedic curricula based around the HCPC SETs (see Table 9.1) and Paramedic Standards of Proficiency and College of Paramedics (2019) curriculum guidance. There will be some variation on where in the programme the students receive some content. For example, some programmes may decide that patient assessment needs to be taught at the end of Year 1, for others it will be in Year 2. Some of this decision-making may result from the partnership arrangement with the ambulance service. This will generally result in a joint decision between the HEI and ambulance trust about what clinical skills will be taught and at what point in the programme it is most appropriate. This will vary from area to area of the UK and from programme to programme. Whatever the case, you can be assured that your programme has been scrutinised by internal university quality processes and the HCPC, as a minimum requirement.

Some of the areas you cover during lectures may be on the brief side. With such a wide range of subjects to cover, academic teams have to decide what subjects will be covered in most detail and what others can be learned via other learning and teaching methods, such as independent and guided study, workshops, recordings, online and simulation. In some situations, there may be guided study provided as a way of extending your knowledge further and exceeding the academic level you need. Clear guidance will be given on this and it is then up to you, as the adult learner, to choose to complete it or not.

Student paramedic comment: The programme I did covered a range of subjects from anatomy to sociology. At first some students questioned the relevance of some topics – why learn about sociology? Once they'd been out on placement and saw how sociology is relevant to the way people live, the situations they get into and how this impacts upon us as paramedics, they realised how useful these subjects are and that the programme had been carefully structured.

I'd also say that at university we weren't just being educated to do a job, we were studying a subject – paramedic science/practice. As a result we gained a far wider and deeper understanding of the paramedic role, not just knowledge of how to cannulate. I feel this gave us the foundation for greater development personally and professionally. University is not simply about training, it's about education.

The wide range of subject areas is one major reason why independent study is essential to your success.

What is independent study?

This may be called different things in different institutions – for example, self-directed study or study time. Independent study is entirely in the hands of the student. Your academic staff can suggest periods of independent study by allocating time during a module/unit; this usually will appear on a timetable. Guided study usually has set reading or a set task or work that needs to be completed and taken to the next lecture. It is different from independent study, where what you do with your time is entirely up to you, as Box 9.1 illustrates.

On some programmes there are set weeks of independent study, on others there are individual days. However your programme is organised, there will be some dedicated time allocated for you to study. Other study will be required on your days off, especially as deadlines approach. But remember you are studying for life, not just to pass modules/units. All of the information you will be gathering is useful for your career development and much of it will be used on a daily basis, not simply learned for an examination and then never used again!

Generally, the most effective way of really learning something is to learn it over a period of time, review it periodically and use your knowledge in practice regularly. This is why academics will advocate reading regularly and not just cramming for deadlines, as this is the material that you forget once the deadline has passed. Cramming may not make you the best paramedic that you can be and you may not realise your potential by using the cramming approach to studies. Being challenged in practice (in a friendly and supportive way) is an excellent way to recall what you know (or have forgotten) and to link theory to practice. I would suggest that any patient that you meet in practice would be useful to write up about consciously for your independent study. An example of this is found in Case study 9.1.

Box 9.1 Do students use independent study?

🎓 **Academic response:** This is really down to the individual and is often directly proportional to a student's prior experience of higher education. Many students who have not experienced university learning before expect everything to be 'spoon-fed' in class. I always say that in university you are 'treated as a grown-up' and we expect you to delve further into subjects we only have time to introduce you to in class. It will be useful for you to ask your tutors to give you broad areas for self-study.

🚨 **Paramedic PEd response:** The more driven the student, the more time I find they devote to self-study. It is the students who really want to be paramedics that tend to go the extra mile with their studies.

🚨 **Paramedic PEd response:** Independent study varies massively depending on the student's enthusiasm and willingness to learn. No matter what the structure of the student's programme of study is, the willingness to learn while on practice varies from student to student. A student who wants to know as much as possible is always looking to broaden their knowledge on things they have seen on placement and will spend their time doing this. Students may spend time before placements researching areas they want to discuss and develop with their mentors. Unfortunately, some students think that the knowledge they need is purely based on what is taught as part of their programme and view independent study as a day off. My advice would be to use independent study time to the best of your ability; you will never know enough.

📖 **Student paramedic response:** My motivation for independent study consisted of equal parts of fascination and fear. I investigated a subject to a deeper level outside of lectures often because I was fascinated by it and had a hunger to learn more, but also because I was dead scared of not knowing enough and failing an exam or essay. This approach may not have been ideal, but it paid off. I got some good grades and a better level of understanding on many subjects than I would have without it.

📖 **Student paramedic response:** Keep reading during break times (Summer/Easter), not tons, but keep things fresh, this will help you when you restart the next term.

CASE STUDY 9.1

Lily is 75 years old. She lives with her husband and she has a long-term history of emphysema. Lily has home oxygen and regularly takes her peak flow reading. She is on numerous medications and really does not like being hospitalised. She has called 999 as her peak flow measurements are lower than normal. Five days ago, Lily was diagnosed by her GP as having a chest infection. Lily has been taking the antibiotics prescribed by her GP for four days now.

Your independent study could be structured in the following ways:

- Understanding the anatomy and physiology of the normal respiratory system.
- Understanding the altered physiology of emphysema and how common it is.
- What is the treatment and management for people with emphysema?
- What are the likely medications Lily would be on and what doses, and how do they work?
- What is a peak flow, what is normal, and what does a change indicate? Are there any local/national guidelines on this?
- How do you document your findings and action?
- How do you assess Lily physically, psychologically and socially?
- Why might Lily not like being in hospital?
- What might be the effect of living with a debilitating long-term condition for someone of her age?
- What help is there that you may be able to access?
- What would you do if Lily refused to go to hospital? What are your responsibilities, ethically and legally?
- Could the care you gave to Lily have been improved? Does the knowledge that you now have mean you would alter her care in any way, and would you do anything differently? On reflection, what have you learned?

As you can see from Case study 9.1, you do not have much information about Lily in the above scenario, yet there are so many questions that can be asked about each patient interaction that you have. These can be examined in as much or as little depth as you individually want, depending on how inquisitive you naturally are and how much you make an attempt to critically analyse situations. It is pertinent to mention the issue of consent when writing about patients in academic work. You will be required to gain consent and maintain confidentiality not only for the purpose of providing treatment but also when writing about patients in your academic work. The policies regarding consent and confidentiality for academic work vary from institution to institution, so you need to be clear what they are before including details of cases in your work. Falling foul of these rules can lead in some cases to a zero mark.

Using your patients to help you study independently is really useful, makes your learning pertinent and real, and most students seem to think this approach is a useful and effective one. Of course, there will be occasions when this approach will need to be supplemented by pure theory and it may not suit all types of learners.

𝒫 Refer to the discussion on learning styles in Chapter 8.

What is guided study?

The term 'guided study' can be used to describe a variety of study methods. Guided study is generally a means of helping the student to focus their attention to a specific area or subject. This can be achieved by asking the student to complete work before a given lecture takes place. Lecturers will generally not cover this material again; they will assume the student has completed the guided study, as referred to in Box 9.2. If your lecturer takes this approach, you may be somewhat lost in the lecture if you have not completed the guided study, as the work you should have done would have prepared you for the lecture content.

As you can see from the responses from the PEds in Box 9.2, guided study is not just a university-based approach. Some mentors/PEds are extremely proactive and embrace a clearly structured teaching role while spending time with their student. This will help to bring the theory to life for the student and affords some excellent learning opportunities. Some guided study can be additional to the university lecture and module/unit content. It may be made up of a series of worksheets/workbooks that

Box 9.2 How useful, or not, did you find guided study material?

🚨 **Paramedic response:** While studying for my paramedic degree, I used quite a lot of guided study, particularly in my first year. I felt it was important to use my spare time wisely to prepare myself for the further two years, which became much busier. It was really helpful that our tutors did this for us as it gave a framework rather than staring blankly at a textbook and not knowing where to begin. Using guided study stood me in good stead for my career; now I'm registered I use a similar framework with any CPD I do, keeping my knowledge and practice up to date.

🚨 **Paramedic PEd response:** To support the use of guided study in university, as a mentor I adopt the following approaches with my students. I initially advise students to highlight any areas of practice they feel they personally need to learn and develop in and suggest independent study, which we can then discuss at a later date using a question-and-answer session to test understanding. To encourage reflection and self-learning I encourage students to keep a record of incidents we attend and advise they do further literature searches and critical reads which I see and we then spend time discussing. I also find out what the student is currently studying at university. I can then, across the course of a number of shifts, focus our discussions, learning opportunities and the student's involvement in cases that are relevant to their stage of study. Letting the mentor have a copy of your timetable so that they know what you are studying allows them to facilitate situations where you can demonstrate your learning and understanding with a real patient, thus fulfilling your potential. I encourage students to be adequately prepared and bring appropriate resources to placements, such as reference books, a realistic plan of what they want to achieve and how they wish to achieve it and a positive attitude to wanting to learn. I like to develop a two-way working process with students, and encourage that as much as I can to help students learn and progress. There is knowledge that you have learned at university, and a good way of consolidating this is to teach it to me!

🚨 **Paramedic PEd response:** Knowing where to direct your study is extremely helpful for a number of reasons. It helps to break down masses of information into bite-sized pieces which stops students from feeling overwhelmed. It can save a lot of wasted time, particularly regarding exam revision. There is nothing more soul-destroying than spending hours revising a particular area only to find that you have concentrated on the wrong things.

🎓 **Academic response:** Guided study material is not an extra, it is key to the content I will deliver in a lecture. Students are directed to read/complete the guided study before attending the lecture; this will form the basis of the information required prior to the lecture and will usually be quite basic in nature. I will not revisit this information in the lecture. I can then concentrate on the more complex aspects of the subject, discuss them and answer any questions the group may have. Students who do not complete the guided study are at a significant disadvantage.

supplement the taught content and help you to appreciate the points made in the lecture, as the other comments in Box 9.2 highlight.

Learning support needs

Many students have individual learning support needs that will have been assessed at their school/college, and they should have the support they require individually detailed for them. If you have declared this on your UCAS form, the HEI will usually have contacted you prior to commencing your studies to discuss your individual requirements and arrangements. All institutions have dedicated staff to assist both student and academics in providing the correct support, as Box 9.3 discusses. Be aware that the way this is managed may be different from what you have experienced to date, so it would be wise to find out how the system in your university works.

If you know you will need learning support it would be wise to ensure your lecturers know about it. As you commence your paramedic programme it may be worth mentioning it to your lecturers, or at least your programme leader or personal tutor. This will enable them to check what has been agreed for you individually, and that it is facilitated for you throughout your studies.

Box 9.3 What kinds of learning support needs do your colleagues have?

🚨 **Paramedic PEd response:** A surprisingly large number of students (and qualified paramedics returning to study) have additional learning support needs, so the first thing to emphasise is that you should not feel embarrassed to ask for support. This may feel like a big deal to you, but it is certainly no big deal to academic staff or colleagues. Additional support can be something as simple as having learning materials made available early, being able to record lectures or having extra reading time in exams. Don't suffer in silence! Support is very easy to arrange and may make a huge difference to the success of your studies.

🎓 **Academic response:** Students who arrive at university with a learning support need are identified early on and receive assessment and support before the term commences. The system is structured and generally works well. Sometimes students will discuss difficulties with their personal tutor, and we can then work with the student to get appropriate assessment, help and support – some issues may have been overlooked or missed at school or college. It is good for the student to finally be able to achieve their potential and realise there is a bona fide reason for their difficulties; it is often a relief for the student and their confidence is boosted.

📖 **Student paramedic response:** There is help with academic work if you are struggling. I have dyslexia and didn't get help organised as early as I could have. Big mistake.

Additionally, some students experience difficulty with studying while at university and their lecturers may advise them to seek support, and this may lead to an assessment of individual learning needs. A student will generally be supported through this process by a person who usually has more experience than your lecturers in this area.

As Box 9.3 describes many students are in this situation. Do not worry about discussing this with staff at your university; they will know how to help you or put you in touch with someone who has the necessary expertise.

CASE STUDY 9.2

Toward the end of my second year I didn't feel that I had progressed to the level that I should have (practice and academically). I decided to re-take Year 2 in the hope of developing my skills and knowledge further. Of course, this made me feel stressed, anxious and affected my confidence, but it was the right decision for me. I talked everything through with the academics, pastoral team and also had the support of a counsellor. I then realised other issues were the root causes of my inability to progress. If I had spoken up sooner, I may have been able to address some of the issues without repeating the year.

Case study 9.2 highlights some of the issues also raised in Box 9.3 and emphasises the importance of talking and getting the right help at the right time.

This chapter has explained what you can expect from your paramedic studies and how you will be studying a broad range of subjects. It is hoped that some useful suggestions have been made to help you understand why studying independently across the course of the year is important and how you can best do this effectively. A percentage of your time in university will be spent learning in simulation, the specifics of this and how to get the most from this type of learning is covered in the next chapter.

References

College of Paramedics (2019) *Paramedic Curriculum Guidance* (5th edn). Bridgwater: College of Paramedics. Available at: file:///C:/Users/ablab/Downloads/Paramedic_Curriculum_Guidance_-_5th_Edition_(FINAL)%20(6)-3.pdf (accessed 12 July 2022).

Health and Care Professions Council (2022) *Standards of Proficiency for Paramedics*. London: HCPC. Available at: https://www.hcpc-uk.org/standards/standards-of-proficiency/paramedics/ (accessed 12 July 2022).

Health and Care Professions Council (2017) *Standards of Education and Training*. London: HCPC. Available at: https://www.hcpc-uk.org/globalassets/resources/standards/standards-of-education-and-training.pdf (accessed 12 July 2022).

10 LEARNING IN SIMULATION

Kevin Barrett and Mark Durell

Simulation is somewhat of an umbrella term, as it ranges from very simple demonstration and rehearsal of clinical or interpersonal skills all the way to complex, multi-day events with other professional groups who are engaging in extremely realistic situations and settings. These may involve professional actors and might be recorded.

Simulation has been a rapidly developing area in clinical education for several years and is certainly a feature of paramedic programmes in the UK; it is very likely that you will meet it on the programme that you begin. The purpose of this chapter is to provide an overview of what simulation is and how it will inform your learning as a student paramedic, as well as offer you advice on how to prepare for learning by simulation.

Typically, simulation approaches involve scenarios that students have to respond to, often in teams, which are observed by the programme lecturers (the 'faculty') who lead the feedback and debriefing. These events are often managed in smaller groups so that the feedback and discussions are easy to manage and so that everyone has a chance to participate.

Why is simulation used in paramedic education?

Paramedic practice is quite unpredictable in nature and many learning opportunities arise infrequently and in an opportunistic manner. This is perhaps not like some other healthcare professions where students can be sent to a respiratory ward, for instance, to learn about peak flow measurements or nebulisers and it is almost guaranteed that they will see these situations. To ensure that students can have exposure to seldom seen but essential elements of care delivery, simulation has a major role to play.

Paramedics use a variety of equipment to respond to urgent and emergency calls, and familiarity with all of these items is important. Simulation can demonstrate their use, as well as alternative approaches to employing

Box 10.1 What is your experience of simulation?

📖 **Student paramedic comment:** There are pros and cons with simulation. You can't get volunteers to come in and have a heart attack on cue for you to practise your advanced life support skills, so the simulation manikin has to do!

The chance to practise with all the relevant kit on a dummy is good as it creates the 'procedure memory' that kicks in when you're faced with the real situation.

We also had a special house on campus which was fitted with cameras and microphones so that students could go into a 'real' home setting and face different scenarios. Each scenario was filmed so that we could all review it after and see what had been done right and what was not so right! This was a great asset and meant we got to practise lots of stuff in as close to a real way as possible.

📖 **Student paramedic comment:** The down side of simulation is that although it is as real as it can be, it's sometimes not real enough. When you go into a real situation you can see, hear and even smell the patient's presenting condition! We use all our senses to gain information, which informs our decisions. In simulation you have to wait to be told all aspects of the patient's presentation, or you have to ask about things which in a real situation would be obvious. This can cause you to miss things or make less than good decisions at times. It's also easier to intubate a real person than a manikin – some things are simpler and easier in real life than they are when working on the plastic people.

📖 **Student paramedic comment:** Simulation is good for teaching you more than the 'how to' of treating patients. In simulation scenarios we discovered the dangers of becoming blinkered and focused on accomplishing some procedure or other at the expense of noticing other things going on around us which were affecting the situation. This was a really valuable lesson for when out in practice.

📖 **Student paramedic comment:** We had a great opportunity to go to a local fire brigade training facility where volunteers acting as patients (with gory make-up) were cut out of wrecked cars in simulated road traffic collisions. This was great in that each scenario was run in real time so you had to go with what was happening, make the right decisions about prioritising and carry out procedures while lots of stuff was going on around you. I was pleased that not all my patients 'died'! The real benefit was that even if you had got something wrong it was not real, but you gained knowledge of what to do differently when it is real. It was really interesting to learn about other professions too and what they can/cannot do in certain situations. Sometimes it's less about the simulation, but appreciating what other professionals can do – this is helpful when you encounter situations, such as childbirth in the community. I know what a midwife is able to do and what they may need my help with. I grew to really like simulation scenarios and learning.

them. The equipment used in manual handling manoeuvres that are required on a daily basis are a good example here. You might be given a scenario that involves access to a patient from only one side (if they are against a wall, for example) or where the space is very confined. So using the gold standard equipment is difficult, and it means you need to consider what steps must be taken and what other equipment might be used instead. Simulation here can reproduce real-life compromises to clinical practice, and you will always be simulating your assessment and decision-making abilities as well as the use of equipment (see Box 10.1).

Safety is a huge part of the rationale for simulation. Simulation is 'error tolerant'. This means that mistakes or slow practice in time-pressured situations are not problematical and become good learning opportunities for yourself and colleagues. The enactments are safe for patients as no-one is actually left in pain if analgesia is not considered, for example, but it is also a safe situation for you because you have the chance to learn new and sometimes complicated aspects of care delivery, knowing that no-one is compromised if a mistake is made.

There is an ethical perspective that correlates to the issues of safety. We should not practise on people who are unwell; there is an ethical maxim called *non-maleficence* which translates as 'do no harm'. Although practice on clinical placement will always be supervised, as a student you want to be in a position where you can contribute to care in a way that is not putting a patient, yourself or staff at any risk. Alongside this, we have to acknowledge that some care interventions, such as cannulation, can be painful, and these are best first learned via simulation; students cannulate plastic arms to become accustomed to the practice.

Aside from the psycho-motor type clinical skills, some communication approaches also require a non-maleficence perspective – breaking bad news, for example. These sensitive situations can be very emotionally charged and there can be social and emotional pressures on clinicians in discussing difficult decisions and asking sensitive questions; rehearsing some of these areas via simulation can be invaluable. Indeed, receiving feedback about communication styles, including non-verbal or body language patterns, is quite a personal issue and beginning this in a structured and relatively private situation is especially helpful.

Many situations that you respond to will be surprisingly complex, and in actual clinical practice it may only be possible for the paramedic that you are working alongside to highlight a few of the areas to concentrate on to support your learning. What simulation allows is for multiple perspectives to be considered, either by repeatedly viewing discrete sections of a response through a video recording, for instance, or by having different members of the faculty deliberately look at different elements of practice. This might mean that your assessment of a patient who has fallen, for example, is considered: the way that you maintain a safe working environment; the way you approach manual handling decisions; the equipment you decide to use; the communication with the fallen person and with your team members; and the thoroughness of your overall assessment of the patient. This is very challenging to manage in real-time clinical practice, but simulation allows a highly structured approach to learning about potentially complex areas of care delivery and can illustrate just how multi-faceted clinical practice can be, even in everyday situations. These non-technical skills are the vital foundations of all aspects of paramedic practice.

In some longer scenarios it is possible to address decision-making and the prioritising and re-prioritising of care delivery. These areas are highly relevant to your developing clinical practice and are quite subtle skills; simulation allows to you to comment and reflect on your own decision-making, what your rationales were and to explore alternatives with expert teachers and peers.

One area that benefits from simulation approaches is called 'interprofessional learning'. This encourages teams of one professional group to learn from another professional group. So you might undertake a set of responses with emergency department nurses to enhance the skill of concisely and accurately providing a handover of a patient, a skill that is being increasingly highlighted as central to good continuity of care and one that is essential to paramedic practice. Additionally, you will discover from the other professionals what they need from paramedics and why.

Often simulation is used to develop your skillset in human factors and crew resource management. This area of practice builds the foundations for both good clinical care but also good working relationships. Crew resource management is concerned with the development of non-technical skills focusing on situational awareness and interpersonal relationships. This element of clinical practice is designed to help you to be aware of your performance and the performance of others to promote a patient safe culture. The aims of including this into your simulation sessions will be to help you build your ability to consider the effect of your own actions and behaviours on the overall safety and outcome for a patient. Considering how you communicate and work alongside colleagues, as well as being reflexive on your own personal experience and state will ensure you are better able to practise as a paramedic.

A key term in simulation is *fidelity*, describing how realistic a situation is. An example of low fidelity is the use of simple manikins, as described by a student in Box 10.2. They are useful in routine skills rehearsals and require little supervision or planning. 'High fidelity' usually refers to more involved situations as described by the academic and paramedic in Box 10.2.

One point that deserves to be highlighted in relation to paramedic practice is that the pre-hospital clinical environment needs to be simulated. It will not necessarily be the case that the skills rooms that many universities now possess (and that you will see demonstrated at open days) will be used all the time; you can expect to be in settings such as the car park, the sports field and the stairwell which present their own problem-solving challenges and are more realistic for student paramedics than the hospital ward. It is worth exploring the meaning of the term 'fidelity' at this point. Fidelity in simulation is a multi-dimensional concept corresponding to the degree of realism created through the selection of simulation equipment, setting, and scenario. Fidelity also refers to the degree of exactness achieved and corresponds to the believability of the experience and relates to several components of simulation. Levels (low, mid, and high fidelity) and types

Box 10.2 What types of simulation experience have you been involved in?

📖 **Student paramedic response:** We did lots of simulation scenarios – anything and everything from cardiopulmonary resuscitation on manikins, to full-scale major incident scenarios with the fire brigade cutting patients out of cars.

Simulation has its drawbacks. We tend to use most of our senses when assessing our patients and a manikin doesn't always look, feel or sound like a real sick person. This sometimes gets in the way of learning. However, you can't arrange for people to come into university and have a cardiac arrest on demand, so simulation is the best way of learning when the real thing isn't to hand. Don't be afraid of it, you are all in the same boat.

📖 **Student paramedic response:** Initially we did not have the opportunity to do much simulation, due to COVID-19, but it is stepping up now and makes a real difference to our learning. It can be daunting, but being prepared and reading notes/researching beforehand means you may not feel an idiot on the day. Knowledge is power in something like simulation.

🎓 **Academic response:** We take our students to a facility that is owned and run jointly by the local council, police and fire service. This is a huge area made out like a town and includes an ED, police station, fire station, law court, shops, restaurants, pubs, roads, houses, vehicles and even a park. We simulate incidents here for students, and feedback has been really great. Students definitely feel the benefit of being away from a classroom environment and the incidents feel more real.

🎓 **Academic response:** Many universities exploit state-of-the-art simulation to develop students' skills and leadership attributes in a safe environment, and it is essential that you engage in these activities. Macro-simulation and practical exercises allow students to explore the relationship between clinical, operational, teamwork and human factors, all of which influence service-user outcome. To add realism to simulated scenarios, moulage (make-up and fake blood) may be used.

🎓 **Academic response:** Simulations can be carried out at various locations to 'set the scene'; in our university we use a mock court-room, mock ambulance, climbing wall and crime scene houses to add realism and replicate the challenges encountered in practice.

My institution has developed a real working 'flat'; it has a working kitchen, bathroom, lounge and bedroom. It is equipped with cameras and the students who are not involved in the scenario can watch what is happening via a TV in a separate room, making notes on a white board in real time. Sometimes we review the recorded footage, some-times not, but it is good to be able to play it back if needed. Students initially feel self-conscious, but soon realise the benefits. Another good thing is that it is for small groups, taking a maximum of eight people at any one time. It generates lots of discussion afterwards, which is really invaluable for all of us present.

🚑 **Paramedic PEd response:** Some years ago I went on a Royal College of Surgeons 'Medicine in Remote Areas' course. One of the exercises was a 36-hour search and rescue simulation in a wood. It was amazingly realistic, with volunteers from the Casualties Union taking part. The injuries looked so real you forgot that it was a simu-lation at all. Amazing!

(physical, psychological, and conceptual) are associated with fidelity (Carey and Rossler 2022). It should not be assumed that high-fidelity simu-lation is always a better learning experience than low fidelity, it depends on what is being taught, for example practising communication skills would be considered low fidelity, but are an essential skill of a paramedic. Simulated assessments will be part of your programme of study they are usually called OSCES. OSCE is the abbreviation for an Objective Struc-tured Clinical Examination; you will see student comments referring to this type of practical examination later in the chapter.

Reflection: Points to consider

What is actually being simulated?

1   Is it the psychomotor skills and developing familiarity with equipment?
2   Is it the decision-making and prioritising/re-prioritising of care?
3   Is it the communication strategies needed in care delivery?
4   Is it the complexities of clinical practice?

Which are the important elements that need to be high fidelity?

1   Is it the setting (for example, an actual railway track)?
2   Is it the equipment used (for example, expensive manikins)?
3   Is it that the debrief relates learning points back to actual clinical practice?

What can I expect from this way of learning?

This approach will support your learning in a number of ways. It is useful to consider your involvement with a situation in terms of being a participant (or responder) in the scenario, a patient in the scenario and as an observer of the scenario, as all present different perspectives.

- **Participant:** as a participant you gain some sense of responding to the clinical scenario, familiarity with equipment and your own decision-making style. This is typically the role in which we expect most learning to occur.
- **Observer:** being one step removed from the practice scenario in this way allows you to become aware of peripheral issues – body language, or how long it takes to offer analgesia, for example – but can also involve you in learning how to offer feedback in some instances. It is useful to be an active observer, consider what your own actions may have been in this scenario, and how you would react to the challenges presented. Being an observer can lead to powerful self-reflection.
- **Patient/casualty:** here you have some experience of being questioned, being carried down a flight of stairs or being pulled out of a car, for example. This is invaluable because you develop sympathy for the fears that people may have simply from being in a carry chair,

but also see how vital it is for patients to be kept informed of what is happening to them.

Typically, a simulation event will consist of the following four stages, with some being more emphasised than others, depending on the skillset or areas of awareness that are being explored:

1   **Scenario briefing.** This can range from being extremely brief and vague (or even misleading, sometimes information given to paramedics responding to a 999 call is incomplete or inaccurate) to a very detailed overview of what is expected and what the intended learning outcomes are specifically trying to address.

2   **Scenario enactment.** This is usually either time-bound (e.g. it is stopped at 15 minutes) or outcome-bound (the response either resolves the scenario or complicates it further). The outcome-bound style of scenario is more complex but also truer to life.

3   **Scenario debrief: questions.** This often begins with the faculty asking the participants how they felt the scenario had run and is frequently structured to avoid any tendency towards either too much negativity or being purely congratulatory, to keep the discussion as objective as possible. Skilful faculty involvement ensures that, no matter how any individual scenario went, the learning experience is positive and participants feel supported and encouraged.

4   **Scenario debrief: feedback.** Normally, the faculty will have kept notes on key learning areas and a timeline of events. The timeline is extremely useful, because often your appreciation of the passage of time, particularly when you are under any form of pressure, can be inaccurate: you might think that you offered a patient oxygen almost as soon as you walked into a room, but to be told that it was after just over five minutes can be a revelation! This illustrates another means through which simulation can support learning; simulation can demonstrate your situational awareness enhancing your consideration of crew resource management. It is easy at first to be so completely engrossed in the performance of one specific element of care that you forget other, essential aspects – for example, did anyone consider the relatives? Did anyone secure the safety of the environment?

Once a group of students are familiar with one another, there is encouragement for some of the feedback to come from those observing, too. It might be that you are given the role of studying body language or the way that medications used have been checked or disposed of, and asked to give feedback on that. This helps develop an approach for feedback to colleagues which is, of course, an unavoidable area of learning and of practice. In these instances, it is understood that students have been asked to undertake the role so that the feedback is a deliberate part of the exercise; no-one should take the comments personally.

⊘ Refer to Chapters 1 and 8 for more discussion around the importance of personal reflection.

It is proposed within the literature around simulation education that about one-third of the time spent on an event is the simulation itself and that two-thirds are taken up with the debrief and discussion around the points raised during the event. These points may be the expected learning outcomes of the scenario, which are often pre-set. Academics may need to facilitate discussion of alternative responses demonstrated in the scenario, which may well be unique to each enactment of a scenario, or be unique to individuals and groups.

Ideally, simulation exercises will be undertaken in small groups, perhaps under ten in a group, so that feedback can be shared in a contained setting. It can be a very supportive way of learning about all aspects of your own practice, even though it can also have a certain intensity. This intensity is managed much better in small groups and can actually help to foster a strong sense of being in a learning community – it is a journey into clinical learning that is being shared and this can be very motivational.

Simulation events frequently see other staff (and sometimes senior students on your course) involved as part of the faculty. The advantage for your learning here is that paramedics and other clinical staff with specialist knowledge can be assembled to help deliver the exercise and ensure that feedback is as contemporaneous and as specific as possible. When senior students are involved, they can address in detail the issues which may affect the student perspective.

Peer debrief is a tool commonly used in simulation. This is where you will be asked to watch the scenario your colleagues participate in before offering your own thoughts or conclusions regarding what you have seen. While honesty relating to performance is important, it is easy to overstep the mark when critiquing so ensure that comments to your peers are supportive and constructive; it can be easy to forget the good parts of performance when offering feedback.

How can I make the most of opportunities to learn in simulation?

When you know that there will be a simulation day or scenario as part of your programme you can maximise what you take from the approach.

- **Be an active participant.** If you are given the scenarios beforehand, study them and clarify areas that you are unsure about. If an illness is going to be encountered, read in advance around that, or if there is equipment to be used that you are unfamiliar with, try and review it prior to the day.
- **During the day, take notes.** A lot can happen in one scenario and you may well want to ask questions of the faculty. Afterwards, to guide your own learning, you will want to follow up with reading around points raised that were either interesting or unclear for you on the day; at university students are expected to be able to direct their own learning. With these points in mind, bring some paper and a pen, or tablet, to make your notes on!
- **Volunteer!** There is always some trepidation at first, but everyone benefits from the lessons to be learned, and well-managed simulations acknowledge that the learning is shared.
- **Ask questions.** Make sure you ask questions not only of the facilitating team but also of your own practice and that of your peers. Simulation is the ideal, safe environment to try new techniques and gain deep understanding of how theory and practice integrate.

As can be seen from the insightful comments from students, paramedics and academics in Box 10.3, the value of verbalising what you want team mates to do before, on arrival, and during a call is a very important skill to learn.

In simulation at university, you will often be asked to verbalise what you are doing, what you are thinking, why you are undertaking a certain assessment or treatment – basically talking the examiner through what you are doing and why. This is crucial during OSCEs – it is the only way

Box 10.3 What advice would you give students to make the most of this way of learning?

📖 **Student paramedic response:** Repetition cements learning: keep practising on manikins and going to scenario days. Just as doing a certain sport creates what athletes call 'muscle memory', so simulation practice creates procedure memory.

Newly qualified paramedic (NQP): I had never relished the concept of simulated scenarios, as they always made me feel uncomfortable and slightly anxious. I actively tried to avoid them prior to starting the paramedic programme. However, my attitude has completely changed. I actively seek to participate in simulated scenarios now, as I have experienced the benefits of practising within a safe environment throughout my time at university, getting valuable feedback from academics and peers and having the chance to discuss practice issues raised by the scenario.

🚨 **Paramedic response:** Working in healthcare, simulation is something you get used to. I have taken part in a large-scale road traffic collisions and major incident simulation. This was incredibly useful as it is, thankfully, not something routinely seen. It gave me a chance to see how I would feel initially managing such a situation, therefore preparing me for this kind of event. Initially, I always feel a bit self-conscious when taking part in a scenario. In my experience assessors try to make them seem as realistic as possible and you soon forget people are watching. Assessment through scenarios continues once you are registered. Most ambulance trusts have an advanced life support scenario as part of their interview process. Further scenarios are used for professional updates throughout your working life.

🎓 **Academic response:** As good as simulation can be, it is not without its limitations. In reality, we can often glean enough information about our patients to conduct a primary survey from the door and make the decision whether or not the patient is time-critical. In simulation this is often not the case. Make sure you ask, ask, ask! If the assessor does not proffer enough information, ask about what you are seeing, feeling and hearing. Get into the habit of verbalising everything. This can be initially very challenging as it feels unnatural and does not happen in practice (maybe it should?), but it is an invaluable skill to learn. It will show the assessor your thought processes and give a good indication of why you are treating a patient in a certain way. I liken it to sitting a maths test – it is not enough to write down the correct answer; you need to show your working out. Even if the simulation is not as real as you would like it to be, remember it is an excellent way of learning a systematic approach to patient assessment and treatment.

Paramedic response: As a newly qualified paramedic (NQP) I was used to verbalising everything in OSCEs and I still try to as a paramedic. I think it is very important point to do so. As an NQP you will work with different crewmates who you don't really know, or know how they work. I found it improved the communication and clarity of what each of us needed to do if I verbalised specific things. For example, before arriving at the scene, I say things like: 'you take the life-pack and I take the wound bag'. Or, if it appears to be a time-critical call, I prepare en route and will verbalise things like 'I'll manage the airway and you do compressions on the chest.' It all comes back to communication but verbalising is perhaps something that is not taught or emphasised enough at university.

Student paramedic response: This relates to verbalising what is going on ... it is really important. At my first resuscitation, as a first-year student, I didn't realise that we had achieved ROSC (return of spontaneous circulation) because no-one verbalised it. In simulation at university, the faculty had verbalised it, so I thought it would be like this in clinical practice. So basically, it is good to rely on what is verbalised in simulation; it is a shame more staff do not verbalise what is going on, and what they are doing in real-life situations. It makes things much clearer for all that are present – which is ultimately better for the patient.

Year 1 student paramedic response: If there is an opportunity to demonstrate or try something new out in the classroom (not necessarily a full-on sim suite), do it. It does not matter what other people are doing – this is your time to develop and gain those skills, so you can be the best paramedic you can be.

an examiner can be sure you understand what you are doing. Going back to the points made above, it is also important that as a paramedic you continue to explain what you are doing and why, especially if you have responsibility for a student. Verbalising your thoughts and actions is also one way to 'invite' your team to add their thoughts to a situation: they may have something to contribute; they may add something you may have not seen, thought of or considered doing. No-one is a mind reader so unless you verbalise what you are doing and why, your team may misunderstand, communication may be adversely affected, and patient outcome may suffer. Communication between professionals is highlighted in Case study 10.1.

CASE STUDY 10.1

Final-year paramedic and midwifery students were grouped together into a number of teams and had to respond to a number of home-birth situations. The students had to rely on each other's skillset, the different equipment they had available and they had to make decisions as a team about moving the pregnant woman onto an ambulance.

The debrief for each team exposed similar issues: that communication was paramount and being clear about who needed to take the lead during separate stages of the scenario mattered to both professional groups and to the safety of the mother and child. This sharing or alternating of the clinical lead role is an advanced and refined area, and simulation allowed some confidence to be developed about strategies that would clarify who ought to be directing care and considering the next step.

Student paramedics were able to develop some confidence that they need not be embarrassed about assessing the woman in labour, something that normal social conventions would prevent, but student midwives were able to be quite clear about the importance of knowing how far the baby's head had appeared and what this meant in terms of imminent delivery. This type of communication across and between disciplines is invaluable and can be accessed through simulated scenarios.

In summary, simulation approaches are, in fact, unavoidable in clinical education. They occur all the time in all manner of guises, from moving and handling demonstrations to physical assessment exams. Whether simulation involves low- or high-tech approaches, what matters most is your own engagement.

References

Carey, J.M. and Rossler, K. (2022) *The How When Why of High Fidelity Simulation.* Available at: https://www.ncbi.nlm.nih.gov/books/NBK559313/ (accessed 28 October 2022).

McKimm, J. and Forrest, J. (eds) (2019) *Healthcare Simulation at a Glance.* Chichester: Wiley-Blackwell

Further reading

The Association for Simulated Practice in Healthcare has a useful website at http://www.aspih.org.uk/

ASPiH is a not-for-profit company limited by guarantee. It is a membership association formed through the merger of the National Association of Medical Simulators and the Clinical Skills Network. It aims to enable a wider sharing of knowledge, expertise, and educational innovation related to simulated practice across the healthcare professions.

11 HOW CAN YOU LINK YOUR ACADEMIC STUDIES AND CLINICAL PRACTICE?

Amanda Blaber

Several points have already been made about the use of reflection, independent study and guided study. All of these recognised approaches should help you make the link between theory and practice.

𝒫 Refer to Chapter 8 for discussion about the use of reflective practice and Chapter 9 for detailed ideas for making the most of your independent and guided study time.

Reflection: Points to consider

1   Think of a time when your studies have directly helped you in everyday life.
2   What worked well?
3   Could you have made more of the learning experience?

It may also be useful to read specific books on study skills and reflection. It is important that you find texts that suit your reading style and that you find informative and interesting; a selection of reading material is provided under the Study Skills texts heading at the end of this chapter.

Handy hints to help you link theory and practice

You are reading this text to learn more about being a student paramedic, so it makes sense for you to read ideas directly from students on this matter, with opinions and additional suggestions from academics and paramedics/PEds.

The comments in Box 11.1 describe a number of different approaches and may give you some ideas and help you understand the importance of making the links between theory and practice.

The strategies highlighted in Box 11.1 clearly illustrate the link between theory and practice. Possessing the underpinning knowledge is part of academic study that needs to be demonstrated in the clinical practice environment. Remember, you should be able to explain anything about a person's assessment, treatment and management to them in a way they can understand – if you cannot do this, your underpinning knowledge is lacking. Equally, you need to be able to explain what you are doing and why to students and colleagues and also acknowledge that you cannot know everything, so there will be occasions you need to refer to textbooks throughout your career.

It is also good to think more widely about sources of expertise and information. Our patients are a major source of information, and they may know their condition in more detail than we do, especially if it is something quite unique and rare. This is explained well by Case study 11.1.

CASE STUDY 11.1

I remember attending a job involving a little girl who had fallen from height. On checking her pupils, I found them to be grossly bilaterally dilated. This just did not make sense as the rest of her signs and symptoms did not add up. It was only when mum arrived and she informed me the little girl had a condition called 'aniridia' (the absence of an iris) that this made sense. It was interesting for me to be able to research this condition when I got home and is a good example of how theory can directly link to practice.

As Case study 11.1 clearly shows, practice and theory are inextricably linked. No matter how long you have been a registered paramedic, there will be things you come across that require you to *hit the books* and remind yourself of something or learn about something new. So never be afraid of

Box 11.1 What strategies would you suggest to link your academic studies and clinical practice successfully? What worked for you?

📖 **Student paramedic response:** I took a couple of relevant books on shift with me so that after each call we attended I could learn more by looking things up like the causes, complications, treatment of the patient's condition. Seeing a patient with a condition you've read about cements understanding, and reading up on things you've seen on placement develops knowledge and decision-making.

I would also keep a note of each call we went to so that I could look up relevant aspects of it later when I could search the literature on it and gain more insight. Obviously, you're also talking with your mentor about each call, getting their reasoning and understanding of it. I found also that my mentors would ask me lots of things about current thinking on treatments, etc. as they knew we were getting the most up-to-date thinking on it in our lectures and they wanted to learn from me as much as I was learning from them. This was a really good aspect of my placement experience. It wasn't just a case of the student sitting at the feet of the master – we shared the learning experience.

🚨 **Paramedic PEd response:** Students often ask why they need to study some subjects in such depth, anatomy, physiology and pathophysiology being the most common. 'Why do we need to know this?' is a common question. When students are on placement and are exposed to a particular medical condition for the first time, they already have a good understanding of exactly what is happening and why. It is at this point that many students have said how glad they were they had the underpinning knowledge to understand what was going on.

🚨 **Paramedic PEd response:** My mentor reviewed patients' conditions with me afterwards and quizzed me on anatomy, physiology, altered physiology, treatment options and medications. This was never done in a negative way. Often, we used to work things out together or she used to teach me certain aspects. As a student, I disliked this approach, mainly because I was self-conscious and really did not want to get anything wrong. How crazy – I was learning a new job, of course I would get things wrong or not know something! But I realise now how this approach really made me go away and learn the things I could not answer and did not know. It is a similar approach that I use with my students now. I also try to widen the scope of subjects to areas such as sociology and psychology, as many of our calls are to people with social or psychological issues. It is not just physical illness that this job is about; as paramedic mentors we need to make sure we assess our students on the holistic range of problems that patients have. Each call usually has an element of physical, social and psychological issues that can be explored and linked to theory.

🎓 **Academic response:** It is a fact that students will engage more with subjects they feel have relevance to practice. As a lecturer I take every opportunity to point out how the academic subjects are relevant to practice and try to give good examples. Don't be afraid to ask your lecturers to point out the relevance of subjects – you may be surprised how even the subjects that are perceived as the driest academic ones have hidden relevance.

Using calls you have attended as starting points for your own study and further research is also a very good way to link academic studies to practice. When one actually sees a medical condition much of the underpinning knowledge will click into place.

learning from your patient; it is not a sign of weakness or lack of competence. If your programme involves block placements, it is wise to try and keep in touch with academic staff at your institution while on placement. This may take the form of occasional emails or more formal one-to-one meetings to discuss your general progress or any specific issue that is of concern to you at the time.

Textbooks will often list signs and symptoms of certain conditions, but it is wise to remember that patients will not present in such a textbook fashion. Symptoms and signs may vary, and your role is often one of a detective, trying to piece together clues that you collect from the patients, significant others and physical data. Often you may need to refer to textbooks to help explain the variation from the normal symptoms/signs that you would have expected, or the interaction of different disease processes.

This will add to your expertise and may help you in the future, with other patients presenting with similar signs and symptoms.

There is nothing drier than trying to learn about the subject from a textbook. Take physiology for example. Learning about the body systems and how they work in normal health is key for any healthcare student to learn. Once you know how the system should work in normal health, then you can move on to learn what happens when things diverge from normal and when people experience ill health.

Let us look at the respiratory system to help explain how you can make your learning more interactive and patient focused. The normal physiology, structures and processes will be taught to you, with you adding to your knowledge via independent study, for example using textbooks, YouTube clips and other interactive tools. Once you have all of this cemented and are clear on how the respiratory system works, you can move your learning onto what happens in certain respiratory conditions.

While on placement you may attend a person who has a diagnosis of asthma and is having an exacerbation of their asthma. Obviously, you will be observing and assisting your mentor, while they assess, treat and manage the patient's condition. During this time, you will observe some signs of asthma as you care for the patient. Your patient may tell you some of their symptoms. Make some notes of your own (while observing confidentiality) such as their observations, what they look like, how they speak to you, and so on. After the call, if there is time, discuss this with your mentor and add to your notes. Using your independent study time, I would suggest you develop this clinical experience into a full academic and practice learning experience and do the following:

- **Write up your patient description.** Possibly including the following: how you received the call, and whether the information you had beforehand was accurate; what they told you; what you observed; previous medical history; how they were assessed and treated (what medications); management of their asthma (guidelines used); what their final destination was (hospital or referral or home).
- **Write yourself a list of questions about things that are not clear to you.** Possibly including the following: what is asthma, and are there different types? How common is asthma (statistics)? How might living with asthma affect a person's life and how may it

make them feel? What happens physiologically to the respiratory system in asthma? Did my patient show *textbook* signs and symptoms? If not, why not? What do I know about assessing the respiratory system? What tests did my mentor undertake on the patient and why? What might this tell us? What are my treatment guidelines for asthma? What medications did we give, what are they called, what are the normal dosages, how do the medications work? And so on …

By using a real-life experience, I hope you can see that learning becomes more relevant, interesting and engaging. Your learning is now about what you have seen, what you observed, what you did and then finding out why all of this was conducted in the way it was from various textbooks, not just physiology texts, but charity websites (in this example, Asthma UK), where you can obtain lay and professional sources of specific information. You will need to use pharmacology sources to explore the usual medications used in this condition and then how the medications work in more detail. Use specific paramedic guidelines to explore the treatment and management options. You may wish to explore psychology and sociology texts to explore how living with a condition like asthma may affect a person's life more generally. If you do this for a variety of patients you have cared for you could end up with a very extensive literature covering various conditions. You will never be able to cover all conditions, but by doing something like this, you will take responsibility for your own study and learning, making it interesting. A student once said to me, 'in my exam (which was about a patient with asthma) I could see Lily, I just recalled exactly what we did when we were with her and wrote it down. I would never have been able to do that had I just read a chapter on asthma from a physiology textbook.' I hope this helps you make learning interesting and engaging.

This aim of this chapter has been to provide you with some ideas about how others have approached linking clinical practice with theory. Do not be averse to trying other strategies. Speak to your colleagues and PEds – they may have some innovative ideas that you can try for yourself. Linking the two together generally also strengthens your ability to study independently and gives you the ability to visualise your patient and not just see, for example, a signs and symptoms table in a textbook. This generally makes it easier to learn and is more interesting for many students.

References

Bolton, G.E.J. (2018) *Reflective Practice. Writing and Professional Development* (5th edn). London: Sage.

Richardson, M. (2019) Reflective practice in relation to pre-hospital care. In A.Y. Blaber (ed.) *Foundations for Paramedic Practice: A Theoretical Perspective* (3rd edn). Maidenhead: Open University Press.

Rolfe, G., Jasper, M. and Freshwater, D. (2010) *Critical Reflection in Practice: Generating Knowledge for Care* (2nd edn). Basingstoke: Palgrave Macmillan.

Study skills texts

Cottrell, S. (2019) *The Study Skills Handbook* (5th edn). Macmillan Study Skills Series. London: Macmillan.

Please use the most recent edition. Stella Cottrell has written extensively in the area of study skills; please investigate her other texts, which include texts on critical thinking skills, dissertations and project reports.

Publishers generally have a series of texts on study skills; please investigate Palgrave, Macmillan and Open University Press publishing houses.

Additional advice

Students also need to examine what is available to them via their university specific resources; this may include study skills sessions run by teaching and learning experts and library technologists (for searching skills). Access and use these expert resources.

PART 4
Placement: Preparing for it and making the most of it

Part 3 of this book has been primarily focused upon your academic studies, but this is inextricably linked to your experiences and learning in clinical practice as a student paramedic. You cannot consider one without the other; consequently there have been some brief suggestions made about the practice environment. Part 4, however, is predominantly related to your experience in the practice environment.

12 IS PRACTICE WHAT YOU THINK IT IS GOING TO BE?

Amanda Blaber and Kim Tolley

Reflection: Points to consider

Before you read this chapter, make a list of the key words you associate with *student paramedic practice experience*.

You will probably be most looking forward to what is commonly called *going out to practice*. Many students find this the most exciting prospect of being a student paramedic. For some, the reality is vastly different than they expected, while others feel very prepared and it is exactly as they envisaged it would be, as highlighted by the diversity of comments made by students. One thing that is certain is that no-one can predict what you are going to see or experience during shifts in any clinical environment, the ambulance service being no exception. Your safety and that of your colleagues is of utmost importance and you will be provided with safety guidance information. Case study 12.1 has been included to help dispel the myth that all ambulance service work is action-packed; it also highlights the importance of communication.

CASE STUDY 12.1

I remember having to tell a 90-year-old lady that we had not been successful in resuscitating her husband. I had been talking to her while the resuscitation attempt was in progress in the room next door. Among so many other things, I knew they had been married for 66 years, knew about their family and how they had met. I found this one of the hardest things to do, yet one of the most rewarding. I had been sitting talking, comforting, explaining, discussing all manner of subjects for over an hour. I had connected with the lady, as I had the time to get to know her. I found it extremely difficult to leave her when it was time for us to go.

For many of the 'non-initiated' the job of a paramedic is all about blue lights and road traffic collisions. This is *not* the case. A huge part of the job is being able to provide comfort and reassurance to vulnerable (often elderly and lonely) people. Some of my most satisfying jobs have been clinically 'insignificant' but I have gone away knowing I made a huge difference to that person at that time.

The emotions explained in Case study 12.1 help to explain the diversity of the role and highlight that while the call was an emergency, the role of each professional attending may be extremely diverse and require very different approaches to the situation.

It may be that not all of your clinical experience will be on a frontline 999 vehicle with blue flashing lights. There is much more to the ambulance service, and answering 999 calls is just one aspect of the service that any ambulance trust provides. Indeed, depending on your programme, you may also spend a significant amount of time in non-ambulance service clinical areas, observing the role of paramedics and other clinical staff working in these areas.

Types of ambulance service placement

Clinical/placement areas that encompass primary, acute, urgent, community and emergency care environments provide the opportunity for learning outcomes to be achieved and can be considered as relevant to the student paramedic experience. This section of the chapter will outline some of the placements considered relevant by the College of Paramedics (2019). You must remember that it is not possible to visit/work in all of the placements listed in this chapter during your time as a student paramedic. The opportunities will vary from university to university and between programmes of study.

Box 12.1 Experiences of clinical placement

📖 **Student paramedic comment:** On our programme each student was allocated ambulance placements at two different base stations, one urban and one more rural, which gave us experience of all types of patients/environments. I thought the rural one would be quiet and uneventful compared to the urban station, but often the quaint town on a Sunday afternoon was busier than the city on a Friday night! I even went to an armed siege, complete with riot squad! It just goes to show you never know what could happen on a shift – that's one of the things I love about the job.

📖 **Student paramedic comment:** We went to a lot of patients with mental health issues. I found that these patients were the ones I felt the most empathy for, as although we could help them with an immediate problem, we felt fairly powerless to make a lasting, long-term difference for them. I'd say we go to more patients with social or mental health issues than patients with trauma. Being a paramedic is not all about running from car crashes to cardiac arrests all day; it's about going to people who often didn't know who else to call; this doesn't mean it's not important or rewarding. You just need to like people and have loads of patience, empathy and a willingness to do the best you can for them.

📖 **Student paramedic comment:** As a Year 1 student I thought we wouldn't be doing much, but I have done loads (in my opinion, not coming from a healthcare background). I also thought the staff may be quite cold, but they have been lovely. Everyone was new at one point.

📖 **Student paramedic comment:** Be aware that you will rarely find out what happens to your patient after you take them to a medical facility.

📖 **Year 1 student paramedic comment:** The types of calls we go to is not what I expected – in respect of the number of people we can leave at home. I was surprised about the emphasis on gaining a patient's consent and assessing their mental capacity before treatment – that was something I had not considered. There is also a huge amount of paperwork/e-paperwork that needs to be completed during/after each call. Wear layers under your uniform in the winter as it can be cold. Calls are very primary-care focused and we take quite a lot of people unnecessarily due to social care reasons, i.e. they are unsafe at home. Be prepared to be out of your comfort zone when going into patients' homes. Some homes are not what you expect, but you need to disguise your shock and maintain professionalism.

As Case study 12.1 and the above student paramedic comments in Box 12.1 illustrate, the patients you will care for may be experiencing crises that you might not have envisaged the ambulance service would be called upon to manage and help with. It is therefore important that programmes address all aspects of care, and do not just focus on physical aspects. To help programme teams achieve this, other professionals with expertise, such as mental health nurses, may be asked for input into your programme. This is something that your mentors/PEds undertaking in-house ambulance service training courses may not have had the benefit of, so make the most of the expertise around you and learn as much as possible.

Student paramedic programmes offer a wide variety of experiences, some of which you may find a surprise. Table 12.1 details the types of placements that the College of Paramedics (2019) recommends as being suitable for student paramedics. Often a programme structure is such that at certain points in the programme it may be more appropriate to undertake certain types of placements. For example, it may be more beneficial for a student paramedic who is undertaking or has just completed their physical assessment module/unit to work with a solo responder for a few shifts, so they can gain more experience and use their physical assessment skills more consistently. Or it may be that your programme includes a few shorter placements in varied areas, such as residential care, mental health services, acute ward environments. Further examples are provided in Table 12.1. It is also important you spend a percentage of your time on an emergency frontline (999) vehicle.

It is worth experiencing the role and pressure of the emergency operation control centre early in your studies and then revisiting it once you have a more comprehensive appreciation of your role. Again, appreciating other people's roles is important to understand their pressures, priorities and working environment. Assessing and taking information without seeing who you are talking to is very different, and requires different communication skills from meeting a person face to face. It is very easy to criticise

Table 12.1 Types of placements that may be included in paramedic programmes

Fundamental care, e.g. residential care, hospice

Patient assessment area, e.g. intensive treatment unit, operating theatre, air ambulance (limited opportunities)

Mental health and learning disability, e.g. crisis team, child and adolescent mental health services, day unit

Children and families, e.g. school nursing, health visitors

Emergency ambulance, e.g. as crew or with solo responder

Hear and treat environments, e.g. 111, clinical hubs

each other, but an appreciation of the difficulties of communication and an understanding of roles are vital for a cohesive and efficient service for patients.

In all ambulance services there are specialist operation units, such as hazardous area response teams, urban search and rescue, baby/neonate emergency transfer units, and helicopter medical services. It is highly probable that students will not be able to secure placements with these specialist teams, but you may have visits or lectures from people from these teams as part of your programme. As you can imagine, these services are small and make up a small part of any ambulance service, so rotating large numbers of student paramedics through them is usually impossible.

Communication skills are an invaluable part of any learning opportunity so this should be at the forefront of your mind with any placement opportunity. Whatever placement experience you have in the local community, acute hospital trust, primary care trust or ambulance service, at some point you will be required to undertake various shift patterns.

Shift work

This was briefly mentioned in earlier chapters, but requires more attention, as it can be the difference between students enjoying their role and finding it too much and giving up their studies. Inevitably student paramedics will encounter shift work at some point in their careers. The vast majority of programmes involve students working shifts from early on, usually Year 1. Some may not involve that much shift work. Whatever your programme does in respect of shift work, it is certain that your first employed role as a paramedic in an ambulance service will expect you to undertake the variety of shift patterns designated by your trust, as the responses in Box 12.2 explain.

Box 12.2 In your experience, what shifts are allocated to students? Does this change when you are registered?

🚨 **Paramedic response:** During my time as a student I had an easy-going mentor that I could text and arrange shifts with. For a placement I needed to give my availability a month or so in advance, and they were still flexible around my part-time job, etc. Since registration, and, more importantly, employment, there is little choice. My current rota has me working three out of four weekends and I'm lucky if I do less than 50 per cent nights in a month. Unfortunately, the unsocial shifts are where the demand is and if you choose to work for a trust where you know you will be relief staff, read your contract thoroughly and understand these implications; it's quite a shock to the system!

🚨 **Paramedic PEd response:** In most cases students will 'mirror' the shift pattern of their mentor. This is usually a full range of shifts following a rota. This can change when a newly qualified paramedic is employed by a trust; in some cases the new staff member will start on a relief line. This can be challenging as the shifts do not follow a pattern and shorter notice is given as to what hours will be required. This said, relief positions are usually only temporary until a permanent line becomes available and are a good way of *getting a foot in the door*.

🚨 **Paramedic PEd response:** A full range of shift work is required throughout the programme of study, and you shouldn't wait until you qualify to do your first night shift or your first weekend or bank holiday. Having said this, take your time to adjust to odd shift times and don't rush into working continuous nights or having quick turnarounds, swapping from days to nights or vice versa. It will take a bit of getting used to, but take it slowly and by the time you qualify you will be set to go. Your shift pattern when registered will be different and may be more intense, but your previous experience of the range of shifts will make the transition much easier.

Box 12.3 highlights the various approaches to shift work that the student paramedic may encounter. The responses also help to explain the variety of shift patterns that you may be expected to work and how this may help to prepare you for employment. The difficulty of shift work should not be underestimated, and the following comments help to explain how important it is to develop your own strategy for coping with shift work.

Box 12.3 Approaches taken and attitudes to shiftwork

📖 **Student paramedic comment:** Shift work is difficult, especially the switch between night and day shifts. I still haven't got used to these – apparently it takes about ten years! It can take a couple of days to reset your body clock after night shifts. Different people have different methods for dealing with it. Some stay up for the whole day after a night shift, others get a couple of hours then make themselves get up – you will find what works for you, but you can feel pretty jetlagged for a while until you find your way of dealing with it.

🔔 **Paramedic comment:** One year into my career I'm fairly used to nights. I have a pattern which I generally follow. Before my first night I try to lie in as long as possible, usually about 10:30, then go about my day as normal, including some form of exercise. I arrive at work about 20 minutes early to ensure there is time for a coffee. I can then sleep solidly between the rest of my nights. If I finish on time, I may even get up an hour earlier, for a jog after a few nights. I struggle more with day shifts as I've never been a morning person! Again, coffee is my answer; I always have a Thermos and a couple of sachets of cappuccino in my bag.

🎓 **Academic comment:** I would disagree with the comment above saying getting used to shifts takes about ten years. I had no problem with early (07.00–14.30) or late shifts (14.00–22.00) or 12-hour shifts (08.00–20.00). However, I never got used to night shifts. We used to be allocated seven nights at a time. I just used to manage them as best I could, and that wasn't very well. I used to dread the rota including them, write off that week of my life and the one following it, as it used to take me three or four days to get back into a regular sleep pattern. Some of my colleagues only worked night shifts, and declined to work day shifts if they had the choice.

Box 12.4 What are the difficulties and/or pleasures of shift work?

Paramedic PEd response: I used to love working night shifts. The world is a totally different place at night, and some of my most interesting and challenging jobs seemed to occur on nights. There also seemed to be more camaraderie between staff on night shifts. Last, but not least, going home to a warm bed on a cold and rainy Monday morning when everyone else had to be up for work was one of my small but significant pleasures!

Paramedic response: There are many pros and cons to shift work. Many people in the ambulance service say they aren't built for 9–5, and this is true for me. The biggest difficulty I have working shifts is missing out on social events, particularly at weekends. You can guarantee if you make plans after work, you'll be so late off it won't be worth attending. I have had a few occasions where this has happened and I've found myself really upset at missing family members' birthdays, etc. Now I've learned my lesson, I rarely arrange to do anything after work; if I do, I warn people involved that I may not actually make it or may get there late. Things that I don't want to miss, I book off with annual leave.

Paramedic PEd response: My favourite thing about shifts is having so much time off. Working a 12-hour day is long, but you do three or four and then the week is yours. I get so much done on my days off, time to myself and to enjoy my hobbies.

There is no one-size-fits-all advice that can be given about managing or coping with shift patterns. The comments from all contributors point to the fact that you need to try it for yourself, as the responses in Box 12.4 help to explain.

The wide variation in personal opinion regarding shift work should be appreciated by the reader having read the comments and responses included in this chapter. Shift work, particularly at night, is a bit like Marmite, you either love it or hate it! You need to make up your own mind.

Reflection: Points to consider

Write down your own list of pros and cons of working unsocial hours.

It is likely that you will have the opportunity to also experience non-ambulance placements while studying as well as ambulance placements.

Wider interprofessional placements

Further to the examples given in Table 12.1, this section will provide further detail of the guidelines for suitable student paramedic placements, provided by the College of Paramedics (2019) for HEIs and NHS ambulance trusts. The list is extensive, as can be seen in Table 12.2, and the

Table 12.2 Types of interprofessional placements that may be included in paramedic programmes

Types of placement area	What can be learned
• Care homes • Ward areas • Hospices	'… to develop the skills and assimilate the principles of what it means to be a healthcare professional: to care for people.'
• Admissions • Emergency department • GP surgery • Urgent care/walk-in centre • Maternity	'… support the development of history taking and assessment skills.'
• Air ambulance • Operating theatre • Intensive treatment unit/high dependency unit	'… develop their assessment, referral, treatment and management of service users who present with critical illness and/or injury.'
• Crisis team • Street triage • Drug/alcohol service • Admissions • Child and Adolescent Mental Health Services (CAMHS)	'… enable learners to develop their assessment, referral, treatment and management of service users presenting with acute and/or chronic mental illness.'
• Admissions units • Health visitors • School nursing	'… to develop their assessment, referral, treatment and management of children who present with acute and/or chronic illness.' Also to learn about normal child development.
• 111 • Clinical hubs	'… to develop their skills with healthcare professionals in non-patient-facing roles to experience clinical decision making in situations where they are not face-to-face with patients.'

2019 guidelines also explain the potential value of the learning experience from these clinical areas. The availability of these areas to student paramedics may depend on a variety of political and local factors and (most crucially) the number of other healthcare students already placed in these areas, as part of their programme of study.

Occasionally, other healthcare students (nurses, midwives) will have the opportunity to work on ambulances, but predominantly these opportunities are afforded to student paramedics. The same applies to student midwives, for example, who need the majority of their practice hours to be spent in midwifery-focused clinical areas. It may be, therefore, that there is not the capacity to accept student paramedics in other clinical areas within your locality. It is very much a situation that varies from year to year, depending on local demand. Your programme teams will work closely with university placement teams and try their best to secure alternative placements where possible.

Interprofessional placements in the wider NHS and/or private sector can help the student to gain an element of insight and witness other health professionals working with various patient groups. Such placement areas detailed in Table 12.2 serve to enhance relationships, teamwork and communication across professions and disciplines and within the workplace. Students must experience interprofessional working to develop the required competencies essential to work within a collaborative workforce.

Table 12.2 lists appropriate interprofessional placement opportunities for the student paramedic. It will not be the case that all students will experience all of the placements listed in Table 12.2. As mentioned above, there will be local variation and, in some cases, limited availability of such placements.

Many of the areas mentioned in Table 12.2 are an opportunity to improve your communication skills with patients of varying ages from very young to very old. In some of the areas the patients you will encounter will not be seriously ill and you will have the opportunity to take your time, assess them and talk to them. This would not be appropriate in areas such as a coronary care unit (CCU) or intensive therapy unit (ITU), but instead there you will see the work that goes on once the ambulance crew has handed over the patient and have the opportunity to extend your knowledge in relation to the specifics of the patient's condition.

There is a wide variety of learning opportunities available by exploring the wider NHS and the roles of other health professionals. The more you develop your knowledge of the NHS as a whole and the services available in your locality, the more you can pass this information on to your patients; you may be able to help them make informed choices regarding their health in the future. Your understanding of what happens in these areas may help to alleviate your patients' anxiety at a point in the future, so these placements are equally as valuable as ambulance service opportunities. Box 12.5 includes responses relating to the benefits of non-ambulance service placements.

Attending any placement can be a stressful experience, so it is important that you feel prepared. Ensure that you are clear about both your responsibilities and those of the registered clinician, in respect of the placement environment and any assessment processes. The following section of the chapter provides some useful suggestions to help reduce the pressure and stress you may feel prior to attending non-ambulance service placements.

Preparing for interprofessional/wider NHS placements

Any change you experience can be a difficult time. Some of these placements will be in Year 1, some in Years 2 and 3; there is enormous variation between programmes of study. This is something to ask about at open days. Going to a different clinical or community area will be strange and a different experience. Your time in these areas may be limited, ranging from a few days to a few weeks; they are unlikely to be any longer. It is therefore important that you are ready to go to the area, have an idea what to expect and start getting involved quickly, otherwise it will be over before you know it.

Reflection: Points to consider

1   Make a list of things you want to see, experience and learn about while you are in your non-ambulance placement. This will depend on the type of area, so think carefully.

2   Talk to other students who have already been to these areas, and focus on what learning opportunities there are.

3   Go to the placement with a clear idea of what you want to learn while you are there. This will help to demonstrate your enthusiasm when you first arrive.

4   Is there a guided study accompanying the placement and is there a student handbook? Ask your lecturers or placement lead.

Box 12.5 What are the benefits of undertaking interprofessional/ wider NHS placements?

📖 **Student paramedic response:** CCU [cardiac care unit] was great as I got to see how the doctors treat cardiac patients from the point the paramedics brought them in, to the point the patient left hospital. This is really useful as it gives you insight into the care a patient will get once you've handed them over and you can use this knowledge to reassure relatives and friends of future patients.

📖 **Student paramedic response:** Maternity was my favourite placement, mainly because the staff were so nice and really enthusiastic towards paramedics getting involved. I got to help deliver 12 babies (including at a Caesarean section) – really rewarding stuff. Lots of paramedics seem scared of maternity jobs, but this placement gave me a confidence that I will be able to handle these jobs well, as and when they come.

📖 **Student paramedic response:** I found that if you put yourself out as a student when on placement in hospitals, offering to help make beds or hand out the patients' dinners (even clean the bed pans) then the staff take notice and really appreciate you being there. This then makes them want to give you their time and create opportunities for you to learn more. Some students didn't do much to help if it didn't include what they were there to do; as a result they didn't get to see much. You get out of placement what you're willing to put in.

🎓 **Academic response:** Wider NHS/interprofessional placements are incredibly valuable not just in clinical terms, but in allowing us to understand what a patient experiences after they leave our care. When we 'deliver' a patient to the ED it is the end of our journey, but the start of theirs (often a very long one). It also gives us an appreciation of the roles of other health professionals and makes for good working relationships in the future.

📖 **Student paramedic response:** It was scary going to children's areas. I have no young children in my family, but I was well supported and learned so much. Some of the communication strategies staff used, I can take to my role and I learned what is a child's normal development at certain ages. It is true: how can you recognise a sick child, if you do not know normal child development?

> **Paramedic PEd response:** I am always so jealous of students being able to spend time in other services/areas of care. It is something I never had in my in-house training. I would have learned so much, that may have made me a better paramedic, things that took years of experience to develop *are laid on plates* for students, if they only knew what opportunities they had. I am surprised at how many students do not value these learning experiences. Don't make their mistake – value these placements.

In order to help you prepare, ask your lecturers and/or placement team for any books and local information provided by the placement. Some placement areas provide information and workbooks for other healthcare students to look at before they start the placement: would this be useful? Talk to your lecturers about what they think you should learn or focus on while in the placement; they may be able to direct you to guided study they have prepared. Some programmes may provide you with clear learning outcomes. The comments in Case study 12.2 and Box 12.6 help to explain the difficulties of attending non-ambulance placements, but also the immense benefits of working with a multi-professional team.

It is difficult to settle in quickly, but a positive, enthusiastic attitude will be noticed by staff and may be the difference between a rewarding and informative experience and one that is lacking in learning opportunities. As Case study 12.2 clearly explains, even a short two-week placement can have an impact on your own individual practice, teamwork and will help to improve your patient care.

CASE STUDY 12.2

I attended an ED for two weeks as part of my student paramedic placement system. I had predetermined thoughts and ideas of what I wanted to achieve from this placement and preconceptions on how I thought an ED would function in comparison to pre-hospital care and being in the back of an ambulance.

The biggest thing I learned from this placement was that although we step in and out of an ED environment on a daily basis with patients and communicate with staff, the lack of awareness and understanding of roles from both sides is huge. I had the opportunity to speak with different staff members to gain an insight into what we all do. We all think that the care we are providing patients in our environment is correct, which it is, but it massively increased my understanding of little things we can do pre-hospitally that will help make the transition of care easier for ED staff and the patient. For example, if we are with a patient who will potentially require cardiac intervention, cannulating a patient on the left-hand side when possible will allow a doctor easier access to perform his intervention as he/she will need to be on the right side of the patient. If we are going to immobilise a patient, removing things from pockets and belts will mean the patient can go for X-rays and scans more quickly and without delay. Additionally, when we write our paperwork, we may use a range of abbreviations that in our environment we all understand, but other people reading our paperwork may not use the same ones, so keeping our language simple stops any confusion.

I also learned just how busy EDs are, and quite simply staff in these environments deal with a hundred things at once. We see one patient at a time, but staff in ED are responsible for the care of a number of patients at any one time. It was also interesting to learn the availability of resources a hospital has – by that I mean that there are specialists available for most circumstances – and how limited we are in the community.

During this placement I gained massive exposure to, and experience of, patient care and developed confidence in my ability to gain a patient history, as this is done repeatedly with every patient. My record-keeping abilities developed, along with my communication skills. Communication varies from when we see patients experiencing their emergency to how they communicate once in a hospital environment, and this was interesting to witness. Finally, my confidence grew in skills, such as taking bloods and cannulating. We attempt these skills in challenging environments under extreme pressure, as the main focus is to deliver emergency and life-saving drugs, but in a hospital you are able to develop these skills in a more relaxed and controlled environment.

Box 12.6 Comments on interprofessional placements

📖 **Student paramedic comment:** As well as ambulance placements we had placements in hospitals. We did a week in a cardiac care unit, two weeks in theatres and two weeks in maternity. Each placement was different. It's difficult to prepare for these placements other than by reading up on the skills you are hoping to practise and develop. You can get a varied response from the staff there, ranging from those really keen to help you to those who might see you as someone getting in the way. Consequently, it can take a couple of days to find your feet on some placements. I struggled with the theatre placement because of this. Everyone was busy getting on with their work and left me to find my own way around, but in the end I met some paramedic-friendly anaesthetists who took me under their wing and taught me loads. I discovered the notice board where they put up the theatre lists detailing which operations were being carried out each day, and worked out a plan of where to be, at what time, to step in and ask to help with cannulating and intubating. I had to be proactive and push myself forward, but it paid off as I developed these skills and also got to observe during some amazing operations. Seeing 'living' anatomy opened up before you is totally different from a textbook diagram or photo of an anatomical specimen.

🎓 **Academic comment:** I had heard many horror stories of how unfriendly theatre staff could be to paramedics on placement. I was determined to make the best of my placement so arrived on my first day in theatre with some large tins of biscuits and a big smile. I pushed myself forward and was friendly to everyone. The result was that I had a great time and was allowed exposure to a whole range of extra experiences such as being allowed to assist on paediatric lists and stay to observe operations.

It is important to notice how the contributor in Case study 12.2 has appreciated the wider role of the ED. Small points about practice have been mentioned too, such as removing keys from pockets, and how this simple act can have an impact on the patient's journey. As the contributor wisely states, understanding and appreciating each other's roles is potentially one of the most valuable lessons that can be learned from non-ambulance service placements.

Reflection: Points to consider

1   At the beginning of this chapter you were asked to write a list of words you associated with student paramedic practice experience. Go back to your list of words and think about them again, in light of what you have read.
2   Were your expectations accurate in the areas that have been discussed in this chapter?

Use of social media while in placement environments

Make sure you remember all the cautions that were mentioned in Chapter 7 about social media. This is crucial when you are on placement. The HCPC (2020) has some top tips for using social media:

- Think before you post. Assume that what you post could be shared and read by anyone.
- Think about who can see what you share and manage your privacy settings accordingly. Remember that privacy settings cannot guarantee that something you post will not be publicly visible.
- Maintain appropriate professional boundaries if you communicate with colleagues, service users or carers.
- Do not post confidential or service user identifiable information.
- Do not post inappropriate or offensive material. Use your professional judgement about whether something you share falls below the professional standards expected of you.
- If you are employed, you will also need to ensure you follow your employer's social media policy.
- When in doubt, seek advice. Appropriate sources might include experienced colleagues, trade unions and professional bodies. You can also contact us if you are unsure about our standards.
- If you think something could be inappropriate or offensive in any way, refrain from posting it.
- Keep on posting! We know that many registrants find using social media beneficial and do so without any issues. There is no reason why registrants shouldn't keep on using them with confidence.

Please remember that you are not a registrant until successful completion of your programme of study. Please also refer to your university guidance on social media use for healthcare students. If in doubt don't post, until you are sure you are within professional and university boundaries.

This chapter has discussed some idiosyncrasies of student paramedic placements, and what you can expect if you are lucky enough to have interprofessional/wider NHS placements included in your programme. The next chapter will consider the care of the patient and the interaction you, as a student paramedic, may have with patients and their families.

References

College of Paramedics (2019) *Paramedic Curriculum Guidance* (5th edn). Bridgwater: College of Paramedics. Available at: file:///C:/Users/ablab/Downloads/Paramedic_Curriculum_Guidance_-_5th_Edition_ (FINAL)%20(6)-3.pdf (accessed 12 July 2022).

Health and Care Professions Council (2020) *Guidance on Use of Social Media.* Available at: https://www.hcpc-uk.org/standards/meeting-our-standards/communication-and-using-social-media/guidance-on-use-of-social-media/ (accessed 12 July 2022).

Review your programme reading lists, guides, workbooks, and information that may be available pertaining to your placement and also social media use.

13 IT'S WHAT WE DO: CARING FOR PATIENTS AND THEIR FAMILIES

Jessica Rimmer

Since its creation in 1971 the role of a paramedic has proven to be an expansive profession that encompasses an array of knowledge and skills. Despite this, the foundation of what we do has, and will remain, the same; we care for patients and their families. Our ability to care is not just demonstrated with a physical act, it is a multifaceted provision that starts from the very beginning of your healthcare career. We, as an ambulance service, are often called on what is the worst day of someone's life. How we manage that event and how we communicate with patients and their families will often leave a lasting impression, long after we have finished our shift. From early on in your student paramedic journey you will have supervised exposure to these events and the way you utilise and learn from these moments will begin to mould how you later provide your own care as an autonomous clinician.

In this chapter I hope to give you some understanding into the complexities of these interactions and provide you with tools to improve the impact you have on people from the very beginning of your paramedic career.

Professional placements

Professional placements are a key aspect of any paramedic course. They provide the opportunity to see and meet patients and families from a wide range of socio-cultural and economic backgrounds in a variety of environments. You will observe how clinicians treat their patients' physical and mental illnesses but also how they communicate with them in a calm, reassuring and professional manner. As a student paramedic you will take an active role within the health service on these placements and it is expected that you will treat all patients with the same level of respect and professionalism as your colleagues.

There are two types of student paramedic placements: frontline ambulance and interprofessional placements.

Interprofessional placements

Interprofessional placements allow you to witness and work with a variety of clinicians within the multidisciplinary team that is the National Health Service (NHS) as a whole. The placements occur in a multitude of environments such as labour wards, emergency departments and primary care units, to name a few. During these placements you will gain a greater understanding of a patient's journey through the healthcare system; you will see how the role of a paramedic can influence this. You will see how clinicians can adapt and mould their communication based on the patient and their environment and learn first-hand how important this skill is. These placements also allow you to increase your exposure to specific fields of medicine that may not be as regularly encountered in the pre-hospital environment and enable you to gain experience to support your new skills.

🔗 Refer to Chapter 12 for more information on types of placement opportunity.

Ambulance placements

Ambulance placements allow you to observe emergency medicine on the frontline. They give you a chance to become familiar with the equipment that an emergency ambulance carries, where to find it and to use it in real-life situations. Your role as a student paramedic is an important and active one. You will be working as part of an ambulance crew and will be encouraged to become part of the team. As you travel through your programme this placement will evolve, allowing you the opportunity to develop your expanding theoretical and practical knowledge base under the direct supervision of a mentor or practice educator (PEd). When you are on these placements they are colloquially referred to as being out *on the road*.

Building a strong relationship with your placement educators is important, as illustrated by the responses in Box 13.1. Throughout your time as a student paramedic, you will be responsible for your own actions but your educator will remain responsible for your clinical decisions and interventions. Having trust and confidence in each other is paramount to both

Box 13.1 How do you decide how much patient responsibility to give a student paramedic?

🚨 **Paramedic PEd response:** It is always a good idea to have a chat before each shift to find out just how much responsibility you are comfortable with and how much your mentor is comfortable with giving you. This seems to initially be decided by how keen and enthusiastic the student is to be involved. Walking in the house first and starting a conversation is a good starting point. As experience progresses, I feel it is important to allow students time and space to build rapport and report findings.

🚨 **Critical care paramedic (CCP) response:** The degree of responsibility given to a student will widely vary based on their clinical knowledge as well as previous experience and exposure. I would expect the level of responsibility given to a student to increase as they go through their training. Nevertheless, the responsibility will never solely rely on the student. I strongly encourage shared decision-making both with the rest of the team on scene and with clinicians able to provide further advice.

patient treatment and the progression of your practical education. During these placements you should only perform skills that you have been officially taught at university. These skills will always be done under direct supervision with support and agreement from your PEd.

Talking to your patient

The ambulance service is in place to make medical treatment available to everyone in the pre-hospital setting. A paramedic aims to create a trusting and calm environment that allows them to assess their patient and give potentially life-saving treatment in a systematic and effective way. This is done by instilling confidence in our patients and your colleagues, reducing their anxieties and being receptive to their needs.

In 2013, Dr Kate Granger MBE initiated an international movement to advocate for patients and create a more compassionate and meaningful relationship between them and their care providers. Kate was taking her own journey through the NHS as a patient herself and found that a lack of communication across all aspects of her care was the main negative take-away point from her appointments. Kate recognised that simply having a clinician tell her their name before moving on to examinations or intimate questions made her feel as though she was being treated as an individual rather than a patient. This improved her confidence in the care she was receiving as well as her rapport with the person involved.

From this simple identification Kate started a global initiative called 'Hello my name is ...' (Granger 2013).

The initiative has four core values:

1   **Communication:** Effective communication that is appropriate to each patient holds significant value and starts with a simple introduction.
2   **The little things:** They aren't so little after all. Personal considerations for each patient are of central importance to the patient journey.
3   **Patient at the heart of all decisions:** 'No decisions about me without me.' Wherever possible patients should be involved in all decisions about their own medical care. Remember, if a patient makes a decision that you would not make for yourself that does not mean their decision is wrong.
4   **See me:** See your patients are people first before a disease or medical condition. Individuals are more than just an illness.

These values extend into the pre-hospital environment, and you can begin to utilise them from your very first day. Things as simple as asking permission to take a seat before beginning an assessment or wiping your boots on arrival at someone's property can make all the difference to how you are perceived by your patients and their families. The ambulance service is an inclusive healthcare facility providing emergency medical treatment to anyone that needs it and, as such, our language should be inclusive too. When we introduce ourselves, it is important to ask patients and their families their names and what they would like to be called.

Pronouns

Pronouns are also an easy and important example of inclusive language. He/she are commonly used pronouns that specifically define a person's gender assigned at birth, but they may not always fit that person's gender identity. They are also not inclusive of people who are born with chromosomes from both genders, known as intersex. For transgender, non-binary, gender non-conforming and queer people, the recurrent use of assumed/ incorrect pronouns can create an uncomfortable environment and has been shown to cause increasing depression and anxiety among members of the LGBTQIA+ (Lesbian, Gay, Bisexual, Transgender, Queer, Intersex, Asexual) community. The legitimate use of pronouns they/them for individuals who do not identify as he/she has been an important and progressive step within society. Please remember that anyone can utilise he/him, she/her or they/them pronouns and it is a fundamental part of patient care not to assume how someone identifies. It is always okay to ask someone what their pronouns are, and you should always listen to and respect their identity.

Using person-first language as opposed to identity-first language is also an incredibly powerful tool. For example: using the sentence 'this is Emily and she is diagnosed with a cardiac condition' as opposed to 'this is a cardiac patient called Emily' allows for patients to feel valued as people before their illnesses.

Throughout your career you will be asking your patients probing and personal questions. It is important that you make your patients feel listened to, respected and involved in their own treatment. This is the beginning of person-centred care. Kate's legacy is one of reassurance, trust and confidence in care. Her initiative is there to be used by all members of the NHS and it reminds us that everyone who accesses our services are, before anything else, people.

It can be quite daunting to meet a new person and strike up a conversation, let alone when they are ill, in pain and need your help quickly. The responses in Box 13.2 may help you develop some strategies to start developing and expanding your communication skills with patients and their families.

> **Important point:** Remember that you may often meet patients in public environments; it is important to consider this when asking personal questions.

Box 13.2 Do you have any tips about how to start a conversation with a patient and/or family member?

🚨 **Paramedic PEd response:** Normally once you have introduced yourself and asked the patient what they like to be called, conversation then begins to flow naturally but usually around their clinical presentation. But once any immediately life-threatening conditions have been dealt with communication will usually shift onto more casual topics. If I am attempting to make small talk and I'm really stuck I use tactics like picking out things in the patient's home to discuss, asking the patient/family about their lives, for example work, family, friends, looking at pictures and using those as a discussion point; also, talking about their pets is a great one.

📖 **Student paramedic response:** Remember that you are in a very privileged position. Unless you explicitly tell them, many members of the public will not recognise your uniform as that of a student. Most people want reassurance and that often starts with simple things like adopting an approachable body language and not standing in the corner. Most patients will want to talk with you. Use their name and show them you are truly listening and always ask family members what relation they are to the patient, never assume. In time this will get easier.

Entering a patient's home

As a pre-hospital clinician you will treat patients in public places, but you will frequently treat people in their own homes. When you enter a patient's property it is important to have an open, non-judgemental mindset but to be aware of your surroundings. You may meet patients whose personal, cultural or religious backgrounds differ from your own and these differences are often reflected in someone's own space. You must remember that just because a persons' home is not the way you would choose to have yours, does not mean it is wrong or unacceptable. You have been invited into their property and therefore you are a guest. You should remain respectful of their personal space and, where possible, gain the patient's consent to touch or move any of their items to better enable you to help or treat them. You do not have a right to be there. If at any point the patient

Box 13.3 How do you find treating patients in their own homes?

🚑 **Ambulance practitioner response:** Treating patients in their own homes comes with its own unique set of pros and cons. Initially, I found the experience of entering someone's home unnatural; assessing a patient in their own environment is not a privilege most healthcare professionals have. I find it allows me to get an idea and a greater insight into the situation just by looking at the wider scene in some cases. Lifestyle choices, eating habits, social or extremist views are all things that can be picked up on from the environment to give me a better understanding of the patient. Treating patients in their own home also presents its own problems in terms of clinical procedures. A pre-hospital setting can prove difficult to perform aseptic interventions and usually doesn't give an abundance of space to work in. I found I had to adapt my ideas a lot when entering patients' homes from the clinical scenarios in training I'd previously been used to. For me one of the pros to entering a patient's home is that it's their own space and they are familiar with it. They will feel more comfortable and more willing to engage with an assessment if they feel relaxed and familiar.

📖 **Student paramedic response:** It has felt daunting at times especially in my first year. You feel like you shouldn't be there and you are unsure what is happening. Progressing in confidence you begin to feel less like a spare part and more comfortable with different incidents and entering patients' homes.

and family ask you to leave you are legally obligated to do so (see Box 13.3 for further insight).

Case study 13.1 highlights the legal issues around assessing a patient's mental capacity and gaining consent. Being in a person's home often entails caring for more than just the patient. This is something other healthcare professionals do not encounter, as Case study 13.2 illustrates.

CASE STUDY 13.1

As a Year 1 student we were called to a patient who was very medically unwell, after my mentor assessed them. The patient's family had called 999. After assessment my mentor said the patient needed hospital treatment. The patient did not want hospital admission. My mentor established (with thorough questioning) that the patient had mental capacity to make an informed decision and totally understood the risks of remaining at home.

Personally, I found it very hard to leave the situation and to reconcile the desire to help with our professional and legal obligations to the patient. I did need to speak to my mentor about this experience. I understand more now, but it still left me sad.

CASE STUDY 13.2

We were called to a cardiac arrest. The patient was a 61-year-old lady. In the house was the patient and her two children who were the same age as me. This immediately made it more relatable for me and I was really out of my depth. I was a Year 1 student, so was not involved in the resuscitation; instead, I found myself being asked questions by the patient's children. This was very awkward and I did not know what to say. All other staff were trying to save the lady's life. A more senior staff member withdrew from the resuscitation and came to help me. She took over caring for the relatives and answering questions. I learned a lot from just listening to what the whole team said, how they said it and their communication skills in general. I wish I had been able to comfort the family more and help the crew more. I learned a lot from this experience.

The six Cs of nursing

The NHS six Cs were published in 2012 and are the cornerstones in a national nursing strategy to improve care. Similar to the 'Hello, my name is ...' initiative, they are designed to be utilised by all members of NHS staff, not just registered healthcare professionals, to inspire workers to put patients at the forefront of what we do.

1   **Care:** Caring is the foundation of the NHS. Each person should receive care that is bespoke to them and this should be consistently available throughout their life.

2   **Compassion:** This is an incredibly powerful tool. Building relation-
     ships between NHS staff and patients is imperative to ensure individ-
     uals receive the care they need. These relationships should be based
     on maintaining dignity and having respect and empathy for people.

3   **Competence:** As a healthcare professional it is our responsibility to
     develop our clinical and practical knowledge continually to maintain
     our standards and deliver care.

4   **Communication:** As previously discussed, communication spans
     across patient and staff relationships and is key to a healthy and
     effective workplace.

5   **Courage:** We need courage to advocate for our patients and help
     guide them through the healthcare system and highlight any issues
     we feel are not being addressed on their behalf. We must also have
     the courage to speak up if we have made a mistake, to admit fault
     and learn how to stop it from happening again. This is called duty of
     candour.

6   **Commitment:** This relates to the commitment we have to consis-
     tently improve the care we provide to patients. Choosing to be a
     paramedic means that we are committing to lifelong learning, keep-
     ing up to date on evolving practices and implementing change in the
     NHS.

Box 13.4 highlights only one person's view. It is important to remember
that all six Cs are important in different ways to different people. They
serve as a reminder of the key values that we should uphold as a healthcare professional.

The effects of COVID-19

The COVID-19 pandemic significantly impacted the care we were able to
give to our patients and their families. This is not just due to the increase
in calls but also the restrictions on who could or could not accompany
patients to hospital. The restrictions placed on visitation within the emergency department resulted in many patients being taken to hospital without a friend or relative. Often these patients were very unwell and the
uncertainty and pain of leaving a loved one put a considerable emotional
strain on patients, families and NHS staff alike. It is understandable that
communicating these limitations was regularly met with anger and frustration. As a result of this, along with many other confounding factors
from the pandemic, several frontline staff experienced compassion fatigue

Box 13.4 Which of the NHS six Cs do you think is important for student paramedics?

🚨 **Paramedic PEd response:** They all apply to students, but courage stands out for me. Integrity is the most important factor when deciding how much responsibility to give to a student paramedic. The student should always be mindful that no matter what happens in an incident, if something does not go right, or if a drug is not checked correctly, etc. then the ultimate responsibility usually lies with the mentor. It is easy to lose the trust of your mentor by being caught out in a lie. If the student does not know something they should admit it and learn from it; if they try to bluff their way through they will quickly be found out and their reputation damaged. Lying about knowledge, or clinical observations can cause fatal mistakes that the mentor ultimately holds responsibility for under their professional registration. If I found that my student had knowingly lied to me, then it would be hard for me to trust them and 'allow' them more freedom and responsibility in placement.

as a result. Physical and emotional exhaustion are common symptoms of burnout and compassion fatigue, and it is why mindfulness and personal well-being are integral parts of being frontline clinicians. It is not possible to care for others effectively if we do not first care for ourselves. Physical activities such as running, walking, swimming, yoga, etc. can help with mindfulness as well as the physical fitness needed to be a healthy paramedic. It is also imperative that you keep track of your own emotional well-being. We often go to difficult and emotive incidents and anyone who works in the frontline emergency services will have had similar experiences. Be sure to talk to your friends, colleagues or managers, both in university and on your placements, and access your local well-being services if you feel you need support. Box 13.5 provides some insightful comments about lasting effects on paramedic practice.

🔗 Refer to Chapters 1 and 18 for more about stress, burnout and resilience.

This chapter has explored the fundamental approaches and key aspects to remember when caring for patients and their families. National strategies have been highlighted that have been adopted in order that healthcare professionals and students develop the skills, attitudes and behaviours

Box 13.5 Do you think the COVID-19 pandemic will have lasting effects on paramedic practice and your own practice?

🚨 **Paramedic PEd response:** A resounding yes. I don't know how it will impact the future generations of paramedics (the ones who will start their training post-pandemic) but I have no doubt that it will have lasting effects on the paramedics who have trained or worked during the pandemic. For the existing workforce, I have never known the ambulance service to have such high rates of stress and burnout. Working through the pandemic has highlighted a lack of preparedness and resilience in the ambulance service as a system. Unfortunately, this has led to staff feeling under-prepared and having to manage patients without adequate training for their condition. This will undoubtedly have a lasting effect on the service and its staff. It is important for staff to be supported in their physical and emotional well-being, now more than ever.

🎓 **Academic response:** The COVID-19 pandemic has definitely forced us to explore new ways of teaching paramedic practice. It has also created some new issues as we struggled to give students placements and exposure to the NHS services. While we are all excited to get back to face-to-face and hands-on learning we have taken away a lot of new skills that will allow us to broaden the way paramedics are educated across the UK. After the cessation of Continuing Professional Development (CPD) during the pandemic, resources have vastly increased conferences, classes, lectures and podcasts being widely available online.

📖 **Senior student response:** COVID has taught me to think positively. It has increased my resilience – going to placement at such a turbulent time was mentally exhausting. Doing university and placement in the second lockdown meant it became the only focus in my life, as there was nothing else allowed outside of work/university and that became very overwhelming. But I survived and feel mentally stronger as a result.

📖 **Senior student response:** I restarted placement when the lockdown was in place. This influenced the type of calls I went to. People did not want to call an ambulance unless it was absolutely necessary and so I found I went to more emergencies than I do now. That has given me an excellent experience of medically seriously ill people, but less confidence with trauma and sports injuries as people were not driving or socialising. It has made me more aware of the importance of infection control and I definitely clean the equipment more and observe hygiene more frequently than I might have before COVID. This has ultimately made me a safer clinician.

that help to make patients' and families' journeys more individualised and personal, while still maintaining professionalism. The next chapter explores the notion of *difficult cases*.

References

Granger, K. (2012) *Hello My Name Is … A Campaign for More Compassionate Care.* Available at: https://www.hellomynameis.org.uk/ (accessed 12 July 2022).

NHS England (no date) *Introducing the 6Cs.* Available at: https://www.england.nhs.uk/6cs/wp-content/uploads/sites/25/2015/03/introducing-the-6cs.pdf (accessed 12 July 2022).

NHS Professionals (no date) *The 6Cs of Care.* Available at: https://www.nhsprofessionals.nhs.uk/nhs-staffing-pool-hub/working-in-healthcare/the-6-cs-of-care (accessed 12 July 2022).

14 ANTICIPATING DIFFICULT CASES

Dan Jarman and Paul Saunders

Perhaps one of the most enticing aspects of the paramedic profession is the diverse nature of pre-hospital urgent and emergency care. Although there are common conditions that may be seen frequently, there are near-endless permutations of patient demographic, environment and acuity which can make the role unpredictable. It is inevitable, therefore, that during the course of your career you will come across incidents that you will find both professionally and emotionally challenging.

In this chapter, we will explore first-hand experiences from student paramedics discussing their perspectives of difficult cases in practice. In doing so, it's important to acknowledge the impact working in healthcare can have upon you. The desire to help others must therefore be counterbalanced by an understanding of the realities of the role so you are prepared to be mindful of your own resilience and well-being.

𝒞 Refer to Chapters 1, 2 and 3 for more on self-awareness, resilience and well-being.

Expectation versus reality

As Box 14.1 explores, some students are concerned about what they may witness while in a clinical environment. Most of the comments received were about ambulance-specific clinical situations. Very few were about situations in other professional areas, possibly indicative of less time being spent in such areas or that these areas are more controlled, less emergency focused and have a larger team of staff available to assist, so students may not feel so exposed, as they do as part of a crew, until back-up arrives.

Box 14.1 Describe some key things that worried or bothered you about incidents you had witnessed

📖 **Student paramedic response:** When I started my first year as a student paramedic, I was worried about how I would feel after seeing a really traumatic injury, or a dying patient. These kinds of incidents were surreal the first time I experienced them, but I found it was often things I didn't expect that stuck with me, or that I found particularly upsetting.

📖 **Student paramedic response:** Sometimes, we would go to patients who were really unwell, and with my mentor, we'd work hard to treat and care for them. That would feel great and so fulfilling, but once we'd handed over our patient to the hospital, there'd often be no feedback about how they were doing, or even whether they'd survived. That sometimes meant I'd find myself worrying about whether I'd done the right things, or just feeling that I didn't have any closure that we'd done all we could for them.

📖 **Student paramedic responses:** Exploring ways paramedics can receive feedback on their patients is a developing area in the profession now, but it took me a while to get used to putting my all into helping someone, then not always being able to find out what had happened to them or know that we'd done the right thing.

Students are often surprised by the experiences in practice that affect them. While significant injuries and dramatic scenes, such as a road traffic accident, can be initially shocking to see, more subtle aspects and smaller details from an incident can also be distressing, as the comments above in Box 14.1 illustrate. As the student paramedic found, the lack of feedback paramedics receive after treating a patient can be a contentious issue in pre-hospital care. There is not always a system in place within the NHS for this to happen easily, so sometimes, especially as a student paramedic, you may struggle to find out a patient's outcome. There are many aspects of care that we have limited control over, and establishing a healthy distance between ourselves and the patients we care for can be a difficult adjustment at first.

Student perspectives

Case study 14.1 comes directly from a student paramedic, exploring a particularly difficult incident attended while on an ambulance placement, and the feelings that the experience elicited.

CASE STUDY 14.1

I went to a job that came through to us as an elderly male who had fallen over at home and was unable to get up. It's not uncommon for us to go to these kinds of incidents so it's definitely fair to say I'd let my guard down. As soon as we arrived, it was clear he was very ill. From the history and a quick assessment, my mentor said it was likely he was suffering from a ruptured abdominal aortic aneurysm. The house was small and difficult to get the patient out of, which allowed me time to build a rapport with the patient's wife and daughter. We managed to speak to a small local hospital, usually reserved for minor conditions, who accepted the fast-deteriorating patient with a view to making them comfortable and allowing the family to be nearby. The patient's daughter hugged me, thanking us for all we'd done, and we left.

The patient's wife was frail, and his daughter wanted to ensure she was okay before following to the hospital. Sadly, however, the moment we pushed the patient into ED on our stretcher, he deteriorated further. We moved into a hospital bay, closed the curtains around us, and I held the patient's hand while he took his last breath. His family hadn't made it to the hospital in time.

At the time, I felt that we'd taken this patient away from their family, to die. I felt that he would have been scared and lonely. I also felt the family would be disappointed in us for not emphasising how quickly the patient might die, causing them to miss their chance to be beside him at the end. I felt shocked. I was just expecting to go to someone who needed help getting off the floor, and I felt helpless that in our best efforts to help them, we just took them to a hospital to die.

This poignant incident demonstrates the complex nature of managing acutely unwell patients in the community. Clinical skill and knowledge is paramount, but simultaneously, emotional intelligence and empathy must guide us to manage expectations and make decisions that not only impact patients, but also those close to them. In order to achieve this, intricate layers of human interaction are required, described in Case study 14.1 between student, paramedic, the patient and the patient's family. It's only human therefore that we may become invested emotionally in an incident, as well as professionally.

While not typically *dramatic* (as many television documentaries show and students initially expect), each incident may be a potentially significant life-event for our patients and those around them. As a student paramedic you may be exposed to these inherently extraordinary situations often, which we should neither forget, nor take lightly. Acknowledging this is important as, if we understand this, we can accept that at times it is normal to feel affected by events (such as in Case study 14.1) when we have invested so much empathy into a single situation.

As previously discussed, the role of the paramedic can be, at times, emotionally demanding. However, it is a role that comes with the privilege of being invited into people's homes to help them at their lowest and often most vulnerable moments. With this in mind, it is possible that there may be occasions in practice that remind you of an experience or situation from your own life.

Case study 14.2 describes a very distressing incident experienced by a student paramedic, and how they were emotionally triggered by what they witnessed. It is undoubtedly a highly emotive and distressing incident for anyone to attend. However, when you also consider the student's personal experience of their brother's suicide, you can see how it is possible to find ourselves in situations all too familiar. Although these circumstances will be different for each of us, depending on our own life experiences, they may be equally as delicate and testing. There may even be moments, as described in Case study 14.2, where a situation *hits so close to home* that you become overwhelmed by what is happening. It is important to acknowledge that this is a normal response and to emphasise the value of having a support network around you, not only as a student but as you go on to qualify.

🔗 Refer to Chapters 1, 3, 6 and 18 for more on support networks and mental well-being.

As a student paramedic you will always be supervised, which means you will not be expected to attend any incident alone or find yourself in a difficult situation without the guidance of a more experienced member of staff. Case study 14.2 highlights how valuable the student found the support of their mentor as well as being able to talk candidly with their colleagues after the incident. This illustrates the significance of being open and honest with your mentor/PEd, making them aware of any worries you may have, so that they are able to support you appropriately. Participating in a debrief after a challenging case promotes open discussions around the care provided and helps to establish any personal or professional needs of those involved. Debriefs provide an opportunity for you to ask any questions you may have in a confidential and respectful environment. The benefits of this include identifying learning opportunities, enhanced teamwork, and most importantly improved staff well-being. Case study 14.2 details how the student found taking part in a debrief was beneficial for their mental health and helped them to start processing what had occurred.

🔗 Refer to Chapters 3 and 8 which highlight the other people, support mechanisms and systems that are available in an academic environment for you to access at any time.

CASE STUDY 14.2

I remember we were being sent back to base for our break, as we had just entered our meal-break window, when the call came through. It was a job I had been dreading and desperately hoping I would not have to attend: a young male patient who had hung himself.

To add some context, my brother had struggled with his mental health for many years and sadly ended up taking his life just a year before I started the paramedic degree. He too had hanged himself, hence my apprehension about attending. I had often thought about what I would do if and when I had to attend such a job. Ultimately, I decided that it would be better to face the situation as a student with the support of my mentor rather than as a qualified paramedic, where I could potentially be a single responder.

I had previously mentioned my concerns to my mentor, and they were aware of what had happened to my brother. I was thankful I had, as it meant we could talk openly on the way to the call, and they were aware of how I was feeling.

We were first to arrive on scene and unfortunately the call was as given. I remember hearing the screams and cries of family members on scene before even seeing the patient. The patient had already been cut down, so we started working on them straight away.

There was a brief moment where I froze – I remember looking over at the patient and seeing my brother's face looking back at me. Luckily, my mentor noticed and said it would be OK if I wanted to leave and wait outside. However, after some reassuring words I decided to stay and help; I felt like I needed to prove to myself I could do it.

We were on scene for a while and managed to achieve return of spontaneous circulation, which meant we then had to transport the patient to hospital. Once the patient had been handed over to the hospital staff one of the senior paramedics gathered everyone who had been on scene for a hot debrief.

I found this incredibly helpful as we all got to talk through the job and what we each did. Some people were visibly upset, including myself, and this allowed for people to comfort and support one another. I feel that this helped me to start processing what had happened, and I felt like I could confide in these colleagues going forward as we had all been through the same thing.

Case study 14.3 details an incident a student paramedic found particularly distressing due to experiencing something similar in their own life. The student identified that they did not feel *right* after the incident, highlighting the importance of understanding yourself and recognising when to access support. However, in this instance the student chose to approach how they were feeling differently; instead of being open about how they were struggling, they endeavoured to deal with it alone. This again is a normal response, and perhaps one you can relate to, but the student describes how this was neither helpful nor healthy for their well-being.

As a student paramedic, we are fortunate to also be present at the end of people's lives. This can be distressing for everyone concerned, but paramedics can make so much difference and your words/actions will long be remembered by the patient's family and friends. Case study 14.4 is from a third-year student, and their reflection on end-of-life care.

CASE STUDY 14.3

I attended a job which came through as a male who had scalded his chest and had called 111 for advice. The call was triaged and resulted in us being dispatched. When we arrived, the patient stated that he accidently tipped a hot cup of tea over himself. However, his story did not totally add up and his partner who was on scene appeared irritated that we were there. There was a strained atmosphere in the home and the patient's partner was adamant that the injuries did not require hospital treatment. Eventually, the partner left the room as a neighbour had knocked on the door wanting to know what was going on.

While assessing the patient we noticed several other bruises on his upper arms, ribs and back. When we questioned him regarding how he scalded his chest ('tipping' a cup of tea as he described would mean the cup would have landed in his lap rather than on his chest), he disclosed that this partner threw the tea over him. He also explained how she often got angry and hit him.

This confirmed my suspicion that he was being abused by his partner, something I too have experienced in the past. I felt my heart rate elevate and my palms get clammy. I found myself reliving memories from my past that I had not thought about in a long time. I had decided not to tell anyone about what had happened to me, but my mentor and crew mate must have noticed something was wrong as they asked me if I was okay. I managed to compose myself and told them I had a headache. I remember staying quiet for the rest of the time we were there as I was not able to fully focus.

This incident made me realise I had not fully dealt with what had happened to me, but I still chose not to tell anyone about how I was feeling – I thought I could figure it out on my own. I was wrong, and over the next couple of months it started to affect my studies and how I was interacting with my peers. It took me almost three months to finally talk to my mentor and tutor about what had happened, and when I finally did, it was the biggest relief ever. I regret not talking to somebody sooner and delaying getting help with how I was feeling.

CASE STUDY 14.4

We had been called to a gentleman in his 70s for shortness of breath. He had a recent diagnosis of terminal lung cancer, but was otherwise fit and well until today. On our arrival he was very unwell, oxygen saturations of 70 per cent and he was very restless. He was not confused, but seemed like he could not get comfortable. I instinctively reached for the oxygen but I was stopped by my PEd.

My PEd had recognised that the patient had entered the dying process. We had a discussion with the patient and his family, about their wishes; the patient wished to die at home. We cared for his needs to make him comfortable.

I was stunned by what was happening. I knew paramedics got called to patients at the end of their lives, but this was the first time I was part of it. My mind struggled to comprehend the fact that this man was alive and by the time we were to leave he would not be. Everything in our education gears us to action, fighting deterioration. I was not mentally prepared for allowing and supporting a natural death. My PEd was amazing – I learned so much from just watching and listening, allowing silence and being comfy with that.

I think about this man on a regular basis, I feel very privileged to have been present at his death, as sad as it was. I know we all come into this job to save lives, but the best thing we could do for our patient was to help him have a good death and support his family through this experience. I had never fully appreciated the importance of that until this moment. I will always be grateful to this man and his family for allowing us to be part of this moment in their lives, and I carry this experience with me to all patients I go to who are at the end of their lives. I attend in the hope that I may continue to support patients at the end of their lives to have a dignified and meaningful death.

The student's honest appraisal of the experience in Case study 14.4 demonstrates the wide range of patient exposure you will have as a student. In certain situations supportive care is the most appropriate option, as shown in this case study. This is a steep learning curve and requires a special set of skills, communication and empathy being at the top of the list.

As you can see from the variety of case studies included in this chapter, your exposure to serious, distressing calls cannot be controlled, so you do need to be strong both mentally and physically, as has been alluded to in several chapters.

The fact that paramedics care for people across the lifespan is highlighted in Case study 14.5. This is something that prospective students need to think about and prepare for as much as possible, by interacting with children from all ages.

CASE STUDY 14.5

As a first-year student in my first placement I was with a crew who were called to a school to attend to an 8-year-old child. The child had arrived at school with bruising around both eyes and a contusion to his head. He alleged that his mother had caused these injuries; the school had called 999.

I was overwhelmed and cannot remember much of the assessment on scene, but I vividly remember the ride to hospital. This small child was surrounded in the back of the ambulance by staff, doing things and asking questions. The school teacher was present, but stood back. I thought it was just a playground accident at first, but I was so shocked and in disbelief when I heard what had allegedly happened.

We learned much later that the child had been taken into emergency foster care.

I spoke to my family about this, as it bothered my head – I am not sure I would do so again, as it bothered them too. I did speak to my PEd, and I used my mental health first-aid tools and resources to help me process what I had witnessed. Now I understand what the paramedic's role in child protection is, I feel much happier and I have additional knowledge from my own reading and researching.

Case study 14.5 highlights that even as a very junior student paramedic you may be involved or witness distressing incidents. Sometimes, because you are so new to the role, it is even more confusing as you do not understand what is going on. In such circumstances, it is even more important to talk to your PEd, to get an explanation, have the chance to ask questions and then do your own independent study. Obviously, talk and access additional help if you need to.

The challenge of assessing and helping patients and their families as they navigate their way through life-limiting conditions, such as dementia, is another aspect of the paramedic role, as Case study 14.6 illustrates. The names have been changed to protect confidentiality.

CASE STUDY 14.6

I was in a car with my mentor and the call came in for an 80-year-old female, non-injury fall. We arrived and were greeted by the patient's husband, Ian. The patient, Sally, was sitting on the floor. As a third year I attended the call and introduced myself; Sally was uttering random words/sentences, unrelated to my questions. Ian informed me Sally had a diagnosis of dementia.

Sally had mistaken a wooden table as her armchair and had slipped off it ending up on the floor. After thorough assessment, Sally had no injuries. Ian was 90-years-old and caring for them both, with no additional help. Ian wanted to talk about Sally as she was and as she is now. Ian told us how Sally was no longer herself and could not express herself anymore. We informed Ian of the potential support that we could get for him (falls service, home help, dementia care assessment) but he refused all our offers of help, saying that he could manage and anyone new in the house may make Sally more agitated and confused.

I found this call emotionally difficult; I think dementia is one of the worst medical conditions someone can have. I felt so sorry for Ian watching the person he loved slowly deteriorate until she was a shell of the person she once was. I felt sad, but so admired Ian for the care and love he provided for Sally. I felt as though I hadn't helped Ian or Sally as much as I wanted to, but I had to respect Ian's choice. I have subsequently spoken to my mentor, friends and family about this call, as it affected me more than I thought it would. I wish I had spoken to Sally more, even though she was unable to communicate with me; it would have been kind of me to *enter her world* and have a conversation with her, even if it was unrelated to why I was there. On a positive note, this call encouraged me to read and learn much more about dementia and its various types, presentations and visual changes that the person experiences. It also helped me understand the emotional toll of long-term caring and how that can affect the life of the carer.

While not a high-stress, emergency call, the situation explained in Case study 14.6 has undoubtably made an impact on the life experience of the student concerned. Difficult cases are not always the critical traumatic incidents, as you might think. Sometimes the emotional response we have to certain situations and people is unexpected and takes us by surprise.

As a student paramedic you will find yourself in extraordinary situations which may incite a variety of extraordinary emotions. It is important to remember that you do not need to navigate these feelings alone. You are encouraged to utilise the support network around you whether that be your peers, colleagues, mentor, tutor, or family and friends. Do not underestimate the value of reflection; engage and contribute during debriefs and discuss cases you find difficult with your mentor. Most importantly, remember to be kind to yourself in this new and unfamiliar environment.

This chapter has used a case study approach to explore some difficult situations raised by student paramedics from their own experiences. We would like to thank the students for trusting us with their experiences and being so open, honest and reflective about these very difficult and emotive incidents; it really is appreciated and we hope the readers will appreciate how hard this may have been for the students concerned.

Of course, this chapter cannot explore every variation of cases that you may see, that may affect you personally and professionally. You are as individual as the people you are called to care for; all your reactions, previous experiences and ways of managing (or not) are unique. It is hoped this chapter has highlighted some common feelings that students experience when faced with difficult cases.

Having explored caring for patients, their families and experiencing difficult cases, the next chapter examines what support is available while you are on clinical placement.

Further reading

Explore the facilities available to you in your place of study. Ensure you know how to access help and have contact details to hand, should you require them.

Talk to your mentor/s about any potential situations that may mirror anything that could potentially trigger a response for you.

See the further reading and references in Chapters 1, 13 and 18 for more information.

15 WHAT SUPPORT IS THERE WHEN ON PLACEMENT?

Amanda Blaber and Kim Tolley

This chapter will outline who is there to help you when you need support; it will also give examples of ways you can contact them. One key message is to make use of the resources available and to talk to those who are equipped to support you.

There are formal support strategies for all undergraduate healthcare students. For student paramedics the HCPC (2017) has a specific section in its Standards of Education and Training (SETs) document relating to practice placements. Table 15.1 highlights the SETs that are relevant to the support available while on placement.

The detail provided in Table 15.1 will enable you to appreciate that your time spent in clinical placement is carefully guided and planned. It is monitored and reviewed by the HCPC and also reviewed by the HEI. Before student paramedics can go on placement, a lot of preparatory work is undertaken by both the HEI and the ambulance trust. Placements require auditing, and staff may need educating, in order to act as effective, supportive practice educators (PEds). In the same way that you should not embark on this career lightly, your HEI and ambulance trust are taking your welfare, education and support needs seriously.

The term *PEd* is specific to paramedic education. When you attend interprofessional placements you may be supported by a qualified mentor. Mentors are registered professionals who have undergone a further period of education and gained a mentorship qualification in order that they can ably support students who come to their clinical area, whether they are nurses, midwives or community staff, for example. For the purposes of this chapter, the focus will be specifically on the student paramedic in ambulance placements and the role of the people who will be responsible for supporting you.

Table 15.1 SETs relating to support in practice-based learning environments

SET number	
5.3	The education provider must maintain a thorough and effective system for approving and ensuring the quality of practice-based learning.
5.4	Practice-based learning must take place in an environment that is safe and supportive for learners and service users.
5.5	There must be an adequate number of appropriately qualified and experienced staff involved in practice-based learning.
5.6	Practice educators must have relevant knowledge, skills and experience to support safe and effective learning and, unless other arrangements are appropriate, must be on the relevant part of the register.
5.7	Practice educators must undertake regular training which is appropriate to their role, learners' needs and the delivery of the learning outcomes of the programme.
5.8	Learners and practice educators must have the information they need in a timely manner in order to be prepared for practice-based learning.

The HCPC SETs (2017) are not student paramedic specific, but when programmes are scrutinised at HCPC validation events, these SETs are examined by the HCPC visitors, and relevant programme documentation is scrutinised to ensure these SETs have been addressed by the HEI and partner trusts.

Reflection: Points to consider

Think about the programmes that you have investigated to date or your own programme if you are already studying to become a paramedic. List the support available from:

- the university perspective
- clinical practice.

Paramedic practice educator (PEd)

The following student comments speak for themselves and really highlight the value of PEd support in the journey of the student paramedic.

Student paramedic comment: I had some amazing PEds during my ambulance placements. In fact, everyone at both stations was really friendly and keen to help me develop. Any time I heard someone talk about 'students' it was during some friendly banter which just reinforced the fact that I was considered one of the team.

My PEds were very supportive. They did more than simply allow me to watch them or occasionally let me mop a patient's brow. They encouraged me to get involved with clinical procedures and patient care (often when they felt I was ready but I wasn't so sure).

They had a confidence in me that helped me to develop as a student. We would debrief after most jobs and talk about what we could have done differently. This was often a two-way conversation; my PEds were always ready to learn from me if I had a good suggestion or some insight from a recent lecture.

Student paramedic comment: Studying, whether for two or three years, can be challenging enough. With paramedic studies you follow the typical university structure of lectures and increasing levels of writing, but you are also thrown in the deep end of a career that you may have very little real knowledge of. This is where your PEd takes you by the hand and guides you through all your questions and eases your fears – or so you hope. This turned out to be the biggest challenge for me. While Year 1 is generally recommended to be a *viewing* rather than *doing* year, it is still a time where you need that extra boost of confidence from those you will be attending in front of in the coming year. The first year goes by so fast, there is no time to lose. I had a poor experience with a PEd whose personality vastly differed from my own, who could not understand the way I worked (or learned) best and soon enough gave up on me. This continued into Year 2. So before I knew it, I was in Year 3, with the pressure on to perform. Unsurprisingly, my confidence took a knock and almost led me to believe I was not right for the job. All because one person got the wrong impression of me, based on their own opinion of who they thought I should have been, or the level I should have been at rather than referring to the practice documentation.

Student paramedic comment: Building relationships throughout placement, finding just one person who shares similar personality style and teaching qualities, or who at least respects your learning style, can be the difference between you just ticking boxes on placement and really experiencing things in the moment, using it to your full potential. With the help of my university and a great previous mentor who I confided in, my confidence slowly grew. Being shown respect as a colleague rather than a student makes all the difference. There are plenty of 'big' characters, as there are anywhere. Some you will work well with and others you will try to work well with; you will not be able to impress everyone while practising as a paramedic, let alone as a student.

As can be seen from these experiences relating to PEds, the role is central to the student paramedic's development of confidence and competence. The College of Paramedics asserts that all education in practice should be under the support and scrutiny of a prepared and educated PEd. The practice education role and quality of practice educators is detailed by the College of Paramedics (2019: 9):

> *Practice Educators must hold professional registration with either the HCPC or another regulatory body; however, professional qualifications and registration with other regulatory bodies need to be appropriate to the practice-based education environment in which they are supervising learners.*

Endorsing such standards helps to ensure ongoing competency and skill development during contact with services users.

These points are echoed by the student paramedic comments above, where the reality of the positive and negative consequences is clearly articulated. Case study 15.1 presents one student's experience of being mentored in more detail.

CASE STUDY 15.1

During my first year undertaking my paramedic studies I got to know and work with my PEd – all was well. I also felt I got to know other staff across the course of the year. I really enjoyed it, felt I was learning and progressing well.

At the beginning of my second year I returned to the station to find my PEd had left. I was assigned a new PEd, and over the course of several weeks, it became clear that we were very different personalities and did not like each other. The way my new PEd worked was very different from what I had experienced in Year 1. My PEd began to see less and less of me, I felt unsupported, lacked direction, confidence and felt my progress stalling. Some of the other clinicians I had come to know well in my previous year had also left the station. I began to dread going to placement, and this must have showed when I was there. I was not my usual enthusiastic self.

At the end of the year I bumped into my Year 1 PEd by accident. There were a few other issues too, but the end result was that my original PEd offered to mentor me until the end of my programme and this was agreed by the university team too. I finished my practice experience feeling confident and positive, very different from how I felt in Year 2.

My PEd always told me there was no doubt I would make a great paramedic; the only thing I needed was self-confidence. When I started my new first job as a paramedic, my PEd told me I could contact him any time if I felt I needed it. We still remain in contact now – years after registration.

I had some negative experiences on my placements but the positives outweighed these. As well as my PEd I have other members of staff to thank for making me welcome, part of the team, and also my programme leader and personal tutor, who always made time for me.

Placement is rarely without issues, as Case study 15.1 describes. The importance of your PEd is well illustrated by the case study and other comments. Other staff on station are also part of the student's support mechanism, whether they are PEds or not. On-station staff are the staff who work at the ambulance station, such as technicians or support worker grade staff. Their involvement is central to the student's experience and development. There is a variety of other people in roles which are designed and intended to be supportive and useful to student paramedics.

It must also be remembered that when you are not in an ambulance clinical environment, you will still be working in a wider team of qualified and support staff, some of whom will hold mentor qualifications from their governing body. They will be competent and confident working with students, so please do not be afraid of seeking their help and advice.

Link lecturers, lecturer practitioners and associate lecturers

Other titles that you may come across are those of link lecturer, lecturer practitioner and associate lecturer. They are different roles, but may also mean different things in different geographical areas. See Box 15.1 for different terminology relating to the roles; it is important that you become familiar with the terminology used in your programme.

As with many of the other aspects in previous chapters, refer to the university programme handbook where there may be a glossary of terms, flowcharts or descriptions of the roles of the staff involved in delivery and support of your studies.

Box 15.1 Can you provide the definition of 'link lecturer' in your location/area?

🎓 **Academic response:** 'Link lecturer' refers to a named university member of staff who is linked to a specific ambulance station/area. This person should be the first port of call for any employee, PEd or student paramedic if they are having difficulties, problems, issues in placement. This named person would also be responsible for auditing the placement area and providing feedback from student and PEd evaluations after students complete their placements.

🎓 **Academic response:** In some localities, the link lecturer can also be called an 'academic advisor' or 'academic mentor'. This is a named member of the university staff who will have had students allocated to them and will be the first port of call for their students should they experience any problems or need any help. Your link lecturer may visit you on placement from time to time making sure that everything is running smoothly. Placements are audited and generally managed by a placements 'lead' who will also oversee the link lecturers and allocate students to them. Students find it valuable to have a named person they can go to if they need anything rather than randomly asking a member of the academic team if they need anything.

🎓 **Academic response:** In our university, link lecturers are referred to as 'zone tutors'. A zone tutor is a member of the paramedic teaching team who is allocated a practice area and provides an important link between the practice setting and the university programme team. The practice mentor and the academic zone tutor are jointly responsible for students who are on placement in their allocated area. The academic zone tutor has many roles, including providing support for practice mentors and students alike during their placement, and briefing and debriefing students before and after placements.

Can you provide the definition of 'lecturer practitioner' in your location/area?

🎓 **Academic response:** A lecturer practitioner (LP) is a paramedic who works some of the time in practice as a paramedic and some of the time in the university, teaching and supporting student paramedics on academic courses. The LP role may also include supporting PEds in practice and potentially visiting students in clinical placement occasionally.

🎓 **Academic response:** Lecturer practitioners can also be known as 'associate lecturers'. These are members of staff who still work in practice but who also come in to the university to teach or assist with practical modules. Many are also on-road mentors.

Academic support

The staff supporting you will be registered healthcare professionals. In most cases, your programme will consist of a mixture of paramedics and other healthcare professionals who will have relevant experience and expertise in the areas they are asked to teach you.

Student paramedic comment: Our lecturers were very good at supporting us academically. I don't think I ever got through all the suggested reading, links to videos of clinical procedures and extra resources, etc. that they all made available to us along with their lectures. They were also available to see if you had a problem or questions about some piece of work you were struggling with. Obviously, they had a vested interest in seeing us do well, but I'd say they were genuinely pleased for us when we achieved things we had been aiming for.

If something cropped up on placement – like a traumatic job – our university lecturers would hear about it and get in touch to check we were all right. When I went to a job which was potentially upsetting for a 'fresh out of the box' first-year student, I found an email from one of my lecturers waiting for me when I arrived home from shift asking if I was OK.

As you will note from the above comments and Box 15.2, on the whole, academics recognise the demands of the student paramedic role. The support is readily available, if you want it. Student paramedics need to remember that their academic staff are also caring professionals. This caring tendency may be experienced by students who undergo difficult times during their studies. It may be that your academic staff feel you need more specialist help and they will be able to help you access this via the university systems and processes.

🖉 Refer to Chapters 7, 8 and 9 for more information on learning support.

Academic support is available to you, but, as has been mentioned in other chapters, a variety of support is given to you by your friends, families, other members of your cohort and previous cohorts. If this is the route you choose to take, make sure the advice you are being given is accurate, correct and not misleading. If you are in any doubt about this, contact someone from your academic team to ensure you have the most up-to-date information

Box 15.2 What would your message to student paramedics be about accessing academic support?

🎓 **Academic response:** Talk to your academic staff – we are not mind-readers. We are here to help, with anything really, but if you do not talk to us, how do you expect us to know you are struggling? It may be a new issue for you, or something you find difficult to talk about, but it is unlikely to be something we have not come across before. Find a way to tell us, write a note/email if you feel you cannot talk to us face to face initially. Ask a friend to help you. Just approach any member of academic staff that you feel comfortable with; it does not even need to be a member of your programme team. Use the university support system; maybe they can support you in speaking to your academic staff. Be brave and we will try our best to advise and help you.

🎓 **Academic response:** While it is in our interest that you do well and have a good experience both in university and on placement, it goes far deeper than this. I am genuinely thrilled to see my students develop, gain confidence and achieve. My students are part of my 'paramedic family' and I am there to support and look after them wherever I can. A lot of staff feel the same way, so never be reticent about approaching us for help. Some of the time we may know you need help with something before you do!

🎓 **Academic response:** Be mindful that as registered profession-als ourselves, if we are told something we often will need to act on it, for example if it involves discrimination to student, staff or patient, care is incorrect, or mistakes have been made. You cannot say 'this is in confidence', because it depends what it is as to whether we need to take action or not. Indeed, you need to carefully read the HCPC Guidance on Conduct and Ethics for Students where it is clear that students need to report concerns over safety, be open when things go wrong, and be honest and trustworthy. Understand these principles and your lecturers will always be able to listen, advise and assist you if you have issues in clinical practice.

available. Your colleagues may have very good intentions, but what applied to their cohort may not be the same for your group.

Debrief

The debrief is a way of discussing and reflecting on practice issues as illustrated in Case study 15.2. It can be undertaken in a formal or informal way; it may often be a two-way conversation with your mentor/PEd. However it is carried out, the effectiveness and educational benefits of the debrief should not be underestimated, as Box 15.3 explains.

𝒫 Refer to the introductory discussion on reflection in Chapter 3.

Box 15.3 Can you provide a brief example of a formal or informal debrief you were involved in and how it helped you, or not?

📖 **Student paramedic response:** I went to a particularly nasty resus in the second year. The patient had a terminal illness but had not signed a do-not-attempt resuscitation (DNAR) form. The crew I was with were unsure about whether to attempt CPR or not, but decided to go ahead. The resus attempt was particularly traumatic for us due to the nature of the patient's condition (fortunately, the patient's family were not in the room). A paramedic arrived to back us up, but we were unable to resuscitate the patient. Afterwards, we had an informal debrief with the paramedic, who clarified that where a patient is in the end stages of a terminal illness and there are clear indications in their patient notes that they will shortly die (and in this case a close relative who could confirm the patient intended to sign a DNAR), we would have been justified in not attempting to resuscitate. This meant we could have spared the patient and ourselves a significantly harrowing experience. The debrief prompted me to study and clarify the law, local policy and expectations upon us as paramedics, in respect of performing CPR on patients with a terminal illness, so that I might act in the best interest of any future patient and in the best interest of my own future mental health.

Important point: Also of particular importance here is the local ambulance service NHS trust's policy on end-of-life care and resuscitation.

🚨 **Paramedic PEd response:** I have always found informal debriefs more helpful than formal ones. This is just my opinion, but I have found that things feel less pressured when informal measures can be taken to address issues that have arisen needing a debrief. Debriefs are useful after an upsetting incident, whether an incident that did not go so well, or one that went like clockwork.

It is important that you also ask to have a formal or informal discussion with someone, to help you reflect on any incident that may have worried you. On occasions, PEds can forget that you are a student and do not consider that the calls you have been to that day are anything out of the ordinary. But, for example, you may not have seen a person who has died before – this will affect you, but may not be something that your PEd would usually debrief. The same adage applies: 'if you do not tell us, we do not know!'

CASE STUDY 15.2

Informal 'hot' debrief

Following a road traffic collision in rush hour in a busy town, where a single patient sustained significant injuries and consequently received a rapid sequence intubation and a finger thoracotomy pre-hospitally, a 'hot' debrief was conducted by the lead clinician outside the ED. Initial concerns, thoughts and feelings were discussed, and I felt happy with the sequence of events and had no underlying concerns. However, this was in essence the end of the incident as far as others were concerned. As days progressed and after I had time to reflect, I had questions which were difficult to find answers to, as the people involved in the incident weren't immediately available. The hot debrief meant that I was not affected emotionally and my questions were purely from an educational and interest perspective.

Informal 'hot' debrief followed by formal planned multi-professional debrief

I attended a paediatric cardiac arrest; this understandably was a highly emotive situation which occurred at the end of my shift. The circumstances of the incident were complex and there was an awful lot of adrenaline flowing through me at the time of the hot debrief. For all concerned our thinking may not have been clear, objective or logical at the time of the hot debrief. I went home and did my own reflection and review of the emergency. Colleagues and staff provided me with support over the next few days while a planned multi-professional debrief was being organised. The planned debrief occurred 10 days later and included everybody from all disciplines involved in the event. This gave us the opportunity to discuss the whole event from the initial 999 call through to the toxicology and scan results. Thorough discussion occurred and a detailed and full understanding was obtained. Wider perspectives were discussed that enabled me to appreciate a more holistic view of the event. It enabled me to bring the event to a close.

In my opinion, the combination of a hot debrief at the time and a following planned debrief was the best outcome and the best solution, enabling closure to highly distressing and emotive incidents.

Formal debriefs in the ambulance service usually occur after specific untoward incidents, such as large-scale accidents. These events will be organised and involve various levels of staff, including managerial staff and specialist staff, such as counsellors and therapists. It is highly possible that the student paramedic is overlooked, not through any malice, but because these events are triggered by internal systems that may not automatically include student paramedics. By keeping in contact with your mentor/PEd, you should be able to participate in any such event and may be given time away from university to take part.

𝒫 Refer to Chapter 14 for more on difficult cases, and Chapters 1 and 18 for more on resilience.

Colleagues, friends and family

As a student paramedic, you will come to recognise the importance of the support available to you from colleagues, friends and family.

Student paramedic comment: At first you tell everyone everything that you've seen and done as you are just excited about being 'out there' whizzing around in a yellow truck! But as time goes on, I started to go into less and less detail about jobs with family and friends. Partly as I wanted to protect family from some of the things we see but also because I found a few friends just wanted to hear 'horror stories' – one friend wanted to know 'what's the worst thing you've seen this week?' every time I saw him. I didn't want the story of a patient's suffering to be a source of pleasure for someone else, so I would say we hadn't been to any eventful jobs, even if we had. And there is confidentiality to seriously consider.

As students, we would lean on each other for support a lot as well as our mentors and university staff. This was because these were all people who had a greater understanding of the work we were involved with and could sympathise, not merely empathise.

One of the support structures on placement is humour. There is a definite 'ambulance humour', which can be quite dark at times. It's used as a coping strategy against stress and it tends to work. However, it is an 'acquired' thing. At first some fellow students were quite shocked to hear some of the jokes that are made in the crew room, only to find themselves cracking the same sort of jokes a few months later when the reality of the job had begun to kick in. Things like this draw you closer together as a team but also build a separation towards some aspects of the job between you and your folks outside. I guess you learn to go to different people depending on what type of support you need.

The student comment above relates to a variety of coping mechanisms and the fact that this changes as time progresses, as your professionalism develops, and as your appreciation of the seriousness of the situations you are witnessing deepens. You may also develop a protective mechanism towards your close family and friends, not wishing to compromise confidentiality or bother them with your worries or concerns. As the student mentions, the style of humour used in the ambulance service and emergency services generally can be quite a shock for people hearing it the first time. It serves a purpose, but should be used with caution, depending on the situation, your location and people accompanying you. As a student paramedic you may witness humour from your practice colleagues, PEds, but your PEd may deem it inappropriate for you, the student, to be the person making the jokes. 'Double standards' perhaps, but they may want you to earn your rite of passage in order to use the humour eventually. Learn to act with professionalism at all times before you get to this point.

𝒫 Refer to Chapter 17 for more on fitting in.

Of course, it goes without saying that any comments in practice should not be discriminatory or offensive. If you have concerns about this, the best thing to do is to read your programme handbook and talk to the university lecturer and/or your PEd, depending on where the incident occurred or who you feel most comfortable talking to about it.

This is covered in the HCPC (2016b) Standards of Conduct, Performance and Ethics, which state that:

> *You must not discriminate against service users, carers or colleagues by allowing your personal views to affect your professional relationships or the care, treatment or other services that you provide.*

You must challenge colleagues if you think that they have discriminated against, or are discriminating against, service users, carers, and colleagues. Again, we refer you to the HCPC Guidance on Conduct and Ethics for Students, your university handbooks and policies, plus the numerous staff you have on hand to talk to should you be concerned or wish to report an incident you have witnessed in clinical placements or academic environments.

This chapter has examined the various types of support available to you generally and specifically while you are on placement. It has touched upon your responsibilities from a conduct and ethics perspective. In discussing this, it is important to mention the value of debriefing incidents that may affect you, however little or large they seem to you. The message is: keep talking.

As well as undertaking assessments of various kinds in a university environment, your competency and knowledge will be required to be assessed in clinical practice; the following chapter addresses this subject.

References

College of Paramedics (2019) *Paramedic Curriculum Guidance* (5th edn). Bridgwater: College of Paramedics. Available at: https://collegeofparamedics. co.uk/COP/ProfessionalDevelopment/Paramedic_Curriculum_Guidance.aspx (accessed 12 July 2022).

Health and Care Professions Council (2016) *Guidance on Conduct and Ethics for Students*. Available at: https://www.hcpc-uk.org/globalassets/resources/guidance/guidance-on-conduct-and-ethics-for-students.pdf (accessed 12 July 2022).

Health and Care Professions Council (2016b) *Standards of Conduct, Performance and Ethics*. Available at: https://www.hcpc-uk.org/standards/standards-of-conduct-performance-and-ethics/ (accessed 28 July 2022).

Health and Care Professions Council (2017) *Standards of Education and Training*. Available at: https://www.hcpc-uk.org/globalassets/resources/standards/standards-of-education-and-training.pdf (accessed 12 July 2022).

Further reading

Read your programme handbook for more information on the roles of clinicians involved with your programme. Familiarise yourself with the titles used and the differences in the roles.

Read your programme handbook about raising concerns (in an academic setting or in a clinical setting); your support and guidance tutor, personal tutor or programme leader will be able to signpost/help you.

Read your ambulance trust's policies related to incident debrief and speak to someone at the trust if you need to, so that you are aware of the processes involved in both formal and informal debriefs in the clinical environment.

16 ASSESSMENT IN PRACTICE

Amanda Blaber and Kim Tolley

All HEI healthcare programmes include assessment of students in the clinical environment. The assessment process varies from institution to institution, but fundamentally it involves skills, attitudes, behaviours and competencies being assessed by a registered professional over a period of time. Usually, the assessment is allocated academic credits, and therefore forms part of a module/unit. In some institutions the assessment of practice is graded, in other institutions the student is assessed and is passed or failed. This is not as drastic as it sounds, as this chapter will explain.

How are you assessed in practice?

Your PEds and a myriad of other ambulance staff are assessing you whenever you are in the practice environment. As the College of Paramedics *Handbook for Practice Educators* (2020) identifies there is a huge amount involved in order to be a successful PEd, assessment being one small part of the wider educational picture. Students' assessment in practice should include:

- encouraging students to adopt critical thinking approaches to patient care
- encouraging independent learning through reflective practice
- promoting and assessing professional conduct
- employing evidence-based practice
- appreciating the importance of audit and research.

Additionally, the Quality Assurance Agency (2013) state that assessment:

- must be set against standards
- must be fair, valid, reliable, timely and purposeful

- can take various forms (points to note from a practical assessment point of view are: verbal questions and answers, practical demonstrations and reflection)
- can inform future development area/needs
- provides a written record.

Most institutions will require your PEds to assess you while you are working in the clinical area. How this is achieved, the people involved and the documentation used will vary from institution to institution. Generally, though, you will need to document events in practice, and provide signatures from your PEd in a formal assessment document that (in line with theoretical work) needs to be submitted to the university on a certain date for analysis.

The institution will make sure that, as the HCPC Standards of Education and Training (2017) state, assessments must provide an objective, fair and reliable measure of a paramedic student's progression and achievement. This is in addition to the institution's own internal quality assurance mechanisms and policies. The programme handbook or central university webpages should detail what you should do if you refer, fail or disagree with an assessment decision. There are clear policies in place and your personal tutor and/or programme leader will be able to assist you navigate the process; hopefully you will not end up being in such a position.

Who assesses you in practice?

Usually it is your named PEd who is responsible for teaching you, supporting you and also assessing you in the clinical environment. These are diverse roles and are one reason why paramedics who want to become PEds require additional educational training and support. It can be difficult for both student and PEd to balance the roles and responsibilities they each have and to get things right all of the time. As the paramedic/PEd response in Box 16.1 shows, the role is not only one of assessment. Indeed, for Dr Vince Clarke to edit a book on practice-based learning on behalf of the College of Paramedics, you should be able to see it is taken as seriously by the profession as academic assessment.

Box 16.1 What have you found is the best way of dealing with the fact that your PEd is also the person assessing you in practice? Does that create any issues? If so, what?

📖 **Student response:** Initially there is pressure to impress, but being yourself is important. The more you relax, the easier the process will become. On one occasion I did have one of my mentors refusing to pass me. The PEd kept going back over one incident; it was a one-off and never happened again. The assessment should be over a period of time and not representative of one specific issue/incident that never occurred again. This was frustrating, but was my only bad experience.

🔦 **Paramedic PEd response:** Initially you may feel you are under constant scrutiny from your mentor. Hopefully, as time goes on and you get to know your mentor, this will feel less and less the case. Although you are being assessed, you are also becoming a part of that ambulance crew and you will work together as a team. Just concentrate on your patients and your job. Your mentor is there not only to assess you, but also to teach and advise.

As alluded to in Box 16.1, there is a vast array of areas, not just skills, being assessed. Your personal behaviour, professional actions, ability to work as part of a team and, of course, communication skills are a few of the many areas that your PEd will be taking note of during your time with them. Assessment can be both formal and informal in nature. Please also read the comments made by student paramedic apprentices in Chapter 4.

Formal and informal assessment

Expect your PEd to use both formal and informal approaches to assessment. Even if you are not working with your PEd, they will ask their colleagues about your progress. While ambulance staff will do their best to help you feel at home and happy in the environment, you will be under scrutiny – although it will not feel this way. Your continued exposure to the clinical environment, in many cases, will form part of your informal assessment. All PEds, as individuals, work differently, and you will have the opportunity to discuss this with them. As the student comment below explains, it is not only about your ability to perform individual skills.

Student paramedic comment: Assessment in practice is also about how you present yourself, your communication skills, and your manner. A paramedic is more than just a person who knows how to take basic patient observations.

How you present yourself and your manner is not something that can be assessed on one occasion, it is an ongoing informal assessment by your PEd about your suitability for the professional role. It should be continually assessed over a period of time.

Formative and summative assessments

There are occasions when your assessment does not count towards your final grade, and others when the assessment is more formal (see the Definitions box).

Definitions: Formative and summative

There are two words that are commonly used in respect of assessment of practice:

1   **Formative** refers to the opportunity to practise. This can relate to academic work or clinical skills. You may be given the opportunity to submit a formative piece of work; you will receive feedback on your efforts, but it will not be given a mark or grade. The same applies to clinical skills and the opportunity to practise them and be given feedback on your progress. The intention is that you act on the feedback provided (either written

or verbal) in order to improve your academic work or clinical performance.

2   **Summative** refers to a more formal assessment. Some academic work will require you to submit it for summative assessment. This work will be given a mark or grade, and you will receive written feedback on your efforts. In some cases, academic work and clinical skills may only be summatively assessed as pass or fail.

Discuss this with your programme team for further clarification if you are unsure about these terms.

How best to carry out summative assessments is a decision for the PEd; this decision is sometimes made in conjunction with the student. The opportunistic nature of paramedic practice means that formal summative assessments are rarely possible to plan. Usually, the procedure or skill will have been formatively assessed by the PEd on the several previous occasions you have demonstrated the procedure (under supervision). Consequently, your PEd is happy to pass you summatively on the next occasion that you encounter the same procedure/skill. As you can see by the student's comment below, it is not the case that once you have passed the procedure/skill you will always perform it perfectly every time.

Student paramedic comment: Don't worry if you get things wrong – you're a student, and your mentor is there to ensure you don't make any serious mistakes. It is an old cliché, but it's true that you learn more from your mistakes than your successes. I had been passed summatively by my mentor on the skill of cannulation. But, one time I forgot to release the tourniquet after cannulating a patient. Their hand was going purple. My mentor reminded me and said afterwards, 'Don't worry about it, now you've made that mistake you'll never do it again – it's a learning curve.' The fact is, I've never left a tourniquet on a patient since.

The learning process, as explained by the student's experience above, is one that has ups and downs. If, however, the student had continued to leave the tourniquet on the patient for too long a period of time, after every cannulation performed, the PEd would have needed to review their decision about the student being competent at the skill of cannulation.

It may be the case that you have met a certain skill only a couple of times during the time you have spent with your PEd. Imagine that the deadline to submit your practice document may be looming and you need to be summatively assessed. Your PEd may decide to be creative and utilise simulation within the practice environment. This will enable your PEd to test your accomplishment of skill competence, test your underpinning theoretical knowledge and your professional behaviour. However, it is crucial that the vast majority of your assessment of practice should take place with patients and not in a simulated environment. Simulated assessments are a compromise and can be used to enable your PEd to fully complete your documentation and may also enable them to provide some additional structured teaching. Many students experience simulations that are additional learning opportunities, organised by their PEd team in the practice environment.

𝒸 Refer to Chapter 10 for more detail on learning in simulation.

What do I do if I don't get on with my mentor/PEd?

As with any situation, people sometimes do not get on and personalities clash, but they still have to work together. You are preparing to work as a professional and, as such, this entails having to work with people you may prefer not to work with. Of course it makes things easier if everyone on the vehicle gets along well as a team, but this does not mean you are anything more than colleagues. Many people work alongside each other in a professional capacity and work well in a team, but may not choose to be friends outside the working environment. Mentors/PEds should keep a professional distance from students, as on occasions it may be necessary to fail a student in practice, and this is made more difficult if friendships are involved. Conversely, the student may not be happy with a PEd's action or decision, and friendships may make this situation more difficult to report and manage for the student paramedic.

Following on from the previous paragraph, on some occasions people may act unprofessionally and it may be necessary to hold discussions between practice staff, the student and university staff, if in the first instance the issues cannot be solved by the student, mentor and/or PEd. Case study 15.1 in the previous chapter describes the student's perspective on some of the consequences of student–mentor relationship breakdown and also the value of PEd support. If, after employing numerous different strategies, the situation is not improving for all parties, it may be wise to recognise each other's differences. On rare occasions, the student para-medic may find themselves moved to a different area or may request to be relocated, if the issues and problems encountered are insurmountable. The vast majority of student experiences in practice working alongside a PEd and other clinical staff are positive in nature. Students report that it is here that their learning, support and personal development are fostered and encouraged.

As with any theoretical work, you need to be fully aware of what is required of you. Assessment of practice is no different. Take the documen-tation/work required seriously, read any handbooks or instructions that are provided for you. Ensure you are clear on your responsibilities and at an early opportunity discuss the assessment process with your PEd. This should enable you both to have a clear vision of how the time spent together should progress and will clarify roles and responsibilities.

The next chapter briefly discusses some ideas on how to fit in to the clini-cal area, specifically within an ambulance service environment. Some of the comments in this, and the previous chapter, perhaps highlight the potential difficulties students have *finding their place* within the clinical environment and beginning to feel settled.

References

Barrett, K. and Nelson, L. (2014) Mentorship and preceptorship. In A.Y. Blaber and G. Harris (eds) *Clinical Leadership for Paramedics*. Maiden-head: Open University Press.

Clarke, V. (ed.) (2020) *Paramedic Practice-Based Learning. A Handbook for Educators and Facilitators*. Bridgwater: College of Paramedics. Avail-able at: https://edition.pagesuite-professional.co.uk/html5/reader/production/default.aspx?pubname=&pubid=0e737f7e-bd96-4888-8f84-7870e2d0e6bb (accessed 12 July 2022).

College of Paramedics (2019) *Paramedic Curriculum Guidance* (5th edn). Bridgwater: College of Paramedics. Available at: https://collegeof-paramedics.co.uk/COP/ProfessionalDevelopment/Paramedic_Curriculum_Guidance.aspx (accessed 12 July 2022).

Health and Care Professions Council (2017) *Standards of Education and Training.* Available at: https://www.hcpc-uk.org/globalassets/resources/standards/standards-of-education-and-training.pdf (accessed 12 July 2022).

Quality Assurance Agency (2013) *UK Quality Code for Higher Education.* Available at: https://www.qaa.ac.uk/quality-code (accessed 12 July 2022).

Further reading

Read your university and practice assessment handbooks relating to practice and the roles/responsibilities of both the student and mentor/PEd.

17 'FITTING IN'

Chris Storey

Starting a new job or joining a new place of work can be stressful. You will encounter a number of new work environments throughout your time preparing for registration, particularly during the first year of your university course. Joining a cohort of other students; attending your first ambulance base on placement; and meeting your mentor and crews you will be working with through the year ahead can be unnerving. Additionally, there may be interprofessional placements such as Emergency Department (ED), General Practitioner (GP) surgeries, or working with mental health services. In each of these situations there is the need to *fit in* and to *find your feet* – a daunting prospect when you might not have had much (if any) previous healthcare experience.

Each of these environments can have subtle differences in how things are done and unwritten rules or traditions in what is acceptable for you as you develop your understanding and awareness.

At university, the rules will be clear on what is expected behaviour for students on a course leading to professional registration (not least in the area of social media use). The Health and Care Professions (HCPC) Guidance on Conduct and Ethics for Students will be impressed upon all students and will underpin your time at university (HCPC 2017).

Hints and tips for fitting into an interprofessional placement

It may be hard to fit into, or build close connections with people in an interprofessional placement due to the limited time you may be there. However, a willingness to get involved in whatever needs doing will open doors for the conscientious student, as the comments in Box 17.1 illustrate.

Box 17.1 What are your top tips for fitting in during a short interprofessional placement?

🎓 **Academic response:** Two students went to a Cardiac Care Unit (CCU) at a local hospital. One told the staff nurse she was only there to learn about ECGs and would not get involved in anything else. The other got stuck in with helping hand out meals to the patients, make beds, take patients to the toilet and generally help the team in their daily tasks. It was the second student who was given the opportunity to spend the day in the cardiac catheter lab watching cardiac stents being fitted and angiograms conducted. The first student was left to sit in the staff room with a file of ECGs. The lesson here is that a willingness to do what needs doing on placement gets noticed and gets rewarded. An elitist attitude ('I'm only here to learn paramedic skills') will close doors.

📖 **Student paramedic response:** It always takes a couple of shifts before you begin to feel you are fitting in. I found offering to make tea whenever the opportunity arose worked wonders. Cake is the currency of acceptance in the ambulance service: buy it, make it, but above all bring it into the station and dish it out – you'll make friends for life!

📖 **Student paramedic response:** It's common sense really; show some willingness to do the tasks you don't have to (like washing-up in the crew room) and word gets round that you're OK. Check the kit bags are all complete on the truck (apart from helping the crew, you get to know where everything is if you suddenly need a particular bag when on a job), be the one who disinfects the trolley, remakes the linen and prepares the truck for the next job – it all works in your favour.

Hints and tips for fitting into an ambulance clinical environment

Entering the ambulance placement and fitting into the team there can be unsettling when first encountered because for many students this is an alien environment that they have not experienced before. If your main under-standing of ambulance culture comes from the numerous TV fly-on-the-wall

Box 17.2 Any advice you would pass on to students about fitting in at their local ambulance station or with a crew?

🚨 **Paramedic response:** Most staff will arrive 15 minutes before their shift start time; this is to check over the ambulance and equipment and to prevent their colleagues being called out for a late job. It's a good idea to do your best to arrive early so they don't have to wait for you. Making tea usually goes down well – if you really want to push the boat out, turn up with cakes or biscuits! Be outgoing, ask questions and be a team player. You are likely to go to various ambulance stations which can be overwhelming – try to introduce yourself each time you meet someone new. It will go down well and you will get a good reputation for being friendly.

📖 **Student response:** Get there before your shift. Be organised, enthusiastic, make it clear you want to learn. Ask questions, when it is appropriate. Be ready and willing to do mundane tasks like cleaning which are also part of the role. Be willing to stay after the shift, build good relationships with all levels of staff, make sure you say hello to them all, including the cleaner – everyone in the team matters.

ambulance programmes you will be mistaken if you think a crew room will be like what you have seen on TV. Comments from paramedics and students on hints and tips on what to do to start the *fitting in* process can be found in Box 17.2.

At the ambulance base station keenness and willingness to get involved in the mundane jobs (like making tea or cleaning equipment) will be rewarded and word will get round that *you're one of the good ones*. It is wise to examine why cultures vary within places of work; the history of organisational culture of the ambulance service is worth exploring.

Organisational culture

The concept of the ambulance service grew out of military operations over hundreds of years. During the crusades (11th century) the Knights of St John were trained in first aid to bring emergency care to wounded combatants. This was further developed in the 1400s in Spain and more radically in 1793 by Dominic Jean Larrey (Napoleon's personal physician) who developed the first ambulances to enter the battle field to rescue wounded soldiers and treat them (Northamptongeneral.nhs.uk; Bravo 2018; Skandalakis et al. 2006).

The ambulance service in the UK was developed through the First and Second World Wars principally as an aspect of the military, though also for assisting the civilian population (Bravo 2018).

With the advent of the NHS in 1948, ambulance services slowly grew and were often staffed by ex-military personnel seeking a second career after leaving the services. Even today, many ambulance trusts actively recruit among military service leavers as they recognise they have many transferable skills (East of England Ambulance Service NHS Trust 2022).

This military history and background of many staff has laid a foundation of military mindset within the culture of some ambulance stations, which can be difficult for the new student to adapt to in order to fit in. However, this culture is slowly changing with the recruitment of younger ambulance staff entering the service as a first career. The number of female paramedics has also grown slowly but steadily over the last few years with 38 per cent of paramedics being female in 2013 compared to 40 per cent in 2021 (HCPC 2013; HCPC 2021). This change in demographic is likely to have an effect upon the traditional culture of the service as it develops further.

Academic comment: The organisational culture of the ambulance service can initially seem daunting. Many people have known each other for years. The higher education route into paramedic practice is still a relatively new one and is taking some getting used to by some people. This will change over time, and it is of use to remember that you are an advertisement for this system.

The use of humour

One feature of ambulance culture is the use of humour. Often this takes the form of what is known as 'dark humour' or 'gallows humour'. The term 'gallows humour' is often associated with William Palmer (The

Rugeley Poisoner) who, in 1856, after climbing the steps of the gallows on the day of his execution, looked at the trap door and asked, 'Are you sure this thing's safe?' (Belarde 2018). Since then, making jokes about often distressing situations has been used as a means of disarming the power of such events and coping with the effects for those caught up in them (Storey 2014).

This is especially true within the ambulance service and can appear shocking when first encountered by new students (see comments in Box 17.3).

Having said this it is important for the student paramedic to understand the rules that exist around humour use in the ambulance service. There is a time and place ...

Goffman (1959) first suggested the idea of boundaries of acceptable behaviour within society. In the context of healthcare this proposes that

---

Box 17.3 In your experience what effects can ambulance-style humour have on students?

🎓 **Academic response:** A new student came to me expressing their concern over some of the joking which took place in the crew room. The student found jokes about death and patient conditions to be shocking and questioned whether crews really cared about their patients' well-being? A year later, after the student had grown in their experience of ambulance work, attending a number of traumatic and emotive jobs, they found that the use of dark humour had helped them to cope with the events they had seen and realised that, in its place, humour was a valuable factor in their resilience.

🚨 **Paramedic PEd response:** The organisational culture of the ambulance service can be a strange animal. Humour, particularly of the dark kind, is common and this can often be a bit of a culture shock to students. Don't judge your colleagues for this. Dark humour is a bona-fide coping mechanism and is common among emergency services personnel. Be friendly and open with people, willing to listen and learn. Don't go in with the attitude that you know more because of your academic studies. Many excellent ambulance staff who do not have academic qualifications or have not reached paramedic level have a wealth of practical experience to share.

emergency workers have 'frontstage', 'backstage' and 'offstage' environments which moderate their behaviour (Williams 2013; Storey 2014).

Frontstage is the 'patient-facing role', or the 'paramedic in public'. This is where the public get their impression of who paramedics are, what they are like, and how they act. The reputation of the profession rests on this.

Backstage is the side of paramedics the public do not see. It's the crew room or environment where only emergency services staff are present. This is where emergency personnel can often reflect together over jobs they have attended and speak frankly about their experiences. It is also where gallows humour will be employed as part of the processing of events.

Offstage is the paramedic (or ambulance staff) when they are off duty, not with other emergency personnel but with their family or friends. Sometimes a paramedic might make a joke which would be acceptable in the crew room but causes surprise or even shock among those who have little experience or knowledge of the ambulance role and the pressures ambulance staff must deal with.

There is an unwritten rule that gallows humour is only acceptable within the backstage environment and never in the frontstage environment where members of the public would not understand or appreciate the purpose of such humour. Gallows humour is also strongly discouraged in the offstage environment when paramedics are with family or friends who might well be outside the circle for understanding the nature or origin of the humour (Storey 2014; Rosenberg 1991).

The student will become increasingly aware of the frontstage, backstage and offstage environments that exist for emergency services personnel and will find (sometimes through trial and error) how to appropriately conduct themselves. A key element of this is not to try to fit in to the crew room environment by using gallows humour yourself before you have gained experience of ambulance work.

> **Paramedic PEd comment:** A student who tried to crack dark jokes in the crew room within the first few weeks of their placement was told clearly that they hadn't been around long enough or experienced ambulance work sufficiently to start coming out with jokes.

Like many work cultures a new member of staff has to earn the right to join in some activities.

By being mindful of the intricacies of ambulance culture the new student should find they fit in quite quickly and are accepted and encouraged by staff in the ambulance service. The vast majority of ambulance staff are keen to help students and support them as they seek to develop.

The main thing for the student paramedic to remember is that the fitting-in process is greatly enhanced through a steady supply of cake!

> **Paramedic PEd comment:** While it is initially alien to students, most will find their colleagues becoming like extended family. The experiences you have with colleagues and the amount of time you spend together will develop into a special bond, the strength of which cannot be underestimated.

However, it is clear that once you have worked at proving yourself as *one of the good ones* and established yourself as a student paramedic within the ambulance team, you will become a member of the paramedic family. This status will change again once you successfully pass your programme of study and become a registered paramedic. Part 5 will explore the transition from student to registrant.

So many of the chapters have mentioned the word resilience, from the beginning in Chapter 1. It is a recurring theme throughout many chapters so it is worth including a chapter related to the more theoretical aspects of resilience, so you can begin to understand the concept, nature and importance of recognising the value personal resilience has in this career, and some useful strategies to use it. This can all be found in Chapter 18.

References

Belarde, J. (2018) Laughing at death: Gallows humour and the physician's psyche. *Synapsis*. March 2018. Available at: https://medicalhealthhumanities. com/2018/03/03/laughing-at-death-gallows-humor-and-the-physicians-psyche/

Bravo, M. (2018) *The history of the ambulance service.* Available at: https://emergencyservices.ie/history-of-the-ambulance-service/

East of England Ambulance Service NHS Trust (2022) *Armed forces to ambulance service, new career same values.* Available at: https://www. ctp.org.uk/focus/recruitment-armed-forces-to-ambulance/502038

Goffman, E. (1959) *The Presentation of Self in Everyday Life.* New York: Doubleday.

Health and Care Professions Council (2013) *Registrants gender split: November 2013. Freedom of information log* (online). Available via online library at: http://hcpc-uk.co.uk/publications/foi/

Health and Care Professions Council (2017) *Guidance on Conduct and Ethics for Students.* Available at: https://www.hcpc-uk.org/globalassets/ resources/guidance/guidance-on-conduct-and-ethics-for-students. pdf?v=637106442980000000

Health and Care Professions Council (2021) *Diversity data report: Paramedics.* Available at: https://www.hcpc-uk.org/globalassets/resources/ factsheets/hcpc-diversity-data-2021-factsheet--paramedics.pdf

Northamptongeneral.nhs.uk (2022) *History of the ambulance service.* Available at: https://www.northamptongeneral.nhs.uk/About/OurHistory/ History-of-Ambulance.pdf

Rosenberg, L. (1991) A qualitative investigation of the use of humor by emergency personnel as a strategy for coping with stress. *Journal of Emergency Nursing* 17(4), 197–203.

Skandalakis, P.N., Lainas, P., Zoras, O. et al. (2006) 'To afford the wounded speedy assistance': Dominique Jean Larrey and Napoleon. *World Journal of Surgery* 30, 1392–1399.

Storey, C. (2014) An investigation into the use of humour by paramedics as a factor in coping with stress and an element affecting resilience against burnout. *Brighton Journal of Research in Health Sciences.* Available at: https://blogs.brighton.ac.uk/bjrhs/2014/10/20/an-investigation-into-the-use-of-humour-among-paramedics-as-a-factor-in-coping-with-stress-and-an-element-affecting-resilience-against-burnout-a-literature-review/

Williams, A. (2013) The strategies used to deal with emotion work in student paramedic practice. *Nurse Education in Practice* 13(3), 207–212.

18 RESILIENCE AND SUPPORT

Abbie Wilkins, Gabriella Tyson,
Aimee McKinnon and Jennifer Wild

What is resilience?

Some people can get over anything. They help someone in distress, are injured, yet pull through to devote even more hours as a paramedic helping to save other people's lives. They juggle two jobs, part-time studies, and raise a family with commitment and focus. Doctors diagnose them with an auto-immune condition and they manage with grace and ease. These people are resilient.

Resilience is what determines how people react to adversity, how it affects the outcomes of their lives. Resilience to stress can be trained and with training, people can become more resilient (see Box 18.1). This chapter is all about what resilience is, the evidence-based tools that improve resilience and how to get them.

Definition: Resilience

Resilience is the ability to maintain or regain your mental health despite experiencing adversity (Herman et al. 2011). It is a dynamic process that can be developed and can change across someone's lifespan.

Our resilience is influenced by a wide variety of factors from our past and present. Some of these influences are fixed, such as age, sex, race, ethnicity, early experiences and traumatic events we may have experienced, while others are more dynamic, such as the strategies we use to respond to difficult events. Some strategies, like leaning on friends, are more helpful than others, such as overthinking or using alcohol to numb uncomfortable feelings.

Box 18.1 What does resilience mean to you?

📖 **Student paramedic response:** It is the ability to bounce back from adversity. Some people will find they have more innate resilience than others. But if you don't it can be developed and there are some useful tools to help you.

🚨 **Paramedic response:** It is the ability to protect yourself against extreme stresses, pressures and insights you see in your profession and the ability to have strategies and plans in place to manage and cope with this accordingly.

🎓 **Academic response:** It is your ability to absorb, manage, cope with, organise and come to terms with anything that is personally difficult for you, without it having detrimental effects on your physical and mental well-being.

Why is resilience important?

Everyone experiences difficult events throughout life but when training and working as a paramedic you may tend to experience more than most. So, what impact might this have upon you? Compared to the general population, emergency workers are at greater risk of developing a severe stress reaction called posttraumatic stress disorder (PTSD). When people develop PTSD, they're more likely to become depressed. Research shows that when paramedics develop an episode of PTSD or depression, they're more likely to take more time off work, to experience poorer quality of life and clinically significant sleep problems than paramedics who do not develop these difficulties. Therefore, it is important to utilise evidence-based tools to build your resilience to stress. Doing so can help to prevent PTSD while also maintaining your mental and physical health (Wild et al. 2018).

Can resilience be developed?

The short answer is – yes! There is growing evidence that resilience can be strengthened and improved.

You can build your resilience to stress in two ways by:

1   increasing behaviours that have been shown to improve psychological well-being, such as reaching out for social support, exercising, extending kindness to yourself and responding to warning signs for stress

2   decreasing behaviours shown to cause mental ill health, such as overthinking the past, using lots of alcohol to cope, avoiding dealing with difficult memories, and thinking overly negatively about your capacity to cope.

Since it is possible to engage in some of the positive behaviours linked to resilience, such as reaching out for social support, while also engaging in negative behaviours, such as overthinking the past, improving resilience to protect against the development of mental health problems includes as a core goal, an emphasis on reducing negative behaviours known to increase risk.

Managing risk

Risk factors can either be fixed (something you cannot change) or modifiable (something you can change). In your line of work, you may be exposed to potentially traumatic events while attending critical incidents and also to the mental ill health and difficult social circumstances of your patients. This is what we call a fixed risk factor. Other fixed risk factors include having had a history of anxiety or low mood, adversity in your childhood, or your own personal traumatic memories.

While it is useful to know that you might be more vulnerable, you might feel worried that there is not much you can do about it. We think it is far more important for you to know about the modifiable factors. These are the things you have control over that will reduce your risk and raise your resilience. We will walk you through some cognitive and behavioural strategies that you can practise day to day, as well as fall back on when your resilience is being tested.

The first strategy is to overcome overthinking, also called dwelling.

What is dwelling?

Everyone chews over the past from time to time. This type of thinking called dwelling is, in simple terms, overthinking: going over things again and again, *dwelling* on problems.

When we're dwelling, we're typically asking ourselves a lot of 'Why?' or 'What if?' questions like 'Why is this happening to me?', 'Why can't I figure this out?' or 'What if I hadn't said that to my supervisor?'. We'll also likely be running through 'If only' statements like 'If only I had made a different clinical decision on that job.'

Definition: Dwelling

Dwelling is overthinking the past. The psychological term for dwelling is rumination. It is defined as repetitive negative thinking about past experiences (Nolen-Hoeksema 1991). In simpler terms, this means negative thinking that tends to go on and on.

Why is dwelling a problem?

Since dwelling is circular thinking, it leads to no plan or action, meaning we're less able to problem-solve effectively when we're engaged in this kind of thought process. During episodes of dwelling, we're much more likely to fast-track our memories to difficult times; this keeps us feeling blue. Research carried out by the University of Oxford found that newly recruited paramedics who had a tendency to dwell were much more likely to develop PTSD within the first two years of employment (Wild et al. 2016).

Dwelling can become a bad habit in response to stress just like smoking, drinking or overeating. The good news is that we can overcome bad habits by teaching ourselves healthy ones. This means disengaging from dwelling when we recognise it. It also means spotting our triggers for dwelling so we can prevent episodes from starting in the first place.

How to spot dwelling

To spot if you're dwelling, ask yourself:

- Is this question in my mind answerable?
- Are my thoughts leading to a plan or action?
- Have I been dwelling or worrying about this for more than 30 minutes?

If the answer to any of these questions is 'yes', then more than likely you're dwelling.

Researchers Lorenz, Beierl and Wild (Lorenz et al. 2019) created a questionnaire for student paramedics that measures the tendency to dwell when faced with stressful scenarios at university or on placement. Here is an example of a situation and the responses the questionnaire measures.

Scenario: You see a patient and recognise symptoms that you learned about in class but can't remember what you have to do next.

What thoughts might go through your mind in this situation?

1   Who can I ask for help?
2   What if I mess up completely?
3   What do I know about these symptoms?
4   Why do I struggle to remember the important stuff?
5   What if I never learn it properly?
6   What can I do to make the patient feel comfortable?
7   Does this mean I'm not cut out to be a paramedic?

What have I learned that I can apply in this situation?

If you answered positively mostly to the odd numbers, well done, you are applying practical thinking to the scenario. If you answered positively mostly to the even numbers, you are probably dwelling in response to the stressful situation. Don't worry, you can use the information in this chapter to help break this habit!

Next steps to overcome dwelling

Once you spot you are dwelling, it's important to interrupt the cycle so that you can choose something healthier. The most immediate and effective way to interrupt an episode of dwelling is to get active. Try to break the cycle with an opposite action:

Sitting down → Stand up

Frowning → Smile

On your own → Telephone a friend

Anything active, even doing a few jumping jacks, is enough to break the cycle of dwelling. Once you've interrupted the cycle, you're better able to take a step back and choose a healthier behaviour – such as telephoning a friend, exercising, reabsorbing yourself in the task at hand or even trying practical thinking, mentioned in more detail in the 'self-talk' section below. Practical thinking is about transforming ruminative thinking (our 'why' thinking) into 'how' thinking ('How can I move forwards?'). What is the next best step to take?

How to prevent dwelling

One of the more effective ways to reduce opportunities for dwelling is to become good at preventing episodes from starting. This means getting skilled at noticing your triggers for dwelling, and responding to your triggers, rather than waiting to respond to a full-blown episode. We do this by creating an *IF–THEN plan* for dwelling (Watkins 2018). The IF part of the plan focuses on your triggers for dwelling, the THEN part of the plan includes effective strategies for responding to your triggers. It goes something like this: IF I notice … (my triggers for dwelling), THEN I will respond with … (specific action from my plan).

When developing an IF–THEN plan, take a detective's approach and consider the different domains where there may be triggers for you. For example, what are the sorts of *situations* associated with dwelling for you? Common situations may include being on your own, commuting, or watching a boring show on telly. Then consider the *physical reactions* associated with your episodes of dwelling. Common ones include feeling tense, irritated or fatigued. Consider the *actions* associated with your periods of dwelling. Typical actions include procrastinating or thinking rather than doing. Then consider your typical *feelings* that precede an episode of dwelling, such as feeling exhausted or overwhelmed. Finally, consider typical *thoughts* that precede an episode of dwelling. Before you spiral into dwelling, are your thoughts more critical, focused on the negative or only on problems?

Once you have made a list of triggers, think through feasible strategies you could try when you spot a trigger. For example, if procrastinating is one of your dwelling triggers, when you spot you're putting things off, you may like to respond by completing one small step of the overall piece of work you're avoiding then take a break. If feeling tense on your commute home from work is likely to spark an episode of dwelling, you may like to schedule a 20-minute burst of exercise before getting in your car to drive home. The important thing is to experiment with what works best for you and respond to the trigger so that you have a chance of halting a full-blown period of dwelling.

Reflection: Points to consider

Don't worry if you think you tend to dwell when faced with a problem. Now that you are aware of it, you can try to disengage from it or prevent it with helpful strategies.

Your focus and self-talk

The next strategy for building resilience to stress relates to focus of attention. It truly does matter what you focus on and how you focus. People who manage stress well choose to focus on what they can do rather than on what they can't.

There are two types of focus: helpful and unhelpful. Helpful focus is the kind of attention that is out of your head and in the task at hand, or in the world around you. This kind of attention, called externally focused, is linked to feeling more upbeat and to more efficient problem-solving.

Unhelpful focus is the kind of attention that has turned inwards to your thoughts, feelings, and sensations in your body. It is also called self-focused attention. It's the kind of attention you experience when you're monitoring how you're coming across to other people. When you feel self-conscious, this is a sign that your focus has gone inwards. This kind of attention is linked to higher levels of anxiety, especially around other people.

So, the second strategy to beat stress with resilience involves shifting your attention from yourself to the outside world.

Any time you spot your focus has shifted to a detailed monitoring of yourself and you're feeling uncomfortably self-conscious, use the following strategies:

1 Look up and around.
2 Notice where you are and who you may be with.
3 If your attention wanders back to yourself, give yourself a break and refocus on what you can see and hear until you are reabsorbed in the task at hand.

The reason unhelpful or self-focused attention causes problems is that it makes you feel self-conscious as though you are the centre of everyone else's attention, which means it will be harder for you to concentrate. It also gives misleading information. When you're self-focused it's much more common to use your feelings to make predictions about how you come across to others. So, if you walk into a full classroom with your head down and your attention turned inwards, monitoring how you're coming across, you'll feel a little anxious. With anxiety coursing through your body, you'll be more likely to assume that everyone is staring at you and that you're coming across badly. But if you walk into the full lecture hall with externally focused attention, looking up and around, you'll discover that your classmates are far more interested in their phones than in you finding a place to sit.

When we're self-focused, it's tough to get accurate information about the environment because our attention has shifted inwards. When we're externally focused, we're much more likely to get accurate information about what's going on around us. You can try it. Next time you're in a busy area, such as a lecture hall or crew room, look down and focus on the feelings in your body. At the same time, estimate how many people are looking at you. Then look up and around. What do you discover? Most people discover that few to no people are looking at them but because they were self-focused, and therefore feeling self-conscious and uncomfortable, it was natural to assume that everyone was staring. When you're self-focused, you lose sight of the task at hand and this means you're more likely to feel stressed, anxious and uncertain as well as more likely to make mistakes.

So, what we focus on and how we focus is incredibly helpful for supporting our resilience to stress. Equally the way we speak to ourselves – our self-talk – can help or hinder our capacity to rise to challenges and cope with situations.

Compassionate self-talk is the next tool that helps to build resilience to stress. Research has shown that when paramedics appraise themselves as being poor copers and have matching critical self-talk, they're much more likely to develop depression over a two-year period. Similar findings were found for journalists. What this tells us is that it absolutely matters how we speak to ourselves. It can be helpful too to recognise our strengths and weaknesses. Rather than responding to perceived weaknesses with criticism or punishing self-talk, respond with active coping strategies. This means if you evaluate yourself as a poor coper, use this awareness as a cue to lean on friends or a tutor in times of stress, rather than turning to self-criticism.

Speaking to yourself with kindness lowers stress hormones and makes you more optimistic as well as a better problem-solver, whereas self-critical talk saps motivation. In a study of almost 200 students, Kristin Neff (Neff & McGhee 2010) and her team looked at different aspects of self-compassion and its links with positive emotions and qualities.

Self-compassion is the capacity to extend kindness towards ourselves in instances of pain or failure; the capacity to normalise our difficult experiences by recognising that people around the world have similar struggles, and that our struggles are a part of the larger human experience. It's also the capacity to see painful thoughts and feelings as passing, rather than identifying with them. Neff and her team discovered that self-compassion was linked to happiness, optimism, positive emotions, and qualities such as wisdom, personal initiative, curiosity, agreeableness, extroversion and conscientiousness.

Her team concluded that self-compassion sustains feelings of warmth, connection with others and a sense of balance or equilibrium. With this frame of mind, you're less likely to dwell about the past. A self-compassionate mindset is linked to adaptive coping skills and could keep people feeling optimistic about the future. Studies show that feelings of compassion for oneself activates the left prefrontal cortex, the part of the brain linked to joy and optimism.

If you're struggling to speak to yourself with kindness, you could first try to think kind thoughts or carry out kind gestures for other people. The act of being kind will boost your mood and put you in a frame of mind where it's easier for you to be kind to yourself.

Definition: Resilience appraisal

The assessment of one's own resilience. Positive self-appraisals can help us deal with difficult situations.

Another strategy to try when you spot your self-talk is self-critical is practical thinking. Practical thinking is characterised by *how* instead of *why* questions. For example, instead of overthinking 'Why is this happening to me?' when you are stressed, transform these thoughts into questions with the word how: 'How can I move forwards?', 'How can I use my time most efficiently?', 'How can I complete this task?'.

Language, the words we choose to describe our experiences, can help or hinder us and influence what we remember. A famous American psychologist discovered that changing how a question is phrased can change how a memory is recalled. So, if you see a minor accident and are asked how fast the cars were travelling when they 'collided', you'll be more likely to give a lower speed estimate than if you are asked how fast the cars were travelling when they crashed.

By transforming the language we use to describe ourselves, we can reduce stress and unwanted memories about stressful experiences. Next time you find yourself spinning with critical self-talk, try to imagine what you would say to a friend in the same circumstances, then speak to yourself in a similarly kind tone. Instead of asking a lot of 'why' questions, try practical thinking, turning your focus to 'how', for example 'how' to move forwards.

Spotting triggers for stress

We saw earlier in this chapter that creating an IF–THEN plan for dwelling is an effective way to prevent episodes of overthinking from starting. We can apply the same tool to help prevent stress from spiralling. First, we think through the sorts of *situations* associated with stress in our lives. Common ones might include exams, practical assessments or long shifts. Then consider the *physical reactions* associated with periods when you have high stress levels. These might include backache, tense shoulders or butterflies in your abdomen. Consider the *actions* associated with high stress. Typical actions include procrastinating or being unprepared. Then consider your typical *feelings* that precede an episode of stress, such as feeling exhausted or overwhelmed. Finally, consider your typical *thoughts* that might lead to periods of high stress. Are they more self-critical or negative?

Once you have your triggers, turn to noting feasible steps you can take when you spot a trigger for stress. For example, if exams are a trigger, what could you do differently when revising that might lower stress levels? One of your actions might be to speak to your tutor or to begin revising earlier than you normally would. Or, if feeling exhausted is a warning sign for potential stress, how might you care for yourself to feel more rested? Do you need to plan some downtime on your days off?

Our triggers are a cue to take more rather than less care of ourselves. The actions you've noted in your IF–THEN plans are ones to try when you spot early warning signs for stress or dwelling.

Planning ahead

Several studies show that making a plan in the evening for the next day and including one enjoyable activity in your plan, dramatically improves mood, well-being and productivity.

Planning ahead is a core tool to build your resilience to stress. Plan your work day and your days off in half-hour chunks and use the plan as a schedule to guide you, revamping and recreating it through the day when you discover that you've underestimated how long it takes to reply to emails, shop for your mate's birthday gift, or write up your project results.

Planning ahead works because it moves routine decision-making to the night before, which frees up mental energy to tackle challenging tasks the following day. Having a detailed plan makes you more productive, meaning you'll be more likely to reach your goals. And, of course, including a fun activity (even for a few minutes) in your plan makes it more likely that you'll do something fun, which improves well-being.

Deal with unwanted memories

It is normal to experience unwanted memories from difficult shifts or times in our lives. But it can be distracting and upsetting when they come to mind. Often spotting the trigger that brought the memory to mind and then focusing on how it is different to the past is enough to break the link between then and now. For example, if hearing a child crying in public brings to mind a difficult call to a child, focus on the differences between the trigger now (hearing the child) and the memory then (the call with the child). The child you hear today may be crying because their father is limiting how many sweets they eat while shopping, whereas the child in the past may have been crying because they were ill and in pain. Then it may have been the middle of the night in a residential area and you were with your crew mates. Now it may be lunchtime and you're with your classmates in a campus shop. Then you were on shift, now you are at university. Then the child was in danger due to illness, now the child you hear is safe, shopping with their dad.

Focusing on differences between then and now helps to unhook the present from the past and give you more control when memories are triggered. The technique called Then vs. Now (Ehlers et al. 2005) helps to reduce the frequency of unwanted memories. But there are times we may need a little extra help.

Who can I talk to?

As a student paramedic you have a host of services and facilities available to you, but you may not realise it, especially if you have not needed them before.

Formal

Students will have the raft of services of the university available to them. Although called by different names in different universities, there will be a formal structure of services and facilities available to students. Ask your lecturers or personal tutor for details, check the web pages or visit the department yourself.

As a student paramedic you will have met staff from the occupational health department who manage students' health needs. This service may also offer support that is specific to your needs and is often an under-utilised resource.

If you are spending part of your studies working for an ambulance trust, you should be entitled to access the same services as employees, such as counselling and occupational health. You may also be able to access clinical supervision as a member of the ambulance trust, if these groups are available in your locality.

The mental health charity, Mind, also have specific resources for emergency workers known as the Blue Light Programme. Their website has a helpful list of up-to-date resources: https://bluelighttogether.org.uk/ambulance/

Non-formal

If you feel you just need an informal social network, there may be reflection groups that run in your faculty, among healthcare students or specifically student paramedic groups. There is also value in peer learning or peer review, where student paramedics from different cohorts meet informally to discuss their experiences, reflect on situations confidentially, and try to make sense of what has occurred in the practice environment. These may be student-led or facilitated by academic or practice staff. However, such groups may not be available in every institution.

Also consider professional forums or special interest groups. These may be open to students via the ambulance trust or within the university. This may enable you to enhance your learning in a certain area and improve your confidence, reducing stress that may occur when caring for certain patient groups, such as newborn babies.

∂ Refer to Chapter 1 for more on practical sources of help and information.

Please now read Case study 18.1, reflecting on the information and *take home* points from the content of this chapter so far. Would having this information and using it, have helped the student in their situation? The case study has been written by a newly qualified paramedic; from the vivid description, you can see that this incident is still very clear in the person's mind, some three to four years on.

CASE STUDY 18.1

In my first year, we attended a call for a 30ish-year-old man who had hung himself. It was my worst fear about to come true. The entire journey I was panicking so much (which is unlike me), I couldn't stop talking, got incredibly sweaty and could feel the stress building up inside me. When we got there, the triage was correct. I remember looking at the patient; for me, it was the most horrific thing I had ever seen in my life. I was so overwhelmed that I decided after the patient was cut down (from hanging position) that I didn't want to stay on scene (I didn't tell anyone this, I just started tidying and packing all the equipment away). I left the scene, got to the ambulance, continued packing up, and started to calm down. After a few minutes I thought I was ready to re-enter the scene, I left the ambulance and went back. A relative came over, put their head on my shoulder and cried and I couldn't help but do the same thing. I decided this was truly unprofessional, so made my excuses and left the relatives together. I spent the rest of the time in the ambulance because I felt it was not fair to act like this in front of the relatives of the deceased; there is a place for emotion with relatives, but I was almost out of control and needed to escape.

All crews that attended had a hot debrief straight afterwards. The best thing I did was to be honest with the other crews and the manager about how much this had affected me. After the shift was over, I went home and phoned a student paramedic friend, sobbing down the phone. I went on shift the next day with the same crew, thankfully, as I was not really myself. I thought I would forget it and move on, but it was completely different.

About 1–2 weeks later I began to have nightmares. I'd wake up at night with an image of the patient. This would happen most nights. Every category 1 emergency would make me incredibly stressed, just in case I had to attend another person hanging. Every time someone mentioned the word 'suicide' or 'hanging' or anything related to that specific patient, I could feel myself going red, my heart rate increased and I would feel really nauseous.

Looking back now (three years plus later) I realise it really affected me for about six months, but I kept thinking to myself 'it'll go away'. I never accessed any help, because I was adamant that I didn't need it. I didn't think that it was affecting me, but those closest to me could see that it was.

After about six months, I noticed I wasn't experiencing the symptoms I have described as much. I was now in the first few months of Year 2. I was on shift and the call came through: 'C1 hanging'. All the feelings and symptoms came flooding back. I wouldn't stop talking, the crew I was with sensed there was something wrong and they asked. I told them what had happened before and they kindly gave me the choice to stay in the ambulance and not to see the patient. I weighed up the pros and cons and decided that one day I am likely to be on my own in a single response vehicle and will have to respond, so I can't have the words 'C1 hanging' come through and feel this way when I may be the lead clinician. I would rather combat it now while I am a student.

At scene, I was exposed to the person's body and the stresses I had before just went. Suddenly I felt okay at seeing this (as much as anyone can feel okay). Had I not attended this call, I probably would have suffered in silence until, either the feelings just stopped me going to placement or I just forgot over time – I don't know which.

With hindsight, there is a *lot* I would/should have done differently. I should have asked for help, sent my tutor an email (if I didn't want to talk) to make them aware. I did nothing, because I was in denial. Looking back, it affected me significantly. Together with the stress of the university course, as well as normal life and other family issues, it had a big impact on my mental health for a good eight months or more. However, I am so glad I was honest at the hot debrief, so at least the practice clinicians were aware. Facing my fears, when I could easily have opted out, was the best thing for me in the end, but it could have been different.

Case study 18.1 illustrates many of the points already discussed in this chapter. If the student had been able to make sense of what was happening and how they were feeling, then they may have been able to instigate some of the self-help tools highlighted in this chapter. As the student recognises, it worked out okay in the end, but they did suffer for nearly a year. They demonstrated their resilience, but they may have been able to expedite the process. This may not always be the outcome, as the next section of the chapter explores.

What if it all becomes too much for me?

Studying to become a paramedic is an exciting and at times challenging period in your life. You may find yourself in situations you have never been in before and helping in ways that you have only just learned about. It can be a very new environment to be in and cause you to consider whether you are cut out for it or if it is the right path for you. While some of these thoughts and feelings are completely normal, if you feel like it is becoming too much, reach out and talk to someone (see Box 18.4). Leaning on others can help you to gain clarity about what is right for you.

Since research has found that emergency workers are at risk of developing PTSD or depression or both, it can be useful to know what the symptoms are, so you can look out for them in yourself and others (see Box 18.2).

After a traumatic event, such as being physically assaulted or witnessing a patient die by suicide, it is common to experience unwanted memories or unpleasant dreams. It is normal to avoid reminders such as people or places that trigger the memory as well as to feel jumpy and on edge. Most people have these sorts of symptoms in the weeks after a traumatic event. If they persist for longer than a month or are very severe and affecting your relationships, work, studies and family life then you may have symptoms of PTSD and may wish to access recommended support. Most people who develop PTSD do recover on their own within five years, or with treatment, within 12 weeks. The National Institute for Clinical Health and Excellence recommends trauma-focused treatment, like cognitive behavioural therapy, for PTSD.

Depression is also a common outcome after difficult events. Wild et al. (2016) found that among paramedics, episodes of depression were related to greater exposure to trauma and stress. But depression can also develop without exposure to trauma – see Box 18.3 for common symptoms.

If you feel like you are experiencing some of these symptoms or that you need support for your mental health in another way, you can speak to your GP or self-refer to your local NHS talking-therapies service online. You can find your local service, called an IAPT (Improving Access to Psychological Therapies) service, by searching online or following the link below:

https://www.nhs.uk/service-search/mental-health/find-a-psychological-therapies-service/

If you feel like you may want to hurt yourself or that you can't keep yourself safe, there are people around who can support you. You can call Samaritans any time on 116 123 or download the 'Staying Alive' app on the app store for practical tools to help you to stay safe in a crisis.

This chapter has explored resilience, the evidence-based tools that may help develop resilience and how/where to access them. There are more resources included in the references on page 289.

Box 18.2 Post-traumatic stress disorder

PTSD can develop after a person experiences a traumatic event. You may experience the event yourself, or witness it happening to others. Emergency workers have higher rates of PTSD than the general population so it can be useful to be aware of its common symptoms:

Memories of the event pop into your mind when you don't want them to or don't expect them to. This memory could be in the form of an image, a sound, a feeling, a smell, or a physical sensation.

- You may have upsetting dreams about the event.
- When you are reminded of the event, you may have a strong emotional or physical reaction to it.
- You may want to avoid thinking about the event or things associated with it.
- You may not be able to remember an important part of what happened during or after the event.
- You may experience a change in how you think about the world or yourself.
- You may be less interested in things or your relationships with others.
- You may feel less able to experience positive feelings.
- You may feel more irritable or angry than usual.
- You may be more watchful or feel on guard a lot of the time.
- You may have trouble sleeping.

Box 18.3 Depression

Depression can present itself differently in different people. Below are some common symptoms.

- Feeling sad, down, or hopeless a lot of the time
- Losing interest in things you used to enjoy
- Feeling tired or having little energy
- Change in appetite – eating too much or too little
- Feeling bad about yourself – that you are worthless, a failure or feeling excessive guilt
- Trouble concentrating on things
- Being fidgety or restless
- Moving or speaking more slowly than usual
- Trouble sleeping or sleeping too much
- Thoughts that you would be better off dead or of hurting yourself in some way

Box 18.4 What advice would you give to students who are really struggling?

📖 **Student paramedic response:** TALK. Who to is entirely up to you … anyone you feel comfortable talking to. They will help initially, but you may need input from people who can help you more than your friends.

🚨 **Paramedic response:** Anyone involved with your education will understand: PEd, lecturer, colleagues, peers … it is a brave thing to do, talking to someone. The first step can be scary, but it is the first step to helping you and no-one will criticise you or think less of you – in fact they will respect you for being honest, open and asking for help.

🎓 **Academic response:** Reach out. If you decide the course or job is not for you, that is ok, remember you are not a failure. You could talk to your programme or personal tutor to explore your options for taking a break from training, transferring to another university course or leaving with a partial certificate; you have gained skills that are transferrable to other careers.

References

Ehlers, A., Clark, D. M., Hackmann, A., McManus, F. and Fennell, M. (2005) Cognitive therapy for post-traumatic stress disorder: development and evaluation. *Behaviour Research and Therapy, 43*(4), 413–431.

Herrman, H., Stewart, D. E., Diaz-Granados, N., Berger, E. L., Jackson, B. and Yuen, T. (2011) What is resilience? *The Canadian Journal of Psychiatry, 56*(5), 258–265.

Lorenz, H. (2019) Improving well-being in student paramedics: Targeting risk factors and predictors of PTSD. University of Oxford DPhil dissertation. Available at: https://ora.ox.ac.uk/objects/uuid:791bf7f3-e042-4295-9334-949e287930b4

Lorenz, H., Beierl, E. and Wild, J. (under review) Development and validation of a measure of concrete and abstract thinking.

Neff, K. D. and McGehee, P. (2010) Self-compassion and psychological resilience among adolescents and young adults. *Self and Identity, 9*(3), 225–240.

Nolen-Hoeksema, S. (1991) Responses to depression and their effects on the duration of depressive episodes. *Journal of Abnormal Psychology, 100*(4), 569–582.

Watkins, E. R. (2018) *Rumination-Focused Cognitive-Behavioral Therapy for Depression*. New York: Guilford Press.

Wild, J., Smith, K. V., Thompson, E., Béar, F., Lommen, M. J. J. and Ehlers, A. (2016) A prospective study of pre-trauma risk factors for post-traumatic stress disorder and depression. *Psychological Medicine, 46*(12), 2571–2582.

Wild, J., El-Salahi, S., Tyson, G., Lorenz, H., Pariante, C. M., Danese, A., Tsiachristas, A., Watkins, E., Middleton B., Blaber, A. and Ehlers, A. (2018) Preventing PTSD, depression and associated health problems in student paramedics: protocol for PREVENT-PTSD, a randomised controlled trial of supported online cognitive training for resilience versus alternative online training and standard practice. *BMJ Open, 8*(12), e022292. https://doi.org/10.1136/bmjopen-2018-022292

Wild, J. (2020) *Be Extraordinary: 7 Key Skills to Transform your Life from Ordinary to Extraordinary*. London: Robinson.

PART 5
Transition to registered paramedic practice

19 ARE YOU READY?

Amanda Blaber

This chapter explores the thoughts and feelings of student paramedics as they come to the end of their period of study. It is easy at this point to feel totally comfortable in your role as a student paramedic: you know exactly what is expected of you, you and your practice educator (PEd) form a team and know most people in your base station/area. Any change to this status quo may make you a little fearful, in addition to the thought that you will soon be completing your studies and need to get a job as a registered paramedic. It's quite common for students in the final year of their studies to experience a temporary reduction in their confidence levels. Any transition in your life is complicated and fraught with worry, so be kind to yourself and expect some anxieties and worries.

Confidence

For some students the loss of confidence does not happen, for others it is associated with their academic work. For the vast majority, it is linked to the clinical area and their performance in practice. It happens to different students at different points, but if you expect it, you can try and manage it, to stop fear and worry getting the better of you. The wise words of a programme leader are retold in the student's comment below.

Student paramedic comment: The words of my programme leader will stay with me forever. One day we were having a few wobbles about finishing our studies, and this is what was said:

In the first year, you were incompetent, but you didn't know it! You were just enjoying flying around in the ambulance on blue lights thinking how fun it all was. Later, you were still incompetent but were beginning to realise it, understanding that you needed to learn a lot. Now you have reached the stage where you are competent, but you don't yet realise it. You know lots of stuff and you can do this job but you lack the full confidence you need. The final stage of the process (stage four) is when you are competent, and you realise it. You can do this job, and though there will always be new things to learn you will have the confidence to meet the demands of the day.

He told us that we were exactly where he expected us to be at that time and that he had every confidence in us. He also said it probably wouldn't be until we had graduated and been registered paramedics for a few months that we would feel we had reached 'stage four'. His chat with us really made a difference. I'll never forget it.

The student nearing the end of their studies will be wiser than they were at the beginning, more aware of their professional responsibilities. That is, of course, scary but it signals that you are taking your role seriously and understand what is expected of you, unlike you ever did in the first year of your studies. Having made it to the final year of your studies is a cause for celebration. The reality check of soon becoming a registered paramedic will probably play on your mind a little; this will be different for all of your fellow students. If you experience a drop in confidence, see Box 19.1 for some advice that may help.

As explained in Box 19.1, you need to have realistic expectations of yourself – you are not going to know it all or have an in-depth knowledge about every illness, injury, and patient condition that you encounter. But what you do have are *the tools* to continue learning, researching, developing, reflecting, and improving yourself as a registered paramedic. Do not forget or negate the wider lessons you learned while in higher education – they will be useful.

𝒫 Refer to Chapter 3 for more on reflection.

Box 19.1 What advice would you give to help students increase their confidence?

🎓 **Academic response:** Gaining your paramedic registration is like passing your driving test. You have met the minimum standard and will really start to learn to drive after you have received your test certificate. Don't expect to know everything just because you have gained your registration and try not to be too hard on yourself. Confidence will develop. You would not be where you are now if you didn't have what it takes!

📖 **Final-year student response:** You should now know why we do everything and the effects treatment has on the patient. Encourage new staff or junior students to ask you questions, so you can explain things to them and test yourself; this should increase your confidence or highlight areas where you need to revise.

The majority of graduates will be applying for employment with an NHS ambulance service; this will require you to undertake a two-year period of preceptorship to enable you to transition to become an autonomous practitioner. During this time you will be provided with periods of support from a registered paramedic acting as your preceptor, some of which will initially be on a one-to-one basis working as a crew. During the preceptorship period you will have to undertake and obtain a practice educator qualification and complete a portfolio of learning designed on a national basis, and implemented by your employer.

Ideas on how to prepare yourself in the last year of study

Having explored the potential loss of confidence, it is wise to investigate the thoughts of contributors about how best to prepare for your final year of studies and the time in practice leading up to registration. The following comment is of course personal to one student, but contains several wider points about study and practice.

Student paramedic comment: In your final year on placement, you really need to step up and push yourself forward to do things. I found at times I was 'hiding behind the paperwork' (at each call someone fills out a form detailing the patient's condition, observations, interventions, etc.). I realised that I had got into the habit of grabbing the clipboard and starting to write at most calls, but this meant I wasn't getting to perform procedures. This may be fine in Year 1 and the start of Year 2, but you need to make sure you're increasingly getting exposure to practice too. I mentioned it to my practice educator and we agreed that I would do most of the attending at calls from then on.

At my other station my practice educator there told me that in the last year that he would just carry my bags and I would attend everything so that I got used to 'being in the hot seat' while he was still there to support me. This was great as I developed a lot of confidence and honed my clinical skills.

I found myself reading loads on clinical skills during my third year – stuff we had been taught in Years 1 and 2 that I wanted to keep refreshing myself on. You can get engrossed in writing your dissertation during Year 3 to the detriment of keeping up to date on your skills knowledge. It's about finding a balance.

You have to put together a portfolio of work showing continual professional development – which you add to throughout your career as a requirement to keep your registration. It's probably best to start this at the end of Year 1 and into Year 2 of your programme, rather than leaving it until the last few months of Year 3 (or 2 depending on the length of your studies) as you need to put loads of stuff in it to show prospective employers. The sort of things they want to see are reflective essays on calls you've been to, courses you may have attended as part of university, or in addition to university, things you've done in support of your profession, etc.

Previous students told us that they took their portfolios to interviews and the interviewers never looked at them. At my interview they made a point of looking through my portfolio, so you never can tell!

The student comment above indicates that the juggling act mentioned in previous chapters continues to the end of your studies. It is wise to reflect on how you are working in the practice environment with your practice educator. As the student above mentions, a note-taking routine had been established with his practice educator that would not have equipped the student well enough once the responsibility for patient care was his alone. The balance between revising clinical skills and theoretical work is something you have been working on from early on in your studies – it is probably more daunting now as the importance of knowing it all becomes more significant, as the advice given in Box 19.2 recognises.

Box 19.2 Advice about your final year of study

🎓 **Academic advice:** Many students go into panic mode in the final year of study. This is completely normal, especially with the pressure of assignments and clinical examinations to face. Remember – you are nearly there. Pull out all the stops for the final push towards registration and ask for support when you feel you need it, even if it takes the form of a good moan over a cup of coffee!

🚨 **Paramedic PEd advice:** If you have a good practice educator they will be letting you take the lead without you really knowing it. You will lead calls, making all decisions and carrying out all interventions, with your practice educator only as a 'psychological safety blanket'.

📖 **Final-year student's advice:** Get stuck in. Your practice educator will not let you make serious mistakes; remember you still have them with you, so you are not alone. Make sure you are proficient in your skills in Year 2, so you can have Year 3 to improve your confidence and practise your decision-making under PEd supervision.

🚨 **Newly qualified paramedic (NQP) advice:** Treat Year 3 as if you have already graduated. Push to make decisions, even if they end up being the wrong ones. Your practice educator will be there to guide you and making mistakes is a normal process. Decision-making is the hardest skill to develop and it will take time; start working on it early and you will be better prepared for the job.

As alluded to in Box 19.2 and in the student's comment, your practice educator will probably have been letting you take the lead for much of your final year and usually you will have been doing well. It seems to be when you start to think about registration that doubt creeps in, and confidence dips a little. Your practice educator should be able to help you with this, provided you let them know how you are feeling. Also remember that you should have a period of preceptorship to complete once you start your first role as a paramedic. This will be discussed in Chapter 20. Sometimes no matter how long you have on a programme of study, you do not feel ready. There are some comments in Box 19.3 on the worries final-year students have about registration as a paramedic.

The worries highlighted in Box 19.3 are commonplace and usual for most healthcare students who are about to register. Sometimes, the only way to dispel these feelings is to start work. You will not always know what to do, but you work in a team. People may not be there in person straight away,

---

Box 19.3 What are your concerns about starting your first job as a paramedic?

📖 I still feel underprepared.

📖 I am concerned that everyone (crewmates) will be looking at me as the lead clinician; am I prepared?

📖 I hope I get a crewmate that I am looking forward to working with.

📖 I'm worried about working shift pattern all the time, with no break for university days or blocks of 'free time'.

📖 I don't know what I don't know … that is a worry.

📖 I doubt myself, my ability and the additional responsibility.

📖 Being the lead clinician is a scary thought, you lose that student safety net.

📖 What if I don't know how to treat/manage a particular patient? How will I manage with drugs, equipment, patient conditions that I have not experienced or used during my education/placement?

📖 How do I maintain my competency without dedicated time for education/training?

but you have access to a wide variety of expertise within your role – use it. Before you can start work you will need to register with the HCPC.

𝒪 Refer to Chapters 1, 6, 12 and 15 for more on support networks.

The next section gives some guidance about this.

Applying for registration

Take advice from your programme team about the best time to apply for registration. The university will usually send a pass list to the HCPC, and your registration form will then be cross-checked with the pass list.

We spoke about the role of the HCPC and your registration in Chapter 7, so do have a look at this information again. These step-by-step instructions need to be closely followed to make sure your application progresses seamlessly.

Once you have applied for your registration, the HCPC aims to review all applications within 10 working days. The following can cause the application reviewing time to take longer:

Declarations

Any issues with declarations can cause delays, so in order to avoid this, look back at Chapter 7 and review any declarations you've made. If you have any questions or worries about them, get in touch with your university for advice.

Professional indemnity

One of the requirements of your registration is that you have professional indemnity. This could be an arrangement provided:

- through your employer if you are employed;
- as part of membership of a professional body, trade union or defence organisation;
- or directly from an insurer.

The College of Paramedics has some very useful information about professional indemnity and what it means for you on their website.

Meeting the criteria

The HCPC cannot process your application without the pass list from the university stating you have satisfied all the criteria to become a registered paramedic, so listen to what your university lecturers say about the process and familiarise yourself with the criteria ahead of time, as highlighted in Box 19.4.

Box 19.4 When is the best time to apply for registration?

🎓 **Academic response:** Most programme staff will advise you about the date when your results and placement hours have been ratified at the academic board. Ask the programme team for advice on the HCPC process, but it is usually quite simple, involving the completion of a form (available from the HCPC website) and completed online.

Portfolio development

As the student comment earlier in the chapter mentions, you may also leave your university with a portfolio. Some programmes will have the portfolio as a credited module/unit; for other programmes it will be an additional piece of work that you should complete before attending prospective employers for interview. Some students say interview panels examined their portfolio, others may not be asked, but taking your portfolio with you to any interview is now widely expected (see Box 19.5).

Box 19.5 Do you need your portfolio for interviews?

🎓 **Academic response:** It is always good practice to take your portfolio with you to any interview you may attend. This is something you will continue with throughout your career and is a condition of your initial HCPC registration and bi-annual re-registration, so it is a good idea to start this early. A good CPD portfolio will go a long way to showing a student's competence and enthusiasm. It can be the one thing that makes you stand out from the crowd at interview.

The reason why portfolios are introduced at undergraduate level is that the content of a portfolio will help form part of the continuing professional development (CPD) record that you are required to keep and maintain as a registered paramedic.

Continuing professional development (CPD)

It is wise to look at the HCPC definition of CPD, as this may differ from other generic definitions or those for other professions.

> **Definition: Continuing professional development**
>
> *Continuing professional development is the way in which registrants continue to learn and develop throughout their careers so they keep their skills and knowledge up to date and are able to practise safely and effectively.* (HCPC 2018)

As can be seen from the above definition, CPD is closely linked to maintaining your registration as a paramedic. The HCPC lists five requirements of registrants in respect of CPD (HCPC 2018) (see Table 19.1).

Table 19.1 HCPC Standards of Continuing Professional Development

Registrants must:
1. maintain a continuous, up-to-date and accurate record of their CPD activities
2. demonstrate that their CPD activities are a mixture of learning activities relevant to current or future practice
3. seek to ensure that their CPD has contributed to the quality of their practice and service delivery
4. seek to ensure that their CPD benefits the service user
5. upon request, present a written profile (which must be their own work and supported by evidence) explaining how they have met the standards for CPD.

Source: HCPC (2018)

Table 19.1 refers to a written profile; you may also hear this being referred to by paramedics as a portfolio. The HCPC guidance is generic to all registrants of the HCPC; it is not specific to paramedics, so you are not being asked to do anything more than other HCPC-registered healthcare professionals. There is no shortage of guidance, should you require it. For instance, the HCPC provides a list of guidance and examples of types of CPD activity (Harris and Fellows 2019), and the College of Paramedics provides expert guidance on preparing and maintaining your CPD portfolio and meeting the HCPC Standards of Continuing Professional Development. Members of the College of Paramedics can keep a record of CPD on their membership profile (College of Paramedics 2022).

The HCPC randomly chooses paramedics to be audited at each renewal cycle. These chosen profiles are assessed by a CPD team, one of whom will be a paramedic. There are three possible outcomes of this assessment:

1   **You meet the standards:** You will stay on the register. The HCPC will write to you and let you know.
2   **More information is needed:** The HCPC will write to you and let you know what further information the assessors need to decide whether you meet the standards of CPD. You will stay on the register while you send more information to the assessors.
3   **Your profile does not meet the standards:** The CPD assessors will decide whether or not to offer you extra time (up to an extra three months) to meet the standards. The HCPC will normally ask you for more information before making this decision.

The HCPC will only audit registrants who have been registered for more than two years (HCPC 2018). They believe registrants should undertake CPD throughout their careers. They also believe that registrants should be allowed at least two years on the register to build up evidence of their CPD activities before they are audited. This time should be spent developing your profile along the guidelines provided by the HCPC. There is also a wealth of information on what counts as CPD and how to organise your profile on the HCPC and College of Paramedics websites. Remember not to leave your CPD until the last minute; try to collect information as you go along, as this will be much less stressful for you if you are chosen to be audited.

Participation in CPD events and reflecting on their value to you and your service users is important in order to maintain your registration. The College of

Box 19.6 What kind of CPD events did you find it useful to take part in during your first year of registration?

🚨 **Newly registered paramedic response:** My professional body – the College of Paramedics – holds many informative CPD days across the UK. This is great for keeping you up to date with current practice and highlighting any changes that will arise in the future. It also shows that you have taken the trouble to attend – that you have been bothered enough. They also provide members with a CPD Hub which contains a large collection of videos, podcasts and links to courses, all of which offers me the opportunity to refresh and update my knowledge and explore new learning. They also provide e-learning modules covering numerous subjects that I can undertake even on my iPhone.

Paramedics works on your behalf to provide a suite of CPD activities, as mentioned in Box 19.6. These are available to both members of the College and non-members, but there is a cost difference. In addition to the College's CPD events, many universities now have student paramedic forums and active student groups which host national study days, so keep alert for these events too.

The requirements on you both as a student and registrant are commensurate with those of a professional, and maintaining your registration is of course a prime way for you to show you are working at the correct standard. While discussion in this chapter has moved from final-year study to the requirements for gaining and maintaining registration, it is important to discuss securing your first employed position as a paramedic. Chapter 20 will continue to offer guidance towards employment.

References

College of Paramedics (2022) *Preparing Your CPD Portfolio*. Available at: https://collegeofparamedics.co.uk/ (accessed 19 July 2022).

Harris, G. and Fellows, R. (2019) Continuing professional development (CPD) pre and post registration. In A.Y. Blaber (ed.) *Blaber's Foundations for Paramedic Practice: A Theoretical Perspective* (3rd edn). Maidenhead: Open University Press.

Health and Care Professions Council (2018) *Standards of Continuing Professional Development.* Available at: https://www.hcpc-uk.org/standards/standards-of-continuing-professional-development/ (accessed 19 July 2022).

Health and Care Professions Council (2020) *Applying for Registration.* Available at: https://www.hcpc-uk.org/students/health-disability-and-becoming-a-health-and-care-professional/applying-for-registration/ (accessed 19 July 2022).

20 GETTING YOUR FIRST JOB

Amanda Blaber

A s has been alluded to throughout the text, the student will experience a series of transitions. One of these is the significant transition from the role of student to the role of employee. Usually, the student is applying for jobs before they have completed their studies, as the process of becoming employed as a paramedic may take several months.

If you want to work for an ambulance service, which one do you want to work for?

In some respects this decision is similar to the one you made when you decided on your choice of university. Assuming that your NHS ambulance trust is employing newly registered paramedics, you will have the choice of applying to the trust where you have been working as a student paramedic or applying to another trust in a different location. The responses in Box 20.1 from the student paramedic and paramedic explain that their decision-making was personal to them, just as it will be for you.

& Refer to Chapters 6, 8 and 15 for more on support networks, and Chapters 1 and 18 for more on resilience.

As the paramedic PEd response in Box 20.1 shows, some students choose to stay within the trust they know and have worked within as a student. However, you may not be working in the same station you have been in previously. For some people this is a positive point, for others a negative one. Some students want to relocate and start with a new ambulance trust in a registered paramedic capacity, as they worry about being still known as 'the student', as alluded to in the comments below. You will need to weigh this up and make the decision for yourself.

Once you have decided on your employment choices, you will need to apply for a paramedic job.

Box 20.1 What things do you consider when applying for your first paramedic role?

📖 **Student paramedic response:** The great thing about being a paramedic is that there are opportunities all over the country, and overseas once you have a few years' experience. I wanted to stay in the area I was educated, not just because I live there but when comparing ambulance trusts I felt that the trust in my area offered more opportunity for development and allowed their paramedics to carry out procedures which other trusts didn't (like intubation). Having learned these skills, I didn't want to lose them.

🚨 **Paramedic response:** When I applied for my first job I discussed my options in depth with my family, close friends, course-mates and tutors. I applied for two trusts, the one where I had been educated and one where I grew up and where my family live. When I was offered both jobs I was faced with a tough decision. One of my tutors advised me to stay within the trust I knew, as they felt this would be easier for my transition to paramedic. I did not take that advice! I went to an unfamiliar trust; my primary reason for this was to be closer to my family. I also wanted to be accepted as a paramedic, not an ex-student, when beginning my first job. The post I was offered in the trust I knew was at the station I'd been on placement at from day 1 as a student. I felt I might still be viewed as a student. This may suit other students. In hindsight I will never know if I made the best decision. I know I made a good decision and the right one for me. I have been really well supported as a newly qualified paramedic. I was fortunate to have an excellent mentor/preceptor and staff have been very welcoming. But I can see the benefits of staying within the service where you have been a student. Familiarising yourself with a new service is stressful at what can be an overwhelming time.

🚨 **Paramedic PEd response:** Many students choose to apply to the trust they have undertaken placement with, as this will have become familiar to them and 'the road they know' over their programme of study. This really is an individual decision and will differ from person to person.

📖 **Student paramedic response:** Due to my student debt, I need to move back home. So I will be working in a different ambulance trust to where I was educated. I have been told that protocols and ways of working are different. I am nervous that in a high acuity situation I will revert back to what I have been used to for the last three years and that this will be deemed wrong by my employer. Ideally, I would not be moving back home.

👨‍🎓 **Academic response:** There are a few things to take into consideration when deciding where to work. Are you happy to relocate or do you want to stay near to home and support networks? All ambulance trusts vary in what they have to offer. Would you like to specialise in the future, and how? It may be that different trusts offer different opportunities and it may be worth taking this into account when you are considering this in years to come.

Job application

Apart from your university interview, this may be the first job interview you have attended. Most job vacancies and applications are managed by the NHS jobs website. It is usual practice that ambulance trusts come and speak to students who are about to qualify. This usually involves a presentation and question-and-answer session. The NHS ambulance trusts will be selling themselves to you, in the same way that the universities do at open days. You will usually be supported by your university at this point, and guidance will be given to you about the job application process.

Advice on preparing your supporting statement

As the student paramedic response in Box 20.2 indicates, the job application process may coincide with final assessments of your programme. For this reason, it is easy to feel pressured and not apply yourself as much as is needed to one or other, but you should keep your eyes on your goal of becoming employed as a paramedic and work at both.

Along with your personal details, employment history and qualifications, most application forms for any role in the NHS also ask you to provide a supporting statement. This is your chance to sell yourself on paper. Just as your university lecturers only had your UCAS personal statement to read before shortlisting you for interview, the same applies to the supporting

Table 20.1 Advice on preparing a supporting statement

Be methodical:
<ul><li>Is where you started different from where you are now?</li><li>What have you learned?</li><li>Skills, personal attributes, knowledge</li></ul>
Be professional
Make sure there are no mistakes
Tell the reader what you want them to know
Have an idea of what the reader wants to hear
Read and highlight the main points of the job description
If there is a list of desirable and essential attributes, use them and ensure you address them in your supporting statement
Use your module/unit content (learning outcomes in your handbooks) to assist your structure
Think about joining relevant associations, professional or voluntary groups, committees, research interest groups, etc.

statement part of your application form. A paramedic job description will be available to you, along with the forms. This is really important. You need to reflect the aspects of the job description when you are writing your personal statement. Additionally, the reader needs to get a sense of who you are. Table 20.1 provides some advice about preparing your supporting statement.

Once you have considered the points addressed in Table 20.1, you will be ready to start writing. Do not underestimate how long it will take you to construct, amend, rewrite and recheck a supporting statement. It is not something that can be rushed, as your future employment may depend upon it.

Once you have written your first draft:

- read it through again
- ask a member of the teaching team to read it as well and make comments
- be critical
- check it; does it:

○ have no mistakes?
○ have a professional focus?
○ have a logical progression?
○ accurately represent what you know and who you are?
○ represent your strengths?

Once you have a second or third draft of your supporting statement it may be ready to send. There will usually be a gap between the closing date for applications and interview dates, during which time you can refocus on your studies. Remember, any job offer will be conditional on you successfully completing your programme of paramedic study.

The following section provides some advice in order to prepare for interview.

Advice prior to interview

There are some practical things that you can do to prepare prior to your interview. These are presented in Table 20.2.

There is quite a lot of preparation for an interview. If you are applying for jobs in more than one ambulance trust, you will be spending a lot of your time on preparation.

As the student response in Box 20.2 explains, there is usually not only a face-to-face interview, but also other tests. The information sent to you by your chosen NHS ambulance trusts prior to interview will provide more detailed information.

Table 20.2 Practical things you can do prior to interview

Review your supporting statement critically. Remind yourself what was written in it.
Devise some questions you think an interviewer might ask you about the content of your supporting statement and the answers you might give.
Think about what you might need to read about before your interview: trust documents, recent important paramedic/NHS-related documents.
Think about questions you want to ask at interview.
How are you going to demonstrate your enthusiasm and commitment to the organisation?

Box 20.2 What advice would you give to students prior to their paramedic interview?

📖 **Student paramedic response:** By the end of your programme – for me this was Year 3 – you are getting fed up with filling out forms and writing personal statements, etc. so the application process can be a little tiring. Also, we had fitness tests to complete and advanced life support scenario assessments, as well as a panel interview.

Having made it so far, the thought of not getting a job offer at the end was a bit of a nightmare – I'd invested so much of my life into getting to that point and just wanted it all over. Fortunately, I passed all the tests and got the offer of a job. I felt like I'd won the lottery!

In the same way that the university course interviewers are looking to see the type of person you are, not just the things you know, so the assessors on the interview day are looking for 'who you are', not simply that you've met the required standard for performing certain skills. You will obviously be nervous, but be yourself as far as you can. Yes, do your homework, practise your skills and protocols till you can do them in your sleep, but show them the person you are. Examples of how you've developed as a person over your three years of paramedic education are just as relevant as examples of the clinical skills you've mastered.

🎓 **Academic response:** Your personal statement is a chance to let your personality and character shine through. Write from the heart and show how you have developed as a result of your education. At interview, just be yourself. You will be nervous, and the interview panel will allow for this. In my experience successful candidates have shown they have warm personalities. Ensure you prepare yourself with a good knowledge of the trust you are applying for too. There is nothing worse than being asked a question about the trust and having no clue as to the answer.

🚨 **Paramedic PEd response:** Be properly prepared! Everybody has their own thoughts on what you will be asked at interview. Think about what you need to know.

It isn't only about trust information, for example how many calls they attend. Interviewers want to know *you* and why *you* should have the position. What makes you better than other candidates? The panel will sit and listen to lots of candidates.

I would suggest doing a simple SWOT (strengths, weaknesses, opportunities, threats) analysis so you are more aware of yourself and think about how you will be a benefit to the organisation. Consider other aspects, the necessities, as I call them, that you need to know to do your job, for example confidentiality, equality and diversity. Be prepared for the practical aspects of an interview. Do you have a fitness test? Are you prepared? Do you need additional clothing? Is there group work? How are you going to function in that group? Are there practical or theory-based exams? Make sure you know algorithms. Bring pens, paper and equipment with you, including your stethoscope. Examine your invitation letter and any other information sent through. Do not assume you know what they are looking for; make sure you *do* know what and who they are looking for.

The advice in Box 20.2 advises you to be yourself. This is hard to do at interview, but preparing and having a strategy on the interview day may help. Box 20.3 covers some main points. These may seem common sense, but at times of stress, simple things can be overlooked.

This chapter has guided you through the process of applying for, and interviewing for, your first job as a paramedic. The comments provided by the contributors relate to their own experiences and thoughts. It is hoped that these provide an insight into the process, but fully investigate this for yourself, in relation to the ambulance trust that you want to work for. Good luck!

Once you have secured that paramedic position the support does not abruptly end, as Chapter 21 explains.

Box 20.3 Some interview tips about the face-to-face or online panel interview

- Arrive early; make sure your internet connection is sound and you can access the links provided.
- Dress professionally (even online).
- If online, unplug or turn off any other phones.
- Reread your supporting statement and highlight questions on it that you may be asked about.
- Practise your responses to questions beforehand.
- Greet the interviewer formally (even if you know them).
- If in person, do not sit down before the interviewer, unless given permission to do so.
- Shake hands on entering the room (if this seems appropriate) and smile. If online, make sure you introduce yourself and catch the names/position of the people interviewing you.
- Try to let the interviewers see a bit of your personality, even if you are nervous.
- During interview, sit quietly, be attentive. If online, try not to fidget or look distracted.
- Do not chew gum, take phone calls, or slouch.
- Ask appropriate questions about the organisation or specific job for which you are applying.
- Avoid a 'What can you do for me?' approach.
- Focus on how your talents, interests and skills fit with the organisation.
- Answer questions as honestly and confidently as possible.
- Try to avoid answering a question by repeating it when you start giving your answer.
- Shake hands at the end of the interview (if in person) and thank the interviewers for their time.

References

College of Paramedics. *Professional Development.* Available at: https://collegeofparamedics.co.uk/COP/Professional_Development.aspx (accessed 13 July 2022).

Health and Care Professions Council. *Applying for Registration.* Available at: https://www.hcpc-uk.org/students/health-disability-and-becoming-a-health-and-care-professional/applying-for-registration/ (accessed 13 July 2022).

Health and Care Professions Council. *Continuing Professional Development.* Available at: https://www.hcpc-uk.org/cpd/ (accessed 13 July 2022).

Health and Care Professions Council. *Getting on the Register.* Available at: https://www.hcpc-uk.org/registration/getting-on-the-register/ (accessed 13 July 2022).

Further reading

Read all documents relating to the job you have applied for and the interview process. If anything is unclear, ask the trust or your university lecturers to see if they can help you.

Research any relevant trust or ambulance-related documents prior to interview.

Review your skills and make sure, if there are practical tests, that you know what to expect. Review relevant notes and texts about these skills or tests.

21 PRECEPTORSHIP

Amanda Blaber

Most HEIs will provide some support prior to completion of your programme in the areas of leadership and what to expect on registration from your employer; this is not standardised across the UK and may be somewhat ad-hoc in nature. Depending on your chosen employer and completing a period of preceptorship, your NHS employer will usually provide an orientation period for new employees. Before discussing preceptorship, this chapter will examine the first few weeks of your employment.

Making the most of your orientation period

The orientation period may be called different things by NHS organisations, such as induction or transition. For the purposes of this chapter the term 'orientation' will be used. Orientation involves raising awareness of the employing organisation generally, reviewing policies, skills, procedures, and mandatory training required by all employees. For paramedics who do not have their emergency driving course, this may also be included as part of their employing organisation orientation. Box 21.1 explores feelings and advice relating to the orientation period that you may find useful.

However long your period of orientation is, it may seem like an extension of your studies, and you may feel like the paramedic in Box 21.1 who just wanted to get out there and do it for real. Or you may still be experiencing a wobble in your confidence. But once you have finished your orientation period you have a period of preceptorship to complete, where you will be supported, as the next section of this chapter explains.

⌀ Refer to Chapters 11, 13, 15 and 16 for more guidance on improving your confidence in practice.

Box 21.1 What advice would you give new registrants about their orientation to their NHS trust?

🔔 **Paramedic registrant response:** Sitting in our NHS trust orientation lectures, I couldn't help thinking about those old Battle of Britain war films where the new pilots who were about to face combat for the first time are being instructed on how to stay alive. The inevitability of being out on shift with 'Paramedic' written on my shoulders loomed very large and I hoped I would last longer than the two-week life expectation of a Spitfire pilot. While being scared of going out there for the first time, there is also a strengthening feeling of 'I just want to get on with it now. I'm not sure that another lecture will give me any more theoretical knowledge than I've already had drummed into me. I need to get out and do it for real.'

I guess you reach the point where you realise that the only way of gaining the confidence you lack is through experience on the job. It's scary and exciting at the same time.

🔔 **Practice educator (PEd) response:** You will usually undergo an orientation session/course on entering an ambulance service/trust. Don't be afraid to ask questions. You will find colleagues a good source of information; do not hesitate to ask them for help. Most people will only be too happy to give you a hand. Remember that although ambulance services/trusts do have differences, the work they do is fundamentally the same and you will have already had good experience of ambulance service culture on placement.

Preceptorship

This term may be new to you. It acknowledges that new registrants in any healthcare profession will be safe and competent, but nonetheless novice clinicians, who will continue to develop their competence as part of their career development (Barrett and Nelson 2014). An official definition is provided by the Department of Health (2010). The HCPC is currently working with Health Education England (HEE) and stakeholders to develop a set of evidence-led principles for Allied Health Professions Preceptorship and Foundation Support that will aim to promote excellence and standardisation in the quality of preceptorship programmes available for all allied health professionals, not just paramedics (see references at the end of the chapter).

This work is in response to data gathered by HEE/HCPC, which has identified that a higher proportion of employees (10 per cent) leave professions within the first five years after registration than at any other time. More worryingly, those leaving within the first year after registration is 11 per cent, hence the need to strengthen the preparation, support and education for those newly registered staff. It is likely that there will be focus in three areas:

1   Support (pre-preceptorship) before entering employment, via the education provider
2   The preceptorship period itself
3   Newly proposed Foundation period (learning opportunities, career support) that will continue into the early years of your career

So, in 2023 expect Foundation Preceptorship principles to be published, pre-preceptorship (possibly called "Step to Work") e-learning for health (eLfH) programmes, excellence frameworks and the AHP Foundation Preceptorship webpages to be released. This is the future. The remainder of this chapter will explore the concept of preceptorship (as it exists at the present time) and the experiences of students on their entry to employment.

Definition: Preceptorship

Preceptorship is *'a period of structured transition for the newly registered practitioner during which [they] will be supported by a preceptor, to develop their confidence as an autonomous professional, refine skills, values and behaviours, and continue on their journey of lifelong learning'* (Department of Health 2010: 11).

It is possible that even with the definition above, the preceptorship role is interpreted differently by organisations, preceptors and new registrants.

The College of Paramedics (2022: 117) describes the differences between the roles of a practice educator and preceptor as follows:

- The preceptor supports a registered paramedic, rather than a pre-registration learner.
- The NQP has successfully completed all academic assessments, whereas the pre-registration learner is still working towards this.
- The skills of a preceptor can be considered to be more akin to those of a mentor rather than to a practice educator.

Knowing the definition of preceptorship, and the role of a preceptor, it is therefore important to explore what preceptorship is not (see Table 21.1).

It is important to note the differences between mentorship and preceptorship, as indicated by points 5 and 6 in Table 21.1. Preceptorship, as indicated by point 4 in Table 21.1, is not viewed as a way to meet any shortfall in pre-registration education, but as a transition phase for newly registered practitioners as they continue with their professional development. Barrett and Nelson (2014) explain that preceptorship provides an opportunity to build the practitioner's confidence in decision-making and further develop their competence for practice. In order for this preceptorship

Table 21.1 What preceptorship is not

Preceptorship is not:
1. intended to replace mandatory training programmes
2. intended to be a substitute for performance management processes
3. intended to replace regulatory body processes to deal with performance
4. an additional period in which another registrant takes responsibility and accountability for the newly registered practitioner's responsibilities and actions (i.e. not a further period of training)
5. formal coaching (although coaching skills may be used by the preceptor to facilitate the learning of the newly registered practitioner)
6. mentorship
7. statutory or clinical supervision
8. intended to replace induction to employment.

Source: Department of Health (2010: 12)

period to be successful, the preceptor is usually an established paramedic, with a minimum of 12 months of post-qualifying experience. In addition to experience, it is recommended that preceptors complete a programme with a university to develop their skills and knowledge of supporting newly qualified registrants (Gopee 2018).

What to expect from your preceptorship period

The process of preceptorship should be structured and form part of the orientation, induction and development of new staff, not necessarily just new registrants. Experienced paramedics who move from ambulance service/trust to ambulance service/trust may also be given a period of preceptorship, although this may vary in its duration or structure from that of a new registrant. The content of the preceptorship programme is usually planned in relation to the professional responsibilities of the paramedic and the needs of the employer, as per the guidance contained within the Department of Health (2010) preceptorship framework document. As with most things, it may not always be what you expected, as the responses in Box 21.2 explain.

The College of Paramedics recommends that all employers should follow this model and offer similar support to any NQP in any healthcare setting (2020: 116).

A preceptor does not, usually, assess the performance of an NQP. Ensure that you establish the preceptorship arrangements available within the workplace, ensure you are happy with the structure/process and that is clearly explained to you. It is important that you are given the support for the transition period from NQP to paramedic. For some people this may take much longer than the *official* preceptorship period but if you get on well with your preceptor, it is likely that they will be on hand for support and advice. We have all been in this situation and generally recognise how unsettling and stressful it can be at times.

Reflection: Points to consider

As a newly registered paramedic, what sort of support and help do you think a preceptor might be able to help you with?

Box 21.2 Was your period of preceptorship what you expected it to be?

Paramedic registrant response: I think preceptorship is heavily influenced by you as a professional. By this point you have successfully passed your studies, you have become a registered healthcare professional, and you have successfully landed yourself a job! So well done! This is your final chance to have direct support right beside you, so make the most of it. We were told all about preceptorship on our orientation to the trust and issued with a book to identify areas to cover during our preceptorship period. I personally found my preceptorship period invaluable. Using this opportunity to learn all you need to know about your new station, you can ask all those questions that you haven't yet asked. You are able to make those first decisions as a registered paramedic, which I found really quite scary, compared to student decisions, but know that there is still someone there to support you. You can iron out any concerns you have and know that other people have been exactly where you are, taking that first step. You are able to highlight areas you feel most confident in and areas you still wish to develop. I would say from the advice we were given about our preceptorship period from the university and from the ambulance services themselves, I had a very smooth transition from student to paramedic and utilised my time to the fullest, achieving all that I wished preceptorship to be.

Paramedic registrant response: Many students think that gaining their paramedic qualification will add extra stress. For me the opposite was true – I found my job a lot less stressful as a paramedic than I ever did as a technician. For one, I had control over situations. Previously, I was forced to back down to the paramedic – even though I knew it was not good practice. I had also been given more skills to help my patients and did not have the stress of having to wait for paramedic back-up to treat my patients. The biggest challenge I found was not having the psychological safety net of another paramedic. The thing to remember here is that you may be lucky enough to be working with an experienced technician who, although not a paramedic, may have years of excellent experience for you to call on.

📢 **Paramedic registrant response:** In a practical sense, transitioning from being a student into full-time work was a change I was not prepared for. Simple things like making sure I had enough food for four shifts in a row, and making sure I had done enough laundry to not have to worry about it in between shifts. I didn't realise how stressful starting work would be or how physically and mentally exhausted I'd be. Having the little things sorted just makes it more manageable.

📢 **Paramedic registrant response:** Being an NQP is as much of a rollercoaster journey and learning curve as being a third-year student. You suddenly become your own version of a paramedic (this changes constantly) incorporating bits of all the people you have worked with and wanted to role model, but also finding yourself. You make all the decisions, advocating for your patients. This does not mean that you are not ready for it. You continue to grow into the paramedic that you want to be. This doesn't happen overnight and doesn't happen because you have left university – it is a process that takes time. It is a good process and things do get easier and you do get more confident.

📢 **Paramedic registrant response:** Preceptorship is another level of tiredness: long shifts, changing crews all the time, no pattern, so much practical learning, responsibility, and driving. The first four months as an NQP have been intense and tiring, but I am beginning to grow in confidence.

The next section of this chapter is dedicated to the views of newly qualified paramedics. It is clear throughout the previous chapters that support networks are vitally important both during and after your studies, therefore the next section contains views from family members. *Family* should be considered in the widest sense and the comments made should be considered with this in mind.

Newly qualified paramedic status

In order to provide a wide range of views on this subject newly qualified paramedics (NQPs) were asked to reflect on their career choice, effects their career has had on them/families and other pertinent questions. The following responses are in the NQPs' own words. Box 21.3 reflects on their career choice.

Box 21.3 Looking back at your younger self, would you choose this career path again?

🚨 **NQP comment:** Yes definitely, although I would have liked to have started younger than I did. There were a number of factors around my own well-being and anxiety which likely would have held me back if I had started when I was younger and before I had a chance to grow and manage these issues. But I would definitely choose the career again.

🚨 **NQP comment:** Coming into the job as an older, mature student was definitely the right decision for me. I have a lot of respect and admiration for younger students in my cohort who studied straight out of school/college. Some of the events we are expected to go to and the situations we need to empathise with and experience, challenge even the most hardy of us and I cannot imagine having to experience these roles as a young 21-year-old graduate.

🚨 **NQP comment:** Yes I would, but as a young graduate it changed my perspective of life, and has made me more grateful.

🚨 **NQP comment:** Absolutely, without a shadow of any doubt! It is the best job in the world, I love the variety, opportunities to learn continually. Each day is different and you never know what you are going to meet. Each shift you can guarantee to make a difference, no matter how small and that's really rewarding.

🚨 **NQP comment:** Yes, I still fundamentally enjoy being a paramedic, the variety from day to day and call to call, meeting people in their own environments, the pace of the job, variety of options available once qualified, all make it a good career. Although there are certainly elements that I do not enjoy and often find stressful, but I am learning to deal with and manage those.

🚨 **NQP comment:** No, I enjoyed the challenge at university, but the constant shift work, unsocial hours and politics of the job itself wore me down to the point of leaving the ambulance service, but I am still a paramedic. I have just started working in primary care, one year after graduation. I know I am lucky to have got the job with not much experience.

🚨 **NQP comment:** My answer is not clear cut. I have moved to another European country now and very few countries recognise the paramedic registration. But with the options available to me at the time, it was the best choice. At university I was involved with the paramedic society; this taught me that if there is something you are interested in doing and it doesn't exist, it doesn't mean it can't be developed – I asked humanitarian aid workers to talk to us.

As can be seen by the responses in Box 21.3, paramedics are working in a variety of areas, not just with ambulance services, and some are moving into other areas within a relatively short period after graduation (although sometimes this is aided by previous work in other health and social care roles). Box 21.4 looks at the good and not so good parts of the role, but it must be remembered that these are only a limited number of views.

Box 21.4 What do you love about your job?

🚨 **Paramedic comment:** I love being out and about (in all weathers). As lead clinician, you are pretty much your own boss (for most calls), being able to care for patients and take time over it. Interacting with such a wide variety of people during a day is great and really interesting.

🚨 **Paramedic comment:** I really enjoy the variety of roles within the workforce – the possibilities are endless. I currently work as a frontline paramedic on a bank basis (I choose my own shifts and when I work) and in a teaching fellow role in an acute hospital trust. These two roles support each other and my skills can be applied to both roles equally.

🚨 **Paramedic comment:** I love the satisfaction of treating and managing a time critical patient, the diversity of calls and teaching students.

🚨 **Paramedic comment:** Whenever you do a *big* job, or a patient/family gives you their genuine heartfelt thanks, it is one of the best feelings.

🚨 It has led me to work in the humanitarian aid sector.

What do you dislike about your job?

🚨 **Paramedic comment:** I hate the politics, pressures and constant watching from the public – it is like they are waiting for you to slip up. The relentless nature of the role can be quite demoralising, as can the lack of career progression within the ambulance service.

🚨 **Paramedic comment:** I hated the politics and lack of welfare from low-level leaders within the ambulance service. I was really angry with how unsupportive they were, the lack of value placed on staff education and continuing professional development and the impact that this may have on patient care, if as a paramedic, you do not undertake this in your own time. I felt undervalued and unseen in a full-time ambulance role, so I made changes and now can concentrate solely on providing great patient care without the political strain when working bank shifts.

🚨 **Paramedic comment:** Patients who do not take responsibility for their health, or treat us as a transport service. I also dislike the low morale of staff, people moaning and not taking control, queuing for hours at hospitals.

🚨 **Paramedic comment:** Nightshifts get harder as you get older.

In previous chapters you have had the benefit of insight from student paramedics. In Box 21.5 there is advice from registered paramedics who have been through a programme of education, so know what being a student paramedic entails.

Box 21.5 What advice would you give to someone who is considering paramedicine as a career?

🚨 **Registered paramedic comment:** Make sure you are doing it for the right reasons. Don't do it because you think it will impress others; the bulk of the work can be frustrating. The adrenaline-fuelled *exciting* calls that you hope to go to and save the day are often the worst days of someone else's life.

🚨 **Registered paramedic comment:** It is a lifestyle and it will impact on every aspect of your life. It changes you as a person (I studied straight from college), it can desensitise you and this can transfer to your personal life.

🚨 **Registered paramedic comment:** Do it – it is an adaptable job, and you can take it anywhere you want. In the next few years, so many opportunities will open up for paramedics. It can help you travel, develop research, leadership or teaching skills and more.

🚨 **Registered paramedic comment:** It is a great job, but if you want to do what you see on TV shows then this isn't it. Prepare to see some difficult things and to have your eyes opened so wide to things you never knew existed or happened. But you will go through this with some of the most amazing and supportive colleagues who will become lifelong friends. And it will be the little things that make the most difference to your patients, not time-critical, Gucci interventions. Do not expect frontline ambulance work to be a lifelong job.

🚨 **Registered paramedic comment:** I have had a few jobs in primary care since graduating (I had plenty of experience in this area as a non-registered clinician before I started my programme). I feel that roles with other paramedics or a close team has been better than working in a small crew or in a clinical room on my own. I prefer working in a team.

🚨 **Registered paramedic comment:** Take the time to look at the wider opportunities for paramedics now; we are not just on ambulances.

The following case study brings to life the acute differences between being a student and the registered paramedic role as an NQP.

CASE STUDY 21.1

Definition and explanation of Pulseless Electrical Activity (PEA):
Cardiac condition, usually identified during resuscitation. Also known
as electromechanical dissociation, it is a clinical condition characterised by unresponsiveness of the patient and impalpable pulse in the
presence of sufficient electrical discharge.

Definition of Return of Spontaneous Circulation (ROSC): This may
happen during a resuscitation activity when chest compressions are
being administered.

This occurred one month into my preceptorship. It was a 12-hour
shift finishing at 18.30hrs. We were driving back to station to finish
our shift when we were asked to back up a crew to help extricate an
89-year-old patient, after a fall, query stroke.

On our arrival the patient's wife and daughter were present, they
seemed relaxed and quite calm. In another room, the crew were performing CPR. We were told the patient was in PEA. Previous medical
history was a cough for a few days, tired today, watching television,
got up, complained of right-sided abdominal pain, and fell to the
floor.

I was asked to administer fluids quickly. I felt calm, but not engaged.
I was watching, I heard the words, but I did not have an understanding of what was going on. More fluids were given to me. I could not
remember how to attach the giving set to the fluid bag. I switched to
take over chest compressions, on the rhythm check, I felt a pulse,
but I did not register the patient had ROSC. I remained task focused,
while the family were made aware of the seriousness of the situation. On ultrasound, the aorta looked very large, highly likely a ruptured abdominal aortic aneurysm. The patient was made comfortable,
transported to hospital where he sadly died.

On reflection, I thought so much about this call. I was not mentally
prepared at all for a cardiac arrest and was taken aback when I saw
CPR in progress. This was my first cardiac arrest as an NQP. I felt out
of my depth with complete brain fog and severely low bandwidth. I
was only able to focus on the tasks I was doing, I made some

mistakes doing these tasks, and all I could think about was the mistakes I had made. The rest of the team were supportive and did not make me feel uncomfortable.

I needed to process this before I could move forward, my confidence had been rocked, so I wrote a reflection and it helped me identify some learning points and to realise that I needed to concentrate on what I did achieve and not just my mistakes. I spoke to the crew who were present a few days later, had constructive clinical discussions and explained how I felt; they helped me discuss what had happened and why, so I felt much better.

A few days later I was in a similar resuscitation situation and I was able to do everything expected of me and did not feel at all out of my depth.

With hindsight I realise that being an NQP in such a situation is very different from being a student. As an NQP I put expectations on myself because it was now my job and I had a duty of care to my patient, therefore I needed to understand what was going on. We cannot anticipate every situation; there are times when we feel completely in control and others when we don't. What is important is to learn from each situation. A university education provides us with the learning tools to do just that and continue learning.

As can be seen from Case study 21.1, there will be times during your NQP period and beyond where you will feel overwhelmed and do not perform well. It is important to recognise this in yourself, talk to other clinicians, understand why (tiredness, too many intense calls, end of the shift, not expecting a time-critical event when all you thought was you were backing up another crew) and learn from the incident to regain your confidence and move forward, rather than ruminate on the things not done well.

℘ Refer to Chapter 18 for more on rumination.

Throughout the book we have referred to the stresses of the paramedic role. It is likely that the stress increases once you graduate and become employed, as you no longer get the enforced breaks of study and the responsibility becomes more intense once you are a registered clinician. It is important to think about coping mechanisms, as Box 21.6 explores.

Box 21.6 What coping mechanisms (positive or negative) have you found helped you cope with the stresses of the role?

Paramedic comment: I run, a lot. Any form of exercise. I also eat a lot, and not always good things. I enjoy meeting up with friends – being outside in nature is so good (but difficult when you are exhausted). Talking to someone I trust does the same job, but you often need someone who understands the role. Having a good cry is useful and what is needed sometimes. Allowing yourself to have emotions is important. Don't punish yourself for having an emotional reaction; acknowledge, accept and live it.

Paramedic comment: I cannot stress enough the value of keeping active enough and getting outside, away from technology. It is easy to become overwhelmed with seeing your non-work friends enjoying their free weekends together when you are stuck in a queue in ED. You need to remember that people just put *the best version* of themselves online and it's not always as wonderful as they make out. Cold water swimming has also been incredible for my own mental health struggles. I find intrusive memories and thoughts melt away when I am swimming, especially during the winter months in my wetsuit at the open-air swimming pool.

Paramedic comment: I have always used exercise to manage stress. In the past year I have learned to book time out for myself, setting time aside that is truly mine to rest and relax. Not working extra shifts is difficult as the money is a temptation, but taking time to look after myself is greater than any financial reward.

Paramedic comment: Socialising with friends, keeping a healthy lifestyle and using my days off productively. Talking through calls with my partner (who is also a paramedic), keeping a learning log and using structured reflective practice techniques.

Paramedic comment: I have a very supportive wife who is a social worker, so she understands. I have a good support network of friends and having utilised counselling previously myself, I am more than willing to use this again, if needed.

🚨 **Paramedic comment:** The really difficult times are when your normal coping mechanisms and stress relievers are not accessible. Taking time for yourself to recover physically and mentally is paramount. The basics really help as this is how we recover: sleep, hydrate, eat nutritiously, exercise, stretch, laugh and love.

Any role in healthcare affects your personal life, but how may it affect your family? It is an important consideration. Box 21.7 shares paramedics' thoughts.

Box 21.7 Has the job affected your personal and family life? If so, how?

🚨 **Paramedic comment:** It can make social gathering difficult, with friends or family – shift work is not really understood by people who have never done it. On the positive side, my friends work shifts, so we can go out during the week together.

🚨 **Paramedic comment:** It is difficult to maintain a relationship. If your partner is also a shift worker, your shift pattern may not match up. If they are not a shift worker, they struggle to understand how it works, the type of work you do and how you cope with what you see.

🚨 **Paramedic comment:** I am tired all the time, which can make me grumpy, short, snappy and sometimes I just can't be bothered to get up and do anything.

🚨 **Paramedic comment:** Realising it is not okay to share all the *ins and outs* of the job with friends and family members who are not in the service. It is unreasonable to expect them to understand the pressures and frustrations of our job and the highly charged emotions that go with them. Having a good friend within the service is invaluable. Very often we just need a listener; we are not necessarily after solutions.

Paramedic comment: You will have to get used to friends and family constantly cracking jokes about *needing a paramedic* whenever anyone falls over or stubs their toe within 15 feet of you!

Paramedic comment: I think sometimes my family, especially my parents have worried a lot about the stress of the job and exposure to traumatic events (and others) on my mental health

In Box 21.8 are some *nuggets* of advice from registered paramedics about qualifying, job roles and attitude while you are a student. Think about what has been said.

Box 21.8 Any other advice you wish to pass on?

Paramedic comment: Paramedics might start off wearing green in ambulance services but it is by no means the only place you can work.

Paramedic comment: Be prepared for *sink or swim* experience when you qualify.

Paramedic comment: Don't moan about a job until *after* you have been. Yes, sometimes the calls can seem annoying and you might hear your mentors question why you are being sent, but at the end of the day you have not heard what that patient has said to the call handler on the phone, and why that has triggered an ambulance response. Call handlers do a fantastic job and you do not realise how much they actually shield you from.

Paramedic comment: Whenever you hope for, or wish for, a more *exciting* job like a trauma or cardiac arrest – often you are actually hoping and wishing for the worst day of someone's life. Remember that!

As educated practitioners, people think to the future, some plan their career path, others see where their career takes them. In Box 21.9 paramedics share their aspirations and this gives you a good idea that there is a wide variety of employment and educational opportunities to choose from.

Box 21.9 What is your next career move?

🚨 **Newly qualified paramedic (NQP) response:** Expedition work.

🚨 **Newly qualified paramedic (NQP) response:** I am on a one-year fellowship, so not sure after that. Different clinical roles and then after five years maybe a PhD and more research.

🚨 **Newly qualified paramedic (NQP) response:** A Masters degree – Paramedic Practitioner in Primary Care.

🚨 **Newly qualified paramedic (NQP) response:** I am a Student Paramedic Practitioner (PP) now. I may go part-time in the ambulance trust and part-time in an urgent treatment centre or General Practice once I have qualified as a PP.

🚨 **Newly qualified paramedic (NQP) response:** I have a job working in a prison on the healthcare wing. I am hoping this will provide a good mix of primary care, general hospital and also trauma response for the prison.

This chapter has discussed the process of moving into employment. There is a variety of support networks available to you as a newly registered paramedic to be aware of and use to your advantage. Guidance and recommendations are available to NHS ambulance services/ trusts relating to the employment of newly registered paramedics. This should ensure that all parties involved are aware of their responsibilities and ensure the smooth orientation and transition from student to registered paramedic. As discussed early in the chapter, the landscape of preceptorship is changing, so please do visit the webpages suggested below.

References

Barrett, K. and Nelson, L. (2014) Mentorship and preceptorship. In A.Y. Blaber and G. Harris (eds) *Clinical Leadership for Paramedics*. Maidenhead: Open University Press.

Clarke, V. (ed.) (2020) *Paramedic Practice-Based Learning: A Handbook for Practice Educators and Facilitators*. Available at: https://collegeof-paramedics.co.uk/ (accessed 19 July 2022).

College of Paramedics (2019) *Paramedic Curriculum Guidance* (5th edn). Available at: https://collegeofparamedics.co.uk/COP/ProfessionalDevelopment/Paramedic_Curriculum_Guidance.aspx (accessed 19 July 2022).

Department of Health (2010) *Preceptorship Framework for Newly Registered Nurses, Midwives and Allied Health Professionals*. London: Department of Health.

Gopee, N. (2018) *Supervision and Mentoring in Healthcare* (4th edn). London: Sage.

Health and Care Professions Council (2022) *HCPC launches new work on preceptorship*. Available at: https://www.hcpc-uk.org/news-and-events/news/2022/hcpc-collaborates-on-preceptorship-programme/ (accessed 19 July 2022).

Health Education England. *National AHP Preceptorship and Foundation Support*. Available at: https://www.hee.nhs.uk/our-work/allied-health-professions/education-employment/national-ahp-foundation-preceptorship (accessed 7 September 2022).

National Health Service eLearning for Healthcare website: https://www.e-lfh.org.uk. This website forms the basis of statutory and mandatory education for registered healthcare staff working in the NHS. There are numerous e-learning subjects available and you will be required to complete these by your employer.

National Health Service England (2022) *The AHP Strategy for England 2022 to 2027: AHPs Deliver*. Available at: https://www.england.nhs.uk/publication/the-allied-health-professions-ahps-strategy-for-england/ (accessed 7 September 2022).

22 IT'S NOT ALL ABOUT YOU. WHAT ARE THE VIEWS OF YOUR FAMILY?

Amanda Blaber

Over many years I have been privileged to speak to family members at the graduation events at the university. On such a special and proud day for all concerned, it has been apparent that family members are also on the journey with the student, from choosing a programme/university, application, interview, throughout the programme and through the ups and downs – they are there supporting you. I wanted in this second edition to give them a voice and explore some of their thoughts, concerns and emotions.

Having explored the honest thoughts and feelings of newly qualified paramedics in Chapter 21, there was some concern expressed about the toll of their role on friends and family. The following are comments from paramedics' family members who responded to set questions, as highlighted in bold in each of the following boxes.

Having been a healthcare student, lived with my parents during my initial education and then shared my employed career with my partner, I am more than aware of how important family is (and I consider this in the widest sense; friends can be equally, if not better than family in certain situations). I consider family to mean anyone you love, trust and share your life with. I think it is really important that students and registered paramedics have some insight into the thoughts and feelings of family members. There is minimal narrative in this chapter, as I believe the responses to the questions in the boxes below speak for themselves.

While this chapter relies on the answers to questions, it provides insight into the concerns, worries and also the positives of having a paramedic within your family. I think Box 22.7 demonstrates the variety of coping mechanisms within a family, some talking more, some talking less but mentioning small things. What is clear is that the thoughts and feelings of family are unique to them, although there are some similarities. The hardship of the paramedic role is appreciated, family members *feel* parts of this with you, because they love you. Alongside this there is a sense of immense pride in their family member, although I am sure whatever your career, they would feel proud of you.

This is the first time I have canvased family members for their thoughts and feelings, I think it has added an extra dimension to the book and I would like to thank those who took time to complete the questionnaires for their valuable insight and honesty.

Box 22.1 Has your loved one's career choice to be a paramedic affected your family life? If yes, please explain how.

family It was hard both mentally and physically. As a result, we have struggled to have quality time in between shifts and on rest days.

family Definitely over the COVID-19 period; it was really hard trying to support and deal with their and our anxieties.

family My partner is often mentally and emotionally exhausted on days off, so we do not do what we used to.

family I have been asked to make more cakes – the ambulance service currency!

family The main effect is that working shifts makes making arrangements to speak and see each other more difficult.

Box 22.2 What was the hardest part of their journey to be a paramedic, for you as their family?

family The university living accommodation and other non-health students being in the same accommodation; they did not respect shift work and tiredness.

family Distance to placement on top of a long 12-hour shift that then overran, having to drive back after such a long day.

family The placement aspect, which could be up to an hour away. I would worry about the travelling after shifts and getting home safely.

family The first six months after starting work, I know they enjoyed their studies, but after graduating, they became suddenly much more stressed, more emotionally tired and less relaxed. This was also on days off.

family Knowing the pressure they were under during their programme and when they had placement and coursework to do – although they coped very well.

Box 22.3 What do you consider the worst parts of your family member being a paramedic?

family Lack of quality time in between shifts.

family Extra stress due to traumatic events happening during their shifts.

family Exposure to infections for them and us (especially worse during COVID-19).

family Lack of support from employer's management team after traumatic calls. All parents expect there to be an importance put on looking after their staff, but this has been extremely lacking in my view. No such issues during their time as a student, when support was always there.

family Quality of crewmates.

family The stress they are under.

family Hearing about certain calls that then stay with me.

family Shift work means we do not see them as much, especially on birthdays and Christmas.

family The idea they may not come home after a shift.

family Low job satisfaction, due to the difference between what they have been educated to do (and want to do) and the types of calls they get sent to.

family The constant overruns and unpredictable shift patterns.

family Knowing that they possibly put themselves in danger, especially during the pandemic; it was worrying.

family Knowing they regularly deal with call-outs that do not really warrant the services of a paramedic, but because of their duty and professionalism they treat them with respect. I worry how this affects them, as it cannot be easy dealing with these types of calls when it stops them attending more urgent cases.

family I worry about how dealing with upsetting/traumatic situations will affect them in the long term.

Box 22.4 What do you consider are the best parts of your family member being a paramedic?

family Sense of being useful to the community, which makes us proud.

family Doing a job that is stimulating and worthwhile.

family A job that always offers some laughs.

family A job to be proud of as a parent.

family The immense pride I have for what they have achieved and what they do on a daily basis.

family I like telling people my daughter is a paramedic; they are always really appreciative and in awe.

family I also work in healthcare and it makes a huge difference to have a partner who understands the stresses.

family It makes me feel safe.

family When they come home and they say they made a difference, I can see how happy and proud that makes them.

family Knowing they have found a profession that has a positive meaning.

family Being proud of knowing that they are helping people as part of their day-to-day job.

family Knowing it is a job they really want to do.

Box 22.5 Do you worry about your family member when they are on shift? If yes, why?

family Not really, maybe if they are on an ambulance car alone at night.

family Yes, for her safety generally.

family Not until recently, but they have been physically assaulted by a patient twice in the past few weeks and I worry about it happening again. How will this affect them mentally and physically?

family I worry about them being involved in an accident on the road.

family A little sometimes, that they may have been involved in a traumatic situation.

family I worry that they could come to harm or become ill due to being in contact with the patients that she cares for, or that the ambulance could be involved in an accident.

Box 22.6 Do you do anything specific to help you cope with this worry? If yes, what?

family Just listen to them.

family I tell myself not to worry and remind myself that they are a strong individual, mentally and physically.

family I talk to my friends.

family They usually give me a rough idea of what kind of a day they have had. If they want to, we discuss specific incidents/calls and look at the strengths/weaknesses of the situation, what they can learn and how to improve next time – so reflect really, but it helps that I also work in healthcare – so I do the same.

family I try to remind myself that most calls are non-traumatic in nature.

family I try not to constantly worry because I know that they are a very capable person, so I try not to overthink too much.

Box 22.7 Do you find your loved one discusses their shifts with you once they get home?

family If I ask how it went, they will say, but it is the funny things mainly or the banter between them and their crewmate. I am grateful for their level of professionalism and censorship.

family They talk about the calls they have been to; it helps them relax.

family We don't discuss their shift – only whether it has been busy or not.

family Not really, they do talk about some issues in a very general way sometimes when we have a catch-up on Facetime or on the phone.

CONCLUSION

In life there are challenges: some we choose to take on and others are thrust upon us. Any student paramedic programme is a challenge. You are studying for a professional qualification and a degree – it will not be a *walk in the park*.

There will be some bumps in the road and this book has been written to help you anticipate what these may be. They will be different for every individual and occur at different times across your three years of study. It is hoped that what this text will do is equip you with the information, knowledge and encouragement to develop your own self- awareness, so you are as prepared as you can be.

It is hoped that if this is the case, you will be ready for the challenge, be ready to study and work hard, enjoy learning in clinical practice and meet role models who you wish to emulate. In addition to making lifelong friends within your cohort, working together with your programme team of lecturers and enjoying your study, try to be successful and achieve your own potential. It is up to you how you meet the challenges of a demanding programme – we have provided some important information, it is up to you now what you do with it. You are in control of your own destiny.

INDEX

Page numbers with 't' indicate tables.

TOP 7

£42.00 A YEAR *or* **£3.50 A MONTH**

STUDENT MEMBE[R]

REASONS WHY YOU SHOULD BE A MEMBER:

01 Discounts on a range of products and services, including books and medical supplies

02 Access to over 500 conference videos on the CPD Hub

03 A quarterly membership magazine 'Paramedic INSIGHT', packed with interesting features, news and advice

04 Free subscription to the College of Paramedics' very own quarterly electronic research journal, the 'British Paramedic Journal' (BPJ)

05 A regular email news digest, keeping you informed of what's going on within the College and the profession

06 Access to our national network of CPD events, discounted for members

07 £5 million medical malpractice and public liability insurance for elective placements and good Samaritan Acts *(T's & C's Apply)*

JOIN TODAY